フォトショップ実戦マスター

Photoshop™ A Designer's Guide

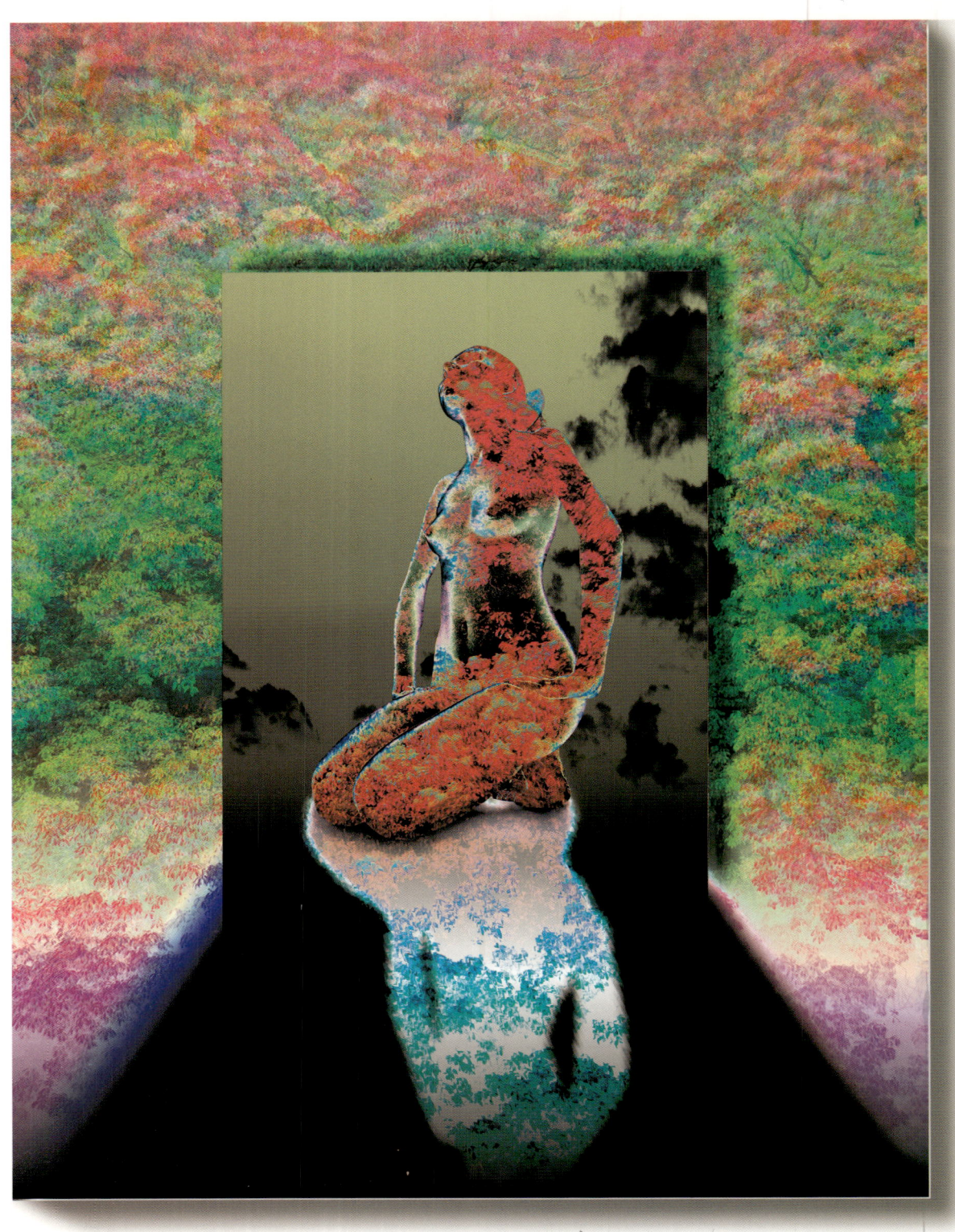

作例１：第７章実習作品のバリエーション、製作のヒントは本文中にあるので挑戦を..........同じ物ができればあなたはプロ！

Work-1　W2173×H2849Pixels　350ppi/17.7MB/RGB........Chap.7

作例2：第6章で紹介している変形作業を実際に応用した例（佐藤製薬イノセアの広告）

Work-2　W2173×H2769Pixels　350ppi/17.2MB/RGB.......Chap.6

作例３：第８章の低解像度データを高解像度に変えた作品のバリエーション
Work-3　W1987×H2911Pixels　350ppi/16.6MB/RGB.......Chap.8

4

作例4：第1章で紹介しているデジタルカメラKodak DCS200mi+ Color Wheel Cameraでの撮影作例
Work-4　W1524×H1012Pixels　350ppi/4.41MB/RGB.......Chap.1　Kodak DCS200

作例5：第8章で紹介しているPhotoCDの最大解像度サイズ16BASEをリサイズせず450ppi/175線で印刷
Work-5　W2921×H1989Pixels　450ppi/16.6MB/RGB.......Chap.8　PhotoCD　16BASE

はじめに

　マッキントッシュ上で使用するペインティングソフトの例にもれず、フォトショップは
わかりやすいインターフェースで、簡単なレタッチやペインティング、データコンバート
等に使っているかぎりはマニュアルを読まなくても使うことができる。

　便利に使っていながら、そのレベルから一歩も前進せずに単なるユーティリティソフト
レベルの使い方で終始している人が多い。

　創造的画像処理ツールとして極めて優れた高機能ソフトを、その能力の数分の一も発揮
させずに終わらせてしまうのはあまりにももったいない。

　フォトショップVer.2.5になってますます高機能化すると共に、マニュアルも前バージョ
ンに比べ格段にわかりやすく丁寧に解説されているので、すべてに目を通しておくことが
フォトショップマスターへの第一歩だ。

　マニュアルを読んだだけでフォトショップを完全に使いこなすことができた人はこの本
を読む必要はない。マニュアルを読んだけれどいまいち理解できなかった、でも画像処理
のエキスパートにはなりたい、という人は是非この本を試してほしい。

　フォトショップを利用して画像処理をしたいと思っているデザイナー、写真家、オペ
レータを読者として想定しているので、マッキントッシュの基本的な使い方、フォト
ショップの基本機能はマスターしていることを前提に解説している。事前に最低限マニュ
アルは読んでおくことをお願いする。マニュアルだけではどうしてもわかりにくい部分、
マニュアルには載っていない便利な使い方等、著者が3年間フォトショップを使い続けて
獲得した画像処理のノウハウを満載してある。

　第2章から第7章まで添付の実戦フロッピーディスクに収録されたデータを使って、本
を傍らに実習すれば、基本的な使い方を高度なレベルでマスターできるはずだ。

　第8章以降は応用編で、掲載したテクニックを読者の作品に生かしていただければ幸いだ。

　作品はRGBモードでのプリンタ出力やカラーポジフィルム出力を前提に記述している。印
刷対応についてはページ数の都合で詳細に記述できなかったが、マッキントッシュのデータ
の取り扱いに習熟した製版会社や出力センターと事前にコンタクトをとって製作すれば、
フォトショップで製作したデータの印刷に関しては、現在まず問題がおきることはない。

　本文中の**斜体太文字**はメニュー名、コマンド名、ツール名、パレット名、キーボード
ショートカット等ソフト内で固有に使われている機能／名称である。

　本文中の画面スナップショットは英語版のプログラムを使用、日本語の解説、動作確認
は日本語版Ver.2.51で行っている。

6

Introduction

Just similar to other painting softwares running on Macintosh, Photoshop is the interface which is easy to execute.

As far as you use it exclusively for simple retouching, painting, or data conversion, you don't have to read its manual throughout.

It is a convenient electronic tool. However, being too convenient, many users have never gone beyond that easiness, using it merely as a simple utility software.

This is a real waste. The excellence in this software is on its high capability as a software for a creative image manipulation. However, not many people have made the use of this high-potential software to its full extent, being satisfied with executing for the very basic application only.

Photoshop Version 2.5 has become more advanced in its technical capability than the version 2.0. At the same time, the manual attached to version 2.5 software has been created in much easier style and in greater detail to understand. If you want to master this capable software, it is recommended to start with reading through the manual carefully.

However, once you read through the manual only once and if you feel that you understand it completely, it is no necessary to take this book with you. Rather, Photoshop:A Designer's Guide is created for those who still have some questions after reading the manual and/or who still want to be an expert of image manipulation making a full use of this software.

Since I have written this book targetting to professional designers, photographers, and operators, readers require the basics of Macintosh technology and Photoshop's functions. It is recommmended that the reader at least read the manual to the end before proceeding. For I intended to clarify those points that are not explained clearly in the manual or to introduce tips and shortcuts that are not mentioned in the manual. In a sense, Photoshop:A Designer's Guide fully covers the result of my achievement for 3 years in the image manipulation.

If you follow the lessons in the chapters 2 to 7 using the attached Instructional Disk, you will master the basics at a high level.

Chapters 8 and beyond cover the practical applications of the Photoshop. We hope you will be able to use those techniques applied to your own work.

All works included in the book are supposed to output to a laser printer with RGB mode or output to 4 color transparencies. Unfortunately I could not make a detailed description about how to apply the scanned data to the actual printing media due to the limited pages for this book. It is suggested you should contact your nearby service bereaus or printing companies before you actually get into the production.

There are currently very few problems for outputting from the disk prepared by Photoshop software.

The **italic bold letters** in the book represent the names of menus, tools, pallets, keyboard shortcuts and other functions properly employed within this software.

目次

Contents

目次

Contents

◆資料／機材提供，協力会社一覧(50音順)
アドビシステムズジャパン (Photoshop Ver.2.5, Photoshop Ver.2.51J)
アップルコンピュータ株式会社 (Macintosh Color Classic)
アルダス株式会社 (Aldus Gallery Effects 1.0E)
キヤノン販売株式会社 (Canon EOS-1)
コダックヴィンズ株式会社 (ProPhotoCD)
大日本スクリーン製造株式会社 (DTS-1030AI,DTS-1015AI)
日本イマプロ株式会社(QCR-Zi,QCS-3200,D4000)
日本コダック株式会社 (DCS200mi,Color Filter Wheel Accessory,PhotoCD)
日本サイテックス株式会社 (Leafscan45)
株式会社ビーピーエス (KAI's Power Tools)
フォーチューンヒル (Andoromeda Series 1 Filters, Fastedit/TIFF, Paint Thinner)
フランクリン・ミント株式会社 (Franklin Mint Precision Models)
ラディウス株式会社 (Photo Booster)
株式会社リングオブファイア (FotoMagic Series 1)
◆
1.MacintoshはApple Computer社の登録商標です。
2.Adobe Photoshopは米国アドビシステムズ社の米国内での登録商標です。
3.その他，本書記載の商品名・名称等は各社の商標および登録商標です。
なお，ＴＭ，Ｒマークは明記しておりません。
◆
本書の内容に関する運用結果については責任を負いかねますので，ご了承ください。

Photoshop : A Designer's Guide
<A Comprehensive, Step-by-Step Manual for Adobe Photoshop>

Copyright© 1994 by Graphic-sha Publishing Co., Ltd.
1-9-12, Kudan kita, Chiyoda-ku, Tokyo 102, Japan

ISBN4-7661-0768-3

Printed in Hong Kong by Everbest Printing Co., Ltd.
First Printing, 1994
Second Printing, 1995

第1章 システム構成

Chapter 1   System Structure

システム構成

System Structure

System Structure

　ハイレゾリューションのデジタルデータを加工処理するためにどの程度のシステム構成が適当なのか頭を悩ましている読者も多いことと思われる。

- ●68030または68040CPUを搭載したMacintoshII以降のコンピュータ
- ●漢字Talk7.1以降のオペレーティングシステム
- ●5MBから8MB（あるいはそれ以上)のアプリケーション用のRAM
- ●24-bitまたは32-bitのビデオディスプレイカードとカラーモニタ
- ●Macintosh対応のスキャナ
- ●PostScript（ポストスクリプト）プリンタ
- ●Adobe認定のアクセラレータ

　以上はAdobeが推奨するシステム構成である。どの程度のデータをどの程度の時間内に処理したいのかによって用意すべきハードは違ってくるが、現在4Ｋ（長辺で4000ライン）レベルで4×5インチのポジフィルムに出力したデータ（1200万画素・RGBで36MB）は十分に実用的なので、このレベルのデータをストレス無くハンドリングできるシステム構成を考えてみよう。

- 1: 68040CPUを搭載したMacintoshII以降のコンピュータ
- 2: 漢字Talk7.1以降のオペレーティングシステム
- 3: 最低30MB以上のRAM
- 4: 24-bitまたは32-bitのアクセラレータ付きのビデオディスプレイカードと15インチ以上のカラーモニタ
- 5: 500MBから1GB以上のハイスピードハードディスク
- 6: 3.5インチもしくは5インチの光磁気ディスクドライブとメディア...........予算があれば
- 7: Adobe認定のフォトショップ2.5専用アクセラレータ
- 8: Macintosh対応のスキャナ（できるだけ高精度のもの）
- 9: ポストスクリプトプリンタもしくはカラープリンタ
- 10: 2台目のサブシステム（メインシステムと同等の構成）

　職業的にフォトショップを使うのであれば"10:"の2台目のサブシステムは重要で、導入時のイニシャルコストに含んでおくべきだ。一人でオペレーティングする場合でも作業効率が大幅にアップするし故障時には有難さを痛感するはずだ。マーフィーの法則ではないがアクシデントはおきてほしくないときに限って起きるものだから。

　Adobe認定のフォトショップ専用アクセラレータも作業効率アップに効果的だ。ラディウス社のPhotoBoosterをQuadra900に装着した実測値は

- ●リサイズ：30MBファイル200%拡大3分（未使用で9分）
- ●回転：30MBファイル199.5°時計回り3分20秒（未使用で7分）
- ●平行四辺形：30MBファイル28.5°右に1分8秒（未使用で2分13秒）
- ●USM：30MBファイル100%2.pix 2分25秒（未使用で7分25秒）
- ●ぼかし（ガウス）：30MBファイル10pix 1分43秒（未使用で7分）
- ●モード変更：30MBファイルRGBからCMYKへ3分20秒（未使用で5分45秒）といったところで、ほぼ2～3倍程度のスピードアップが可能だ。対応するコマンドはモードメニューのRGBからLab、RGBからCMYK、イメージメニューの角度入力回転、マウスで回転、拡大・縮小、平行四辺形、台形、画像解像度、フィルタメニューのぼかし、ぼかし（強）、ぼかし（ガウス）、ぼかし（移動）、輪郭以外をぼかす、シャープ、シャープ（輪郭のみ）、シャープ（強）、アンシャープマスク、エンボス、輪郭検出、カスタム、ハイパス、選択範囲メニューの境界をぼかす、以上22コマンド。

I'm sure there are many readers who are wondering just what sort of system is required to handle high resolution digital image processing. Here are some parameters:

* A Macintosh II or newer model with a 68030 or 68040 CPU.
* System 7.1 or a newer operating system.
* From 5MB to 8MB (or more) of application RAM.
* A color monitor with a 24-bit or 32-bit video display card.
* A Macintosh-compatible scanner.
* A postscript printer.
* Acceleration products bearing the *Adobe charged* logo.

Above is the system recommended by Adobe. Depending upon what kind of data you wish to process in what length of time, the required hardware will differ. Let's assume a fairly practical job: a 4K (4,000 line) level file of a 4x5 inch color transparency (12 million colors, RGB 36MB). What would it take to handle and output this without stress?

1. A Mac II or newer model with a 68040 CPU.
2. Operating system 7.1 or newer.
3. No less than 30MB of application RAM.
4. A 24 or 32-bit video display card with accelerator and a 15-inch or larger color monitor.
5. A 500MB to 1GB high speed hard drive.
6. A 3.5 or 5-inch magneto-optical disk drive and media
....if you can afford it.
7. Acceleration products bearing the *Adobe charged* logo
8. A Macintosh-compatible scanner. (As high-resolution as possible)
9. A postscript or color printer.
10. A sub-system of the same configuration as your main system.

If you are going to use Photoshop for work applications the second system is very important, and should be included in you initial budget. Not only does it make work more efficient with two systems, but it will save you from misery if your main breaks down. It's not Murphy's Law, but it always seems like accidents strike when you most fear them.

The special Adobe-licensed accelerator for Photoshop will also improve your efficiency. Below are some measurements with a Radius PhotoBooster equipped Quadra 900.

Resize: a 30MB file enlarged by 200% in 3 min. (Ordinarily 9 min.)
Rotate: 30MB file 199.5 degrees CW3 min./20 sec. (Normally 7 min.)
Skew: 30MB file 28.5 degrees right 1 min./8 sec. (Normally 2 min. 13 sec.)
USM: 30MB file 100% 2 pix 2 min./25 sec. (Normally 7 min./25sec.)
Gaussian Blur: 30MB file 10 pix 1 min./43 sec. (Normally 7 min.)
Mode change: 30MB file **RGB** to **CMYK** 3 min./20 sec. (Normally 5 min./45 sec.)

　As you can see, the accelerator improves time by 2 to 3 fold. Commands handled include, under the **Mode** menu, **RGB** to **Lab** and **RGB** to **CMYK**; under the **Image** menu **Arbitrary Rotate**, **Free Rotate**, **Scale**, **Skew**, **Perspective** and **Image Size**; under the **Filter** menu **Bluer**, **Blur More**, **Gaussian Blur**, **Motion Blur**, **Despeckle**, **Sharpen**, **Sharpen Edges**, **Sharpen More**, **Unsharp Mask**, **Emboss**, **Find Edges**, **Custom** and **High Pass**; and, from the **Select** menu **Feather**. All of the above 22 commands are covered.

メモリについて

About Memory

予算との兼合いだがアプリケーション用のメモリをどれだけ搭載できるかは、作業効率に圧倒的な影響を与える。

作業するデータが36MBだとすれば最低限その3倍の108MB、できればその5倍量の180MB用意すれば、通常の作業はほとんどメモリの範囲内で行われるので快適だ。もちろん漢字Talk7でメモリの32ビットアドレスをオンに設定しておくのが前提だが。

右図はQuadra950で比較的価格のこなれた背の高いコンポジットタイプの16MB SIMMを12個、4MBのSIMMを4個搭載した経済的な大容量メモリ構成例である。

システム7はアプリケーションメモリの割り当てが100MB以下に制限されている。ファインダー上でファイルメニューから**情報を見る**コマンドでメモリ必要条件の使用サイズを99,999KB以上にすることはできない。

シェアウエアソフトのAppSizer (Peirce Software 719 Hibiscus Pl., suite 301 San Jose, California 95117 U.S.A／Nifty-Serve MACLIFEフォーラムにアップロードされている)をインストールしておくと制限を超えて設定することが可能になる。下図がその設定画面である。

フォトショップのメモリ推奨サイズは5,120KBだが最低でも6MB以上割り当てておきたい。36MBのファイルを開くのにかかる時間は割り当てメモリが5,120KBで3分、6MBで1分35秒、36MBで1分20秒、42MBで1分16秒、108MBで36秒である（Quadra900での実測値）。

必要十分な容量以下なら6MBでも42MBでも大差無いことがわかりであろう。逆に5,120KBと6MBの大きな差にも気がつかれたと思う。ちなみに最小サイズの3,072KBではこの大きさのファイルを開くことは不可能だ。

フォトショップのパフォーマンスを上げるためには、コントロールパネルのメモリを開いてディスクキャッシュ容量を最低単位の32KBに設定しておくことと、システムの仮想メモリを切にしておくことが重要だ。パフォーマンスが上がるだけではなく無用なトラブルの防止にもなる。また、こまめに**保存**してメモリを開放すること、クリップボードにいつまでも大きなファイルをため込んでおかないこと（小さな選択範囲をコピーしなおす）、作業の切れ目ごとにフォトショップを終了、立ち上げなおしてフォトショップの仮想記憶ディスクを開放するのも効果的だ。システムエラーの起きる確率が格段に減るので習慣にすると良い。すくなくとも朝立ち上げたフォトショップを夕方まで連続で酷使するような使い方は、最後に保存できずに泣くことになるので避けたほうが良い。

作業領域のみを切取り小さなファイルにして**別名で保存**、加工処理後元のファイルを開いてペーストするのもスピードアップに効果がある。チャンネルごとに加工するのもよいし、カラーコレクションなどはリサイズした小さなファイルで確認後、設定を保存しておいて実画像にそのカスタムデータを呼び出して実行すれば極めて効率的な作業を行うことができる。

Of course it depends upon your budget, but the amount of application-usable memory on your computer has an overwhelming effect on performance. If you are working with a file of 36MB you'll need three times the memory, 108 MB, to handle it, and preferably five times the amount, or 180ME. Then you should have no problems handling any job you care to attempt. Of course you'll have to have your System 7 32-bit addressing turned "On".

Shown above is a Quadra 950 loaded with 12 high profile 16MB SIMMs and four 4MB SIMMs; a large volume, economical memory configuration.

Normally, System 7 won't allow more than 100MB of application memory. On the Finder's File Menu Get Information Command you'll see that memory can only be set up to 99,999 KB.

If you install AppSizer shareware (Pierce Software, 719 Hibiscus Pl., Suite 301, San Jose, Ca. 95117 U.S.A.) you can set your memory above this level. Shown below/left is the AppSizer menu.

Photoshop's suggested meory size is 5,120KB, but you ought to give it at least 6MB. To open a 36MB file takes 3 minutes with 5,120KB, 1 min./35 sec. with 6MB, 1 min./20 sec. with 36MB, 1 min./16 sec. with 42MB, and 36 sec. with 108MB. (Figured on a Quadra 900.)

As you can see, the difference is not so vast between speeds with 6MB and 42MB, but the difference is quite noticable between 5120KB and 6MB. Note that a 36MB file cannot be opened with 3,072KB, the manufacturer s minimum suggested size.

To improve Photoshop's performance, it is important to open the Control Panel memory and set Cache Size to the minimum, 32KB, and to turn the system's Virtual Memory "Off". Not only will performance be improved, but troubles will be avoided. It's also good to Save frequently, in order to open up memory,to keep your clipboard small, to shut down Photoshop after finishing each job, and to restart, to open up Photoshop's virtual memory. Doing this will decrease by orders the number of system errors you experience; make it a habit. Running Photoshop from morning to night, without rest, will only result in waste and tears.

If is also faster to cut out the area you need to work on, save it as a separate file, do your work, and then repaste it to the main image. It's also fine to work on separate channels, and extremely effective to use small files from Color Collection and the like to resize and make custom settings for use in images you are currently working on.

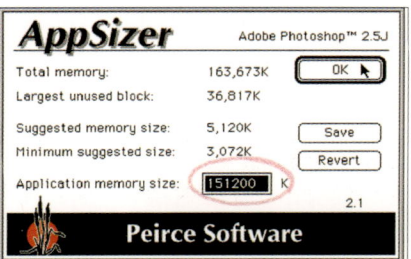

データの記録媒体について

Data Recording Media

フォトショップを使う場合のハードディスクは2つの役割を担うことになる。1つはデータを記録保存する本来の役割であり、もう1つはアプリケーションメモリの不足分を補うための仮想記憶としての役割である。

この2つを完全に分離して考えないとトラブルの元となる。常に高解像度のデータを扱うのであれば仮想記憶を担当する仮想記憶ディスクはスピード優先の高速ハードディスクを専用に用意すべきだ。

毎回作業に入る前に中身が空であることを確認して（ときどきイニシャライズすると良い）使用する。中に1つでもファイルがあるとフラグメンテーションをおこしていて、必要な連続空き容量を確保できない場合がある。

予算があればシリコンディスクを使うのがベストだ。通常扱うデータの3倍から5倍の容量が必要とされているので、4Kレベルのデータ（4096×3072ピクセル36MB）であれば180MBあれば良いことになる。

8Kレベルのデータ（8192×6144ピクセル144MB）を扱うのであれば720MBの仮想記憶ディスクが必要になる。

専用のSCSI IIボードを利用するTwinDiskArrayシステムは原理的には倍速になりそうな気がするが、実際のところは30%ほどスピードアップするだけだ。Quadraの内部SCSIを使う内蔵タイプのTwinDiskArrayシステムは単独で使う場合には良いのだが、外部SCSIにMOやスキャナなどをつなぐと途端に動作が不安定になるので避けたほうが賢明だ。フォトショップの仮想記憶ディスクとして使うハードディスクはアクセスが激しいので、消耗品と考えて高価な製品ではなく、なるべく安くて高速で単純なハードディスクの購入をお薦めする。

システムとプログラムソフトは専用に100～200MB前後の信頼性を優先したハードディスクを別途準備したほうがよい。

データの記録保存用には1GB程度のハードディスクと3.5インチのMOの2本立てが良いのではないだろうか。作るデータの内容によって違ってはくるが、4Kレベルの写真画像の合成作業でもあっという間にデータは増えていって300MB～400MBくらいにはなる。同時に2～3点の作業を進めることを考えると1GBは必要だ。

入出力センターへのデータの受け渡しには現在最も互換性のある3.5インチMOが最適だ（8Kレベルのデータは倍密度の3.5インチか5インチのMOが必要になる）。メディアの価格も年々こなれてきているので遠からずフロッピー並みの気軽さで使えるようになるはずだ。保存したデータの安全性はフロッピーの比ではない。2年間使ってきて社内データの損傷事故は1度もない。社外データで読めなかったり、データが壊れていたりという事故はあったが、最近持ち込まれるデータで読めないケースはほとんどなくなっている。各社のドライバの互換性がほぼ取れたという事だろう。

JPEGの最高画質で圧縮して4Kレベルの写真画像が10点前後保存できるので、テープバックアップに比べて簡便だという事も含めて保存用にも最適なのではないだろうか。

JPEG圧縮は最高画質で圧縮するとデータによって圧縮率に差が出るが3分の1から5分の1の容量になる。解凍した画像は元データと比較してもまず差はわからない。完全なロスレスではないがロスレスに準ずるものとして、製作終了後の保存用には便利に使える。専用のアクセラレータボードを使えば圧縮解凍のストレスは感じないですむ。

Hard disks play two roles when using Photoshop. One is their normal duty of saving data. The other is to supplement application memory when your computer doesn't have enough on-board memory. This is called Virtual Memory.

If these two roles aren't thought of quite separately problems will result. Normally, if you are using high resolution data, you should use a high-speed hard disk as the Scratch Disk for Photoshop's Virtual Memory. Before starting work, make sure that this disk is empty (even go so far as to initialize it occasionally). If just one file is contained in it, fragmentation will occur, and you might not have the space required to handle your work.

If you have the budget a silicon disk is the best. You will be handling three to five times the normal amount of data, so if you are working at the 4K level (4096x3072 pixels, 36MB) 180MB is probably the best. If you're handling 8K level data (8192x6144 pixels, 144MB) you'll need a 720MB scratch disk.

Theoretically, a twin disk array run off the SCSII port will give you double the speed, but in reality performance is only about 30% faster. It might seem advantageous to employ the Quadra's internal type twin disk array, but then you can run into instabilities with your external SCSI hook-ups, such as MO drive and scanner. It's wiser to avoid that. Because your scratch disk will be run very hard it's probably best to think of it as something you'll eventually replace; get a single drive that's as fast and cheap as possible. That's the best advice.

For your system and programs, purchase a 100-200MB drive that you can really trust, and use it for no other purpose.

Both a 1GB hard disk (or thereabouts) and a separate MO drive are advisable for storage of your data. In no time a 4K level composite photo image can grow to 300MB-400MB. Now consider working with three such composites over the same period of time; already you've hit 1GB.

As for input centers, currently the most popular form of passing data is on 3.5-inch MO disks. (For 8K level images, you'll need to use double density 3.5 or 5-inch MO disks.) Media prices are common down, and it probably won't be long before MO disks are being tossed around just like floppies. Anyway, saving to MO disks is incomparably safer than saving to floppies. In two years of office work we've not had a single accident. There have been instances of unreadable or disrupted data arriving from outside, but recently we've seen almost nothing we couldn't read. Most of the drivers are now pretty compatible.

About ten files compressed to the 4K level from high resolution JPEG images can be contained, and back-up is easier than with tapes, so they are also ideal for archiving.

High resolution JPEG images lose a bit of quality in compression, depending on the data, but can be shrunk from 1/3 to 1/5 their original size. Upon returning them to their original size its nearly impossible to see the difference. If you don't mind the slightly lower resolution its a good way to save images, and with an accelerator, the task of unfreezing is pretty painless.

出力について

About Output

入力の前に出力の解説を持ってきたのには意味がある。写真画像の取り込みに際しては、最終画像データの出力形態と出力機が決まっていないと、精度の高いスキャニングはできないからだ。

何に使うのか、何で出力するのか決めずに漠然と画像データを作っている人も多いと思われるが、アナログデータと違ってデジタルデータは作ってしまった後でサイズや出力形態を変更することは困難か結果が思わしくないことが多い（特に低品位のデータを高品位に出力することは不可能だ）。

きれいな画像データを出力するためには、最初に出力形態、出力機、画像サイズ、モードを決めること。

出力形態が4×5インチのポジフィルムであれば出力機は専用のフィルムレコーダーでRGBモード、サイズは4K,8K,12K,16Kなどであり、最低の4Kモードで出力する場合、スキャニングは4096×3072ピクセルのRGBデータとして取り込まねばならない。

4Kレベルのデータをフォトショップでリサイズして8Kレベルで出力してもあまり意味がない。出力センターが喜ぶだけだ。8Kで出力するのであれば8Kでスキャニングしなければならない。フォトショップが扱うビットマップのデジタルデータとはそういう性質のものだ。

出力機は出力センターによって使っている機種が異なる。4×5出力用にはSolitaire 8xpかImapro QCR-zi/Premiumを使って4K,8Kモードで出力サービスを行っているところが多い。どちらの機種も超高精度のモノクロCRTを使ってカメラとフィルターを通してスポット光をフィルムに露光する仕組みで、使い勝手は別にして出力結果に大差はない。

それより1ランク高精度な出力を行っている所はKodak社のLVTやMacdonald Dettwiler社のFire1000、大日本スクリーン製造のCLP-300等フィルムに直接レーザー光やレンズで収束した光を使って描き込む方式で500dpiから最高3000dpi前後の出力に対応している。使用フィルムは8×10以上のサイズで4×5インチの出力でも価格は安くない。

最近コダック系のプロラボがプレミアイメージエンハンストメントシステムを使った入出力サービスを始めている。出力は1000dpiなので4×5インチで4000×5000ピクセル（実効画面サイズで約3760×4750ピクセル）のサイズに対応している。価格は精度のわりに安い。カラーフィルムの取り扱いに慣れたプロラボが行っているサービスなので、既存の入出力センターの出力結果にあきたらない読者は、試してみる価値があるのではないだろうか。

カラープリント出力についてはIRIS SmartJet、Victor Trueprint、Fujix Pictrography、Kodak XLS8300、3M Rainbow等A4〜A3サイズで300dpi前後の解像度、RGBモードのものが多い。反射原稿として十分入稿可能なレベルにあるので利用価値は高い。300dpi A4サイズで実効画面サイズはおよそ2200×3200ピクセル 20MB程度になる。

印刷に関して今回は詳しく取り上げられないが、日本では150線ないしは175線で印刷されることが多いので、印刷用のデータは線数の2倍300〜350ppiでCMYKモードでスキャニングすること、出力には4色分解出力に経験の深い出力センターを使う。製版・印刷会社系の出力センターを選べるのならそれにこしたことはない。データ作成時に必要な注意事項さえ守れば、いまやMacintoshから4色分解出力、印刷することはなんら特別なことではない状態になっている。

There is a reason for discussing output before input. You can't do precision scanning for high resolution output without first determining the kind of output format and equipment you will be using.

There are probably many people out there who are creating data with no clear idea what they will be using it on, or what they will be outputting it on. But unlike analog work, altering size and output format on a finished digital image in order to match to output equipment often leads to unexpected and undesired results. (It is virtually impossible to output low resolution images on high resolution equipment and get good results, for instance.)

In order to output beautiful image data, first you must determine output format, then equipment, then image size and mode.

If your output format is 4x5 inch positive film your output equipment will be a special film recorder and output will be in RGB mode, with size options of 4K, 8K, 12K, and 16K. When outputting in the lowest 4K mode, scanning must be done at 4096x3072 pixels with RGB data.

It is meaningless to take 4K level data and resize it in Photoshop to output at the 8K level. Only the output center will appreciate your work. If you want to output at 8K level then you must scan at the 8K level. That's what Photoshop's digital bitmapping is all about.

Output centers use various makes of equipment. Many services offer either Solitaire 8xp or Imapro QCR-zi/Premium for outputting in 4 and 8K mode. Both use and ultrahigh -precision monochrome CRT and a spot beam to expose film, and achieve similar results, depending on the operator.

A step better than these are the Kodak LVT and MacDonald Dettwiler Fire 1000, and Dai Nippon Screen's CLP-300, all of which use direct lasers and lenses to bundle light and write at 500dpi to 3000dpi. The minimum film size is 8x10, and even at 4x5 output, they're not cheap to use.

Recently, Kodak-family pro labs have begun to offer premium image enhancement system output services. Output is 1000dpi, which in 4x5 positive means 4000x5000 pixels (in actual image size 3760x4750 pixels). Price is based on precision. The labs are naturally staffed by film professionals, so those who have tired of other output centers might find some value in them.

For color print output there are the IRIS SmartJet, Victor Trueprint, Fujix Pictography, Kodak KLS8300 and 3M Rainbow, all of which print out at around 300dpi, and mostly in RGB. Since output of this resolution can pass as film paste-ups its cost is high. An actual image for a 300dpi A4 size print will be about 2200x3200 pixels and 20MB.

Also on the subject of printing, but somewhat beyond the scope of this discussion, it is the case in Japan that printing is more often done at 175 lines than 150. For printing data the number is doubled, from 300 to 350ppi. If scanning is done in CMYK, then a very experienced output center must be used, such as a printing or color separation company's outlet. However, if the necessary parameters are followed, there is no reason why these services could not output four color separations from your Macintosh data.

スキャニングで画像の品位が決まる

前段で出力の形態が決まらなければ精度の高いスキャニングはできないと述べた。逆に言えばスキャニングした時点でそのデジタルデータの性格、品質は決まってしまう。生まれながらにして品位の低いデジタルデータは後からフォトショップでいくら加工してもその品位を高めることはできないのだ。

品位の低さを特徴にした作品づくりをするのではないかぎり、スキャニングは必要十分な条件で行うようにしたいものだ。

画像の品位はスキャナの絶対性能（ハードソフト両面）とオペレーション能力で決まる。いかにオペレーターの能力が優れていても、レベルの低い機械でスキャニングしたものはそれなりの物でしかない。プレゼンテーション用であれば普及機で十分だが、印刷用にと考えるなら予算の許す範囲で最大限良いものを導入すること。半端なものをいれるくらいなら普及機にしておいて、印刷用のスキャニングは入出力センターに依頼する方が良い。

次ページ以降に筆者の経験の範囲で良いと思われるデスクトップスキャナ及び入力機器を紹介しておく（35mm専用機、製版専用機は使用経験がないので言及しない）。

きれいなスキャニングのための原則

● きれいなデータをスキャニングする（特にフィルムの粒状性）。
● 最終出力サイズでスキャニングする（後でリサイズしない）。
● 印刷用には使用線数の2倍の解像度でスキャニングする。
● 最終出力モードでスキャニングする（印刷用にはCMYKで）。
● 出力機のガンマにマッチしたガンマでスキャニングをする。
● 適切なダイナミックレンジを選択する。
● 適切なシャープネスを選択する（ポジ出力用には弱めにかける）。
● 適切なカラーバランスを設定する。
● ゴミ汚れ指紋等をきれいに清掃してスキャニングする。

通常、ビットマップ（ラスタデータ）のポジ出力やプリント出力の場合はその出力機の解像度と出力可能な最大サイズ（ピクセル数）が分かれば良い。ガンマ設定のできるスキャナの場合、ポジ出力機に対応するモニタのガンマは2.2なので入力のガンマは0.45に、プリント出力機に対応するモニタのガンマは1.8なので入力のガンマは0.56にする（Imaproの推奨値、同社の専用スキャナドライバーは精度の高いよく練られたものだ）。最大出力可能サイズの範囲内で出力したい実寸を割り出しスキャニングする。

出力結果を印刷用に使うのでなければ出力機の解像度の50%程度の解像度で作成しても見た目には問題ない。ほとんどのプリンタはフォトショップの画像解像度コマンドで解像度とサイズを設定しておけば、プリンタの出力解像度と関係なく指定した寸法で出力される。

ポジフィルム出力用のフィルムレコーダーはデータの設定解像度に無関係で画像データの絶対値である縦横の画素数（ピクセル数）と選択した出力機の出力モード（4Kモード、8Kモード等）で画像の出力寸法が決まる。

印刷用のデータは特別な理由がない限りCMYKでスキャニングしてCMYKで加工処理する。画像解像度は分解フィルム出力線数の倍を基準として決定する。150線であれば300ppi、175線であれば350ppiで良い。写真など自然画の場合は150線で200ppiにしたからといって急激に画質が落ちるというわけではない。

We just stated that you cannot achieve high precision scanning without first determining your output equipment. Said conversely, you decide the character and quality of your digital data at the moment you scan it. A lowborn digital image cannot be born again no matter what you do with it in Photoshop.

Unless you are out to make a body of work from low resolution images there are a number of factors you must consider when scanning.

Image quality is going to be determined by the operating ability and performance capabilities of your hardware and software. No matter how good the operator is, he won't be able to do magic with low level equipment. For presentations there is plenty of adequate equipment, but when it comes to printing purposes, the best affordable equipment is required. Rather than go half way, one should make do with a low end scanner for office purposes, and have final, high-resolution products scanned at a service. On the following pages the author introduces the desktop scanning and input equipment that he has had experience with. (35mm equipment and film separation machines are not mentioned, as he has not used them.)

Rules for Clean Scanning
* Scan clean data. (Especially film grain)
* Scan at the same size as final output.
* Scan at a resolution double the number of lines when scanning for film.
* Scan in the same mode as final output.
* Scan at a gamma matching the output equipment gamma.
* Choose the ideal dynamic range.
* Select the ideal sharpness (Weaken it when scanning for posi film.)
* Clean the scanner of all fingerprints and dirt before working.

In most print and posi film output situations for bitmap (rasterdata) output it is enough to know the highest resolution and output size (pixels) of the equipment. In cases where the gamma setting can be adjusted, where the monitor gamma is 2.2 for posi output, the input gamma is 0.45, and where the monitor gamma for print output is 1.8, the input is 0.56. (Here the recommendations are for Imapro's high resolution driver.) If the output size is within the limits of the maximum output size, scan at the same proportionate size on the scanner.

If the output is not for printing, in most cases you can scan at 50% resolution and not notice the difference in output. Most printers will output at the correct dimensions regardless of what resolution the printer is set to if you set the image resolution and size with Photoshop's Image Resolution command.

Image sizes for posi film output will be decided regardless of the data resolution settings on film recorders, based instead on absolute vertical and horizontal data (pixel) settings and the selected mode (4K mode, 8K mode, etc.) of the output equipment.

Unless there is a special reason to do otherwise, data for printing should be scanned and handled in CMYK. Image resolution is set at double that of film separations; if 150 lines, then 300ppi, if 175 lines, then 350ppi. But photos and scenic paintings which are set at 200ppi for 150 lines should not appear dramatically worse, either.

Scanning Decides Your Image Quality

スクリーン線数と出力解像度

印刷などハーフトーンスクリーンを使う出力についてはポジフィルム出力ほど単純ではない。

画像を形成する解像度の単位がpixels per inch＝ppiで、スクリーン線数の単位がlines per inch＝lpi、出力解像度がdots per inch＝dpiで、この３つの解像度が相互に関連している。ppiとdpiは単位としては同じなので混同して使っているケースが多い。どちらの単位として述べているのか判断する必要がある。

ポストスクリプトプリンタやイメージセッターでの出力は、出力機の解像度とスクリーン線数によって出力できる階調数が左右される。

（出力解像度÷スクリーン線数）^{2}＋1＝出力階調数

フォトショップの最大出力階調数が8bit 256階調なので256階調表現できる出力機の解像度は、使用するスクリーン線数の約16倍必要という事になる。150線であれば150×16＝2400dpiだが、この2400dpiはハーフトーンスクリーンを使って256階調表現するのに必要な出力機の解像度dpiであって画像の解像度ppiではない。150線で出力するのに必要な画像解像度は150×2＝300ppiだ。この関係は面倒だがしっかり理解して頭の中に入れておいてほしい。

製版業界ではRes（レゾ）12とかRes14といった解像度表現をすることが多い。この単位は1mm当たり何ラインかということで、Res12は12×25mm＝300dpi、Res14は14×25mm＝350dpiに相当する。

現在発売されている高精度デスクトップ型スキャナは大きく分けて受光素子にフォトマル（光電管）を使用したドラムスキャナとCCDを使用したフラットベッドスキャナがある。サイテックス社のLeafScan 45等は形態からはフラットベッドと言いにくいが。

受光素子の性能と構造上、現在のところドラムスキャナのほうがハード的に取り込み画像の品位は優れている。ただコンピュータ用品はハードだけでは性能が決められないので、ソフトの良くできたCCDスキャナの総合性能はドラム型をしのぐ場合もありうる。

イマプロのQCS-3200は実効解像度が1600dpiで4.88"×17"のスキャニングができ、縦方向は実効、横方向のみインターポレーションによる半疑似モードでは3200dpiで同寸法をスキャニングできる。600dpiモードでは12"×17"（A3サイズ）の反射・透過読み取りが可能だ。

サイテックス社のSmart340に肩を並べる性能といって良いが、価格ははるかに安い。Smart340のスペックは読み取り範囲、反射12"×17"、透過10"×17"、拡大率20〜250%（最大8000画素3CCDアレイ）。

同じサイテックス社のCCDスキャナLeafScan 45は次ページに解説してある。製品写真は4×5ポジを同製品でスキャニングしたものだ。

ドラムスキャナは大日本スクリーン製造のDTS-1015AIが最も普及している。解説は次ページにしてあるが、製品写真とこの本のほとんどの作例データはDTS-1015AIでスキャニングしたものだ。上位バージョンDTS-1030AIが発売されてDTPドラムスキャナの定番になりそうだ。

イマプロでもScanmaster D4000を発売している。10"×10"の反射・透過原稿の読み取りを4000dpi各色12bitでスキャニングできる。原稿を張込む時、水平垂直を出すのに便利な専用のドラム置き台が附属する。

OptronicsのColorGetterも新しくⅡシリーズになってCMYKの直接入力に対応した。35mmから11"×15"までの反射・透過原稿を最高4064dpi各色12bitでスキャニングすることができる。重量は100kg近くあってデスクトップタイプとは言いにくいが。

Screen resolution & output resolution

It is not as simple to discuss halftone screens and other output devices as posifilm output.

The unit by which Image resolution is measured is ppi = pixels per inch, while the screen resolution are measured as lpi = lines per inch , and the output resolution as dpi = dots per inch. All these measurements are mutually related. And though dpi and ppi units are the same, and are of used interchangably, it is necessary to use the correct term in each given situation.

It makes a difference in postscript printing and at the imagesetter, where output devices's resolution and screen resolution need to be adjusted for tonal range.

(Output resolution ÷ screen resolution)^2 +1 = output tonal range

Photoshop's maximum scale adjustment for output is 8bit 256 scale, so the resolution of 256 scale output equipment will be about 16 times the number of screen resolution. If there are 150 lines that's 150 x 16 = 2400dpi, but this 2400dpi is the necessary resolution for a halftone screen to output 256 scale images, not the resolution of the image itself. For output at 150 lines the necessary image resolution is 150 x 2 = 300ppi. This relationship is difficult but must be understood.

Resolution is often expressed in the prepress as 12 or 14 Res. This refers to the number of lines in 1mm. Res12 is 12x25mm=300dpi, Res14 is14 x 25mm = 350dpi.

Generally speaking, the desktop scanners currently on the market can be divided into drum scanners, which use photon receivers and photomultipliers, and flatbed scanners, which utilize CCD. Flatbed scanners, such as the LeafScan 45, by Scitex, are called so because of their shape.

Because of their construction and photomechanism, drum scanners now produce the better quality images, at least from the hardware standpoint. But computers are not all hardware, and overall performance has much to do with software, too. There are now flatbed systems which compete in overall performance with drum scanners.

Imapro's QCS-3200 produces real 1600dpi resolution in 4.99" x 17" scanning, or 3200dpi in real vertical with in half-suspected mode horizontal interpolation. 600dpi mode scanning is also possible at 12" x 17" (A3 size), good enough for large-size photostats and transparencies.

The Scitex Smart340 offers the same capabilities, but at a much lower price. Specs include reading size of 12"x17" reflective, 10"x17" transparency, with enlargement from 20-200% (Max. 8000pixels 3CCD allay.)

Scitex also offers the LeafScan45, which is introduced on the next page. The picture of the product was scanned with the same machine.

Among drum scanners, the most popular is Dainippon Screen's DTS-1015AI. The specs are given on the next page. Most of the shots in this book were scanned with a DTS-1015AI.

The new 1030AI looks to become the next industry standard.

Imapro Corp. also markets the Howtex Scanmaster D4000, which scans 10"x10" in either prints or transparencies at 4000dpi and 12bits per channel. It also has a convenient attachable drum for horizontal film loading.

The new Optronics ColorGetter II series now offers CMYK. It handles 35mm to 11"x15" in prints or transparencies at a max. 4064dpi at 12bits per channel. But because it weighs close to 100kg it can't really be called a DTP model.

製版専用機の機能を使いやすく凝縮.....DTS-1015AI&1030AI

The DTS-1015AI and 1030AI : Film Separation Capabilities for the Desktop

製版用機器の日本におけるトップメーカー大日本スクリーン製造(株)がDTP用に専用機の機能を凝縮して使い易くまとめあげたのがテーブルトップタイプのドラムスキャナGenascan DTS-1015AIだ。入射原稿、反射原稿とも読み取り可能。読み取り最大サイズW：145mm×H：150mmなので4×5インチ以下専用機と考えれば良い。最大解像度は2500dpiで35mmフィルムの読み取りにはちょっと不満が残る。最新バージョンのフォトショップ用プラグインドライバはCMYKカラー，RGBカラー，グレースケールモードとも完全に対応しUSMの使い方も明快になって使い易くなった。オプションでネガフィルムへのAI対応も可能だ。

DTS-1015AIの上位バージョンがA4サイズまで対応してドラムが着脱可能になったGenascan DTS-1030AIだ。最大解像度は5200dpiになり35mmフィルムの読み取りも十分な余裕を持って行なうことができる。

付属するAI機能はかなり高機能で通常の使用状態ではほとんどマニュアル設定をする場面はないだろう。これだけ高精度の物が手軽にデスクトップでビギナーでも使えるようになったのは素晴らしいことだ。ドラムスキャナというと専門的な高度な知識が必要でとても素人に気軽に扱えるものとは思えなかったが、認識を新たにしてくれた。

4×5サイズィルムからの読み取りでは1015も1030もスキャニング結果に大差はない。右図はDTS-1015AIに4×5ポジフィルムを装着したところである。

これで価格が手の届く範囲であれば言うことがないのだが..........

For print film separations the top equipment maker is Dainippon Screen Mfg. Co.,Ltd., who has managed to shrink its film separation technology into a tabletop drum scanner, the Genascan DTS-1015AI. It reads both prints and tranparencies at max. size of W:145mm,H:150mm, so its handles sizes under 4x5inch. Max. resolution is 2500dpi for 35mm film, which is a little low for full satisfaction, but it handles CMYK, RGB and Gray in Photoshop Ver. 2.5, and has a full, easy-to-use USM. An option is AI for negative film.

The next version of the DTS-1030AI will read up to A4 size, and have a detachable drum. Max. resolution will be 5200dpi, which is plenty for 35mm film.

The AI function is pretty high, making it almost unnecessary to refer to the manual. That beginners should now be able to utilize such high-tech equipment on the desktop is really wonderful. Drum scanning is normally thought of as an art for experts only, but the reality appears to be changing fast.

In 4x5 inch scanning there is little difference in quality between the 1015 and the 1030. Below is the DTS-1015AI with posi-film attahed.

If this system were only within everyone's budget there would be nothing more to say....

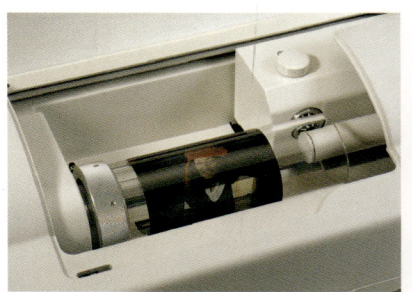

ビギナーにも使いやすいLeafScan45

For Beginners the easy LeafScan45

サイテックス社のDTP用CCDポジフィルムスキャナがLeafScan45である。最大4×5インチサイズのフィルムをポジ、ネガとも読み取ることができる。読み取りモードはRGBカラーとグレースケールのみでCMYKカラーには対応していない。USM機能も持っていない。読み取りは各チャンネル当たり16bitで読み込んでいるので階調のなめらかさが素晴らしく美しい。フォトショップ2.5Jは16bitの取り込みに限定的ではあるが対応しているので、専用のプラグインソフトを使えば8bit変換をせずに各色65,536階調で取り込みが可能になる（1993年10月現在のプラグインドライバでは16bitを8bitに変換して取り込んでいる）。最大解像度は4×5インチで1200dpi、35mm横位置で2540dpi、35mm縦位置で5080dpi（縦位置用のネガキャリアはオプション）6×6、6×7、6×9は2540dpiである。プラグインドライバのインターフェースがわかりやすく、引伸機メーカー、ベセラー社製のしっかりしたネガキャリアとあいまって、ビギナーにも使いやすく仕上がっている。

Scitex's CDD posifilm scanner for DTP is the LeafScan45, which reads both positives and negatives up to 4x5 inches in RGB and Gray, but offers no CMYK mode or USM function. Reading is 16bit per channel, so gradation is smooth and quality beautiful. 16bit is the limit in Photoshop Ver. 2.5, but it handles the input, so if you use the plug-in you won't need to drop down to 8bit, and can achieve 65,536scale per channel. (As of Oct. 1993 16bit drivers were still being offered in the package.) Resolution is 1200dpi for 4x5, 2540dpi for horizontal 35mm, 5080dpi for 35mm vertical (a vertical negative carrier is optional), and 2540dpi for 6x6, 6x7 and 6x9.

The plug-in driver interface is easy to understand, and with the well-designed Bessler negative carrier, this is a convenient system for beginners.

実用期に入ったデジタルスチールカメラ........DCS200

Digital studio cameras make the scene

Kodak社のDCS200はNikon F801S 1眼レフカメラの裏蓋部分を改造して14×9.3mmのCCDセンサを装着した携帯性に富んだデジタルスチールカメラである。1524×1012ピクセル約160万画素の解像力で読み取り、ハードディスク内蔵モノクロ専用機のDCS200miとカラー専用機のDCS200ciに分かれ、それぞれにハードディスク外付けタイプも発売されている。ストロボ、デイライト、タングステンに対応しており感度はモノクロでISO100～400、カラーで50～200である。画像サイズはモノクロで1.5MB、カラーで4.5MBで、内臓80MBのハードディスクには52カットの画像が記録できる。別売で80MBの外付けハードディスクがある。28mm、F2.8 AFレンズが標準レンズとして付属している。

右図はオプションのColor Filter Wheel AccessoryをDCS200miに装着して3ショット高精度静止画像を撮影している風景である。下図がその操作画面で作例は口絵ページに掲載されているので参照されたい。DCS200ciで撮影したカラー画像よりワンランクアップしたカラー画像を得ることができる（動体撮影には使えないが）。DCS200はすでに相当台数が出版・報道関係に普及、活用されている。チラシのカット用に採用したところも現れている。

Kodak's DCS200 utilizes a Nikon N8008S single-lens body and a 14x9.3mm CCD sensor. This hybrid digital studio camera reads at 1524x1012 pixels for gradation of 1.6 million and comes in two models, either monochrome or color, both of which can be purchased as hard disk internal or external attached models. Strobe, daylight and tungsten photography are handled, with monochrome sensitivity ISO100-400, and color ISO50-200. Image size for monochrome is 1.5MB, for color 4.5MB. The 80MB internal hard disk comes with 50 cuts. A separate 80MB external drive is also for sale. Standard lens is a 28mm, F2.8 A-focus.

The picture above shows a DCS200mi with a Color Filter Wheel being used to take three high resolution still shots. At left is the screen showing the page frame where the shots will appear. With this system you an achieve one level better color image performance than with the DCS200ci. (But you can't use it for moving shots.) The DCS200 is already commonly used in news and publishing. It's especially suited to cuts for flyers, etc.

さらに高精細 Leaf Digital Studio Camera

サイテックス社のハイエンドデジタルスチールカメラがLeaf Digital Studio Cameraである。2048×2048ピクセルの解像力で読み取り、モードはRGBカラーとグレースケール。CMYKカラーには対応していない。読み取りは各チャンネル当たり14bit（16,384階調）で読み込んでいるので階調はなめらかで美しい。カメラ自体はモノクロなので、カラー写真の場合はレンズ前にRGB 3原色分解用のカラーフィルタを連動させ、1つの被写体に3回露光、1枚のカラー画像を得る仕組みである。

ストロボかデイライトに対応し感度はISO300相当、露光時間は125分の1から1秒までの範囲に対応している。CCDの有効エリアは30×30mmなのでかなり短いレンズが標準となる。

対応カメラはMamiya RZ67、Hasselblad 500EL、553ELXシリーズ、ビューカメラのSinar、Cambo。1枚のモノクロ画像は4MB、カラー画像は4MB×3チャンネルの12MBになる。

Kodak DCS200の3倍以上の価格だが、得られる画質は相応に高精度なものだ。カタログ類の撮影には十分実用になるレベルと言って良い。

1ショットでこの程度の画像取り込みができるカメラが、導入しやすい価格で出てくればかなり普及するのではないだろうか。

For even higher resolution the Leaf Digital Studio Camera

Scitex's high end digital camera is the Leaf Digital Studio Camera. Resolution is 2084x2084 pixels, and modes are RGB and Gray. There is no CMYK. The scanner reads 14bits per channel (16,384 gradations) for an extremely smooth, beautiful image. The camera itself is monochrome, so the lens must be set with color filters in RGB mode for consecutive takes; three exposures produce a single color shot.

Exposure equivalent to ISO300 handles daylight or strobe, with exposure time variable from 1/125 to one second. The CCD area is only 30mmx30mm, so the standard lens is pretty short.

Compatible cameras include the MamiyaRZ67, the Hasselblad500ELX, 553ELX series, and Sinar and Cambo view cameras. One monochrome image requires 4MB, color 4MB x three channels, for 12MB.

It's three times the price of the Kodak DCS200, but the high resolution enables you to do very fine images. Quality is certainly high enough for catalog photo work.

If a single shot camera with this level of precision comes out at a more affordable price it will probably win wide popularity.

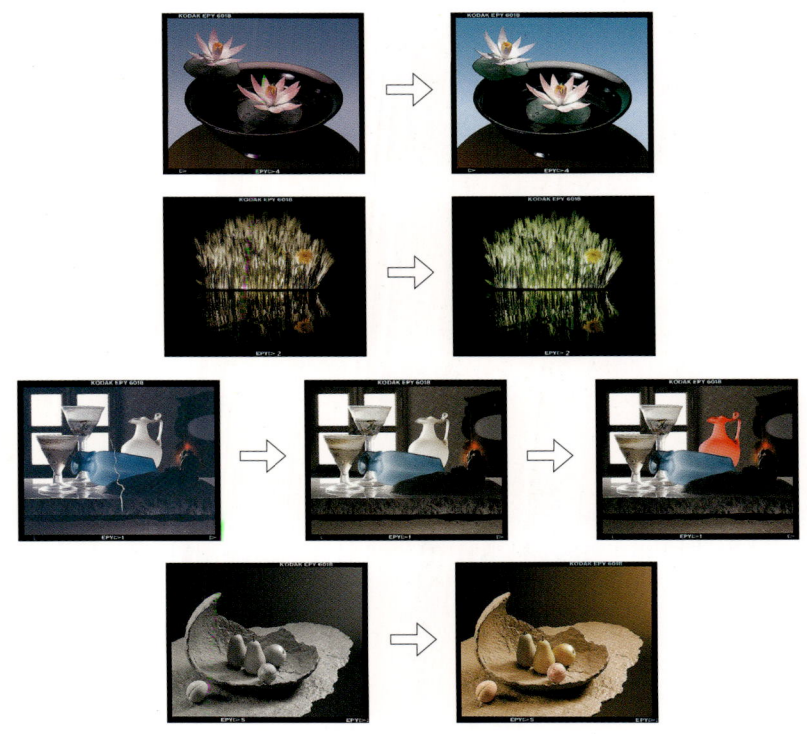

第2章　カラーコレクションテクニック

Chapter 2　Color Corrections Techniques

カラーコレクションテクニック

モニタキャリブレーションがすべての始まり！

　絵を描くときに用紙やキャンバスの地色に無関心な画家はいないはずだが、モニタの色には無関心なCGアーティストが多いのはなぜだろう。購入したままで何の調整もされていないモニタは色温度が7000〜9000K°でかなり青いかグリーンに偏っており、淡色はその影響を大きく受けて表示されている。人間の目はホワイトバランスを自動的に取るのでモニタだけを見ていれば、違和感はないが実際の色とはかけ離れた状態で、色評価をしていることになる。それが作成イメージと出力結果の相違の最大原因だ。もちろんRGBからCMYKへの変換プロセスや、各出力機の性能も重要な要素だが、我々製作現場の人間にとってはキャンバス代わりのモニタに見えている配色こそがすべてなのだから。

　フォトショップ添付の「ガンマ」コントロールパネルか同等のユーティリティを使ってきちんとキャリブレーションをとるのが最初の作業だ。マニュアルの第15章に詳しい作業手順が書かれているので参考になる。

モニタキャリブレーションの手順

1．モニタの置かれた環境を整備する(環境光のコントロール)。
2．モニタの明度、コントラストをハード側で調整固定する。
3．コントロールパネルから「ガンマ」を開く。
4．ホワイトポイントを調整する。
5．カラーバランスを調整する。
6．ブラックポイントを調整する。
7．キャリブレーションの設定を保存する。
8．環境設定のモニタを設定する。
9．環境設定のインキを設定する。
10．添付ディスクのイメージファイルを*開く*。前ページの印刷を参照して。
11．上記3〜9の手順をイメージファイルを対象にもう一度実行する。

Everything begins with monitor calibration!

There is probably no painter who would begin his work without considering the color of his paper and canvas, so why is it so many CG artists are unconcerned about the color of their monitor? At time of purchase the color adjustment is 7,000-9,000K, tending toward either blue or green. The influence on the display of pale colors is particularly strong.

The human eye automatically adjusts white balance, so when you see an image on the monitor the color will appear fine. But in reality, the difference will show. This is the largest factor contributing to a difference between created image and final output. Of course, the change from RGB to CMYK and output equipment performance also have an effect, but this doesn't change the fact that for those working in the production area, the coloring of the monitor is the key to everything.

The Gamma CDEV utility, which is included with Photoshop, allows you to calibrate your monitor. This is your first job. Refer to Chapter 15 of your manual for detailed instructions.

Monitor Calibration Procedure

1. Arranging the environment around the monitor. (Lighting control.)
2. Adjusting the brightness and contrast controls on the monitor.
3. Opening "*Gamma*" on the *control panel*.
4. Adjusting the *white point*.
5. Adjusting the color *balance*.
6. Adjusting the *black point*.
7. Saving the calibration settings.
8. Setting *Monitor set-up*.
9. Setting *Printing inks set-up*.
10. *Open* the Image File on the disk. Refer to the printing on the previous page.
11. Follow procedures 3 - 9 again on the Image File.

１．コントロールパネルからガンマを開く。ターゲットガンマを印刷を含めたプリント出力には1.8に、ビデオ出力やカラーポジ出力には2.2に設定してスライダで微調整する。

２．プリント用紙と同じような白い紙を用意、「白」のボタンをクリック、RGBの3つのスライダを動かして、モニタが同じ白を表現できるように調節する。

３．「カラー」のボタンをクリック、RGBの3つのスライダを動かして、グレーチャートの全階調がニュートラルグレーになるように調節する。

1. From the *Control Panel* Open *Gamma*. Inlcuding *Target Gamma*, set print output at 1.8, and video and color posi output at 2.2. *Adjust* with the slider.

2. Prepare paper which is the same color as your printer paper. Click the *White Pt.* button, then move the three RGB sliders, trying to achieve the same whiteness on your monitor.

3. Click the *Balance* button and move the three RGB sliders, adjusting the gray chart to achieve a neutral gray.

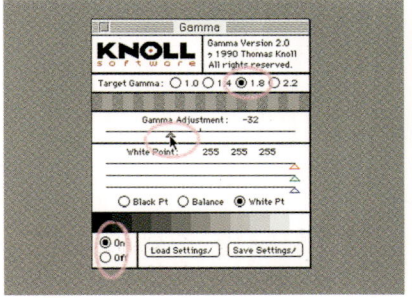
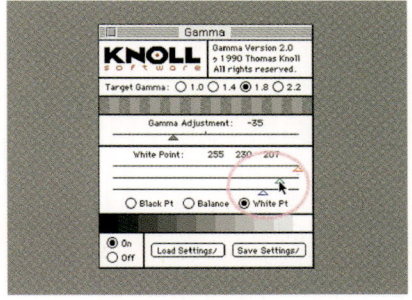
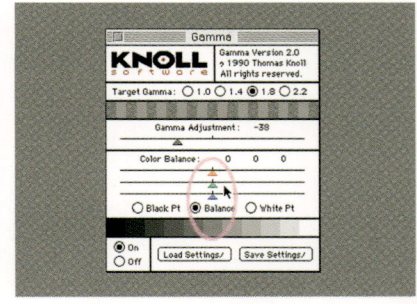

Color Correction Techniques

カラーコレクションについて

　添付ディスクのイメージファイルはガンマ1.8でほぼ下段のスナップショットのモニタ設定で製作されている。モニタキャリブレーションがきちんと取られれば、ほぼ23頁の印刷された画像に近い状態で見ることができる。

　画像のカラーコレクション（カラー補正・レタッチ）はモニタのキャリブレーションが取れていない限り正確に行うことは不可能だ。

　各社から各種各様のカラーマッチングシステムが普及し始めているが、現状はすべての機器に対応しているわけではないし、それなりのコストもかかるので、自分が使う出力機器に合わせてモニタのキャリブレーションを取りカスタムガンマ設定を保存、出力機に合せ切り替えて使用する作業は必要だ。

　フォトショップは豊富なカラーコレクション方法を備えている。バージョン2.5になって新登場の**バリエーション**コマンドはもっとも使いやすく今後のカラーコレクションの主流になっていくだろう。

　トーンカーブコマンドは慣れが必要だがもっとも細かく自由自在に補正することができる。写真撮影では補正不可能なハイライトマゼンタ・シャドウグリーンなどのカラー補正も可能だ。精密なカラーコレクションがしたいなら**トーンカーブ**コマンドのマスターが必須である。**レベル補正**コマンドはハイライトレベル、シャドウレベル、中間トーンの３点で全体と各色ごとの補正が、自動と手動の両方で調節できる。出力コントラストを下げることもできる。スキャニング画像の最初の調整には大変便利である。**色相・彩度**コマンドは色変換に力を発揮する。**トーンカーブ**コマンドとの組み合わせで、ほとんどどんな色にでも変換することができる。**明るさ・コントラスト**コマンドと**カラーバランス**コマンドはカラー補正にはなるべく使わないほうが良い。データが乱れて後の修整がしにくい。

About color corrections

Settings for the monitor in the Gamma 1.8 image file are shown below in snapshots. If you achieve correct monitor calibration, your image will appear about like the one shown on page 23.

Image color correction (Supplementing, Retouching) can only be done with accuracy if the monitor is correctly calibrated.

Every company in the field now puts out its own color matching system, but none of them yet works for all equipment. Therefore, you must do the calibration for your own equipment and save your customized Gamma settings, and adjust your output equipment to match.

Photoshop contains a rich repetoire of color correction methods. With Ver. 2.5 an easy-to-use **Variations** command has appeared. This will no doubt become one of the most popular color correction methods.

It takes time to master the **Curves** command, but it offers one of the most accurate and powerful methods of supplementing color. In photography, normally impossible corrections as highlight magenta and shadow green can be done. For fine color corrections, a mastery of **Curves** is essential.

With **Levels,** three settings - highlight level, shadows and middle tones - can be used to adjust the entire image or a particular color, either manually or automatically. Output contrast can also be reduced with **Levels**, and it is extremely convenient for making initial adjustments to scanned images. **Hue/Saturation** shows its strength when changing colors. Used with the **Curves** command, it allows the replacement of almost any color with another. One should never use the **Brightness/Contrast** or **Color Balance** commands for correcting colors, as they will disrupt your data and make repairs very difficult.

４．「黒」のボタンをクリック、RGBの３つのスライダを動かして、シャドウ部の色調を調節する。シャドウ部の色調は画面にあたる環境光の影響が大きいのでモニタの天面に遮光用のフードを装着すると効果大だ。

4. Click the **Black Pt**. button, and move the three RGB sliders to adjust the color in the shadow area. The shadow color adjustment has a major effect on the lighting in the display, so it may be wise to use a shade over the top of the monitor.

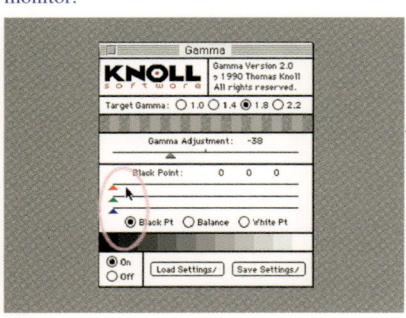

５．フォトショップを起動し、**ファイルメニュー**の**環境設定**から**モニタ**を選択、使用しているモニタの種類を選択、ガンマ補正値を入力、ホワイトポイントは6500°K、**RGB色度座標**にモニタの種類を、**環境光(照明)**に室内照明の状態を選択する。

5. Select **Monitor Setup** under **Preferences** on the **File** menu, setting to the monitor you are using and inputting the Gamma correction values. Set **White Point** to 6,500, **Phosphorous** to Monitor, and **Ambient Light**, for the interior room lighting.

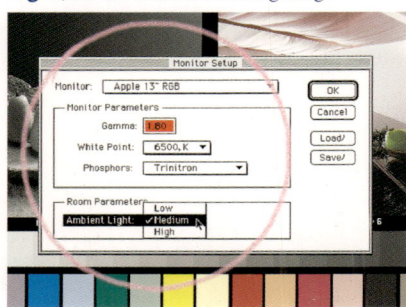

６．**ファイルメニュー**の**環境設定**からインキを選択。使用する出力機の**インキ**の**色特性**を選択する（初期設定は SWOP Coated）。この設定は画像のモード変換時に大きく影響する。

6. Select **Printing Inks Setup** under **Preferences** on the **File** menu. Select **Ink Colors** for the output equipment you will be using (original setting is Swap-Coated). This setting is important when you switch image modes.

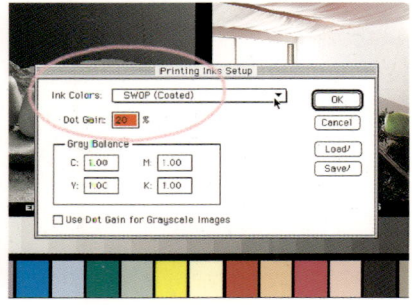

使いやすいバリエーションコマンド

Easy-to-use variation commands.

Wrong FileのNo.4画像、全体に暗くかなりマゼンタかぶりをしている。冒頭のキャリブレーション用ファイルNo.4にどこまで近ずけられるか、バリエーションコマンドを使って挑戦してみよう。

Wrong File No. 4 shows an image which is dark overall and tinted magenta. Let's use the *Variation* command to see how close we can come to the Calibration File No. 4 seen at the outset.

イメージメニューの色調補正からバリエーションを選択。全体の明るさを調整するためにラジオボタンを中間調にして、右上の明るくの画像を見ながらちょうど良い明るさになるようにスライダを調整する。明るくの画像をクリックすると現在が明るくなる。左2段目の緑(G)の画像を見ながらちょうど良い色味になるようにスライダを調整後、画像をクリックするとマゼンタかぶりがぬける。

Select *Variations* under *Adjust* on the *Image* menu. To adjust overall tone, set the radial button to *Midtones*. Then, watching the upper right side of the image, move the slider to adjust the image to the desired brightness. Click the Image *Lighter* button to make the entire image lighter. Now watch the two-layered image at the left as you use the *More Green* Image slider to achieve better color. Click the image to add the magenta coloring.

作業を始める前に156ページを参照しながら添付ディスク中のWrong Fileを4つの画像に分割して別々の名前で保存しておく。バリエーションコマンドはEFI社のCachetと同じようなインターフェースを持っている。濃度、カラーバランス、彩度を中間調、シャドウ、ハイライト別々に調整できる（結果としてコントラストの調整もできる）。しかもこれからすることの結果を見ながら選択できるので、初心者にも非常にわかりやすい。色というものは非常に微妙で、並べて比較すると違いが良くわかるが、単独ではかなり偏っていても気がつきにくいものだ。微調整が必要な場合は次ページのトーンカーブコマンドと組み合わせて使用すると良い。

Before beginning your work refer to page 156, then select Wrong Files from the extra disk, separating the files into four. Name and *Save*. The *Variations* command uses the same interface as EF's Cachet. You can make midtone adjustments to darkness, color balance and intensity (and, ultimately, to contrast.) But we are going to see the results of these functions as we work, which will be extra helpful to beginners. Color is a very elusive phenomenon. One can see differences easily enough when comparing, but set alone, different qualities are much harder to notice. One cannot make extremely fine adjustments with this command; when they are necessary use *Curves* command, which is discussed on the next page.

7．イメージメニューの色調補正からバリエーションを選択する。全体に明るくするためにラジオボタンを中間調にしてスライダを調整する。右上の明るくの画像をクリックすると現在が明るくなる。

7. Choose *Variations* from *Adjust* on the *Image* menu. Set the radial button at *Midtones* to increase overall brightness and use the slider to make the adjustment. Click the *Lighter* button to increase the brightness of the image.

8．同様に左2段目の緑(G)の画像をスライダ調整後、クリックするとマゼンタかぶりがぬける。すべて結果を見ながら選択できるので非常にわかりやすい。

8. In the same way, adjust the image below with the *More Green* slider, and Click on the image to increase the Magenta. You can see all the results as you work, which is very convenient.

9．ラジオボタンでシャドウをオンにすると明るく以外はすべて限界外で選択不適当であることが分かる（限界を表示をチェックしておくこと）。

9. Set *Shadows* "On" with the radial button, which inactivates all settings except *Lighter*. (Check beforehand with *Show Clipping*.)

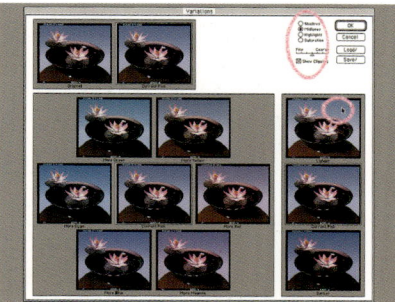

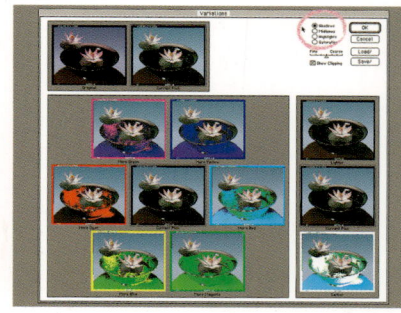

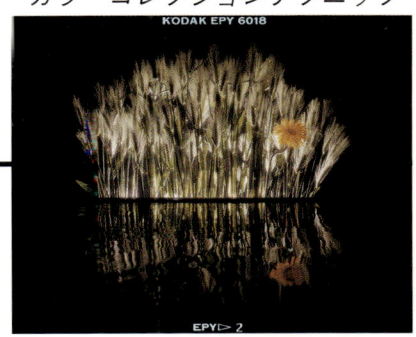

精度の高いトーンカーブコマンド

High-precision tone adjustment with Curves command.

トーンカーブコマンドはもっとも精度の高い画像補正が行なえるコマンドである。ビギナーには分かりにくいインターフェースだが、プロはほとんどこれ一本で画像補正を行なっているので、プロを目指す読者は是非マスターして欲しい。

バージョン2.01の階調補正メニューにあった階調補正グラフコマンドがバージョン2.5になって消えてしまったと思ったらカスタムマップオプションと名を変えてトーンカーブコマンドに同居している。以前作った補正用の階調補正もそのまま使うことができる。トーンカーブコマンドに精通することがカラーコレクションマスターへの近道だ。

Curves is the most precise command for making color corrections. The interface is difficult for beginners to understand, but pros use it all the time to make adjsutments. Anyone who is aiming for the top should definitely master Curves.
It might appear that the Arbitrary command of Ver. 2.01 has disappeared from Ver. 2.5; in fact, it now lives together with Curves as the Aribitrary Map option. And the correction map can still be used in the same way.
At any rate, proficient handling of Curves is the path to mastery of color corrections.

Wrong FileのNo.2画像、色温度のかなり低い照明器具を使って、露出をアンダーに撮影したような画像である。本来緑色の麦が枯れたようになっている。

The image in Wrong File No. 2 uses an image with lighting that brings out insufficient color warmth. It might have been an underexposed photo. Now it looks like green barley that has withered.

イメージメニューの色調補正からトーンカーブを選択。10図及び11図の要領で色補正を実行する。
（添付ディスクのトーンカーブフォルダー内のカスタムマップを読み込みすると上記の設定を自動的に行う）。

Choose Curves from Adjust under the Image menu. To adjust the overall brightness set the Channel to RGB, indicating Input: 120 and Output: 135 for the middle periphery, and Input: 8 and Output: 0 for the shadows. Next, to remove red, set the Channel to Green, setting the central area periphery to Input: 114, Output: 182, and the Shadows to Input: 32, Output: 79. (The automatic settings in the Barley-Curves file on the disk are the same.)

カスタムマップオプションで色変換した画像。

The image adjusted with Arbitrary Map option.

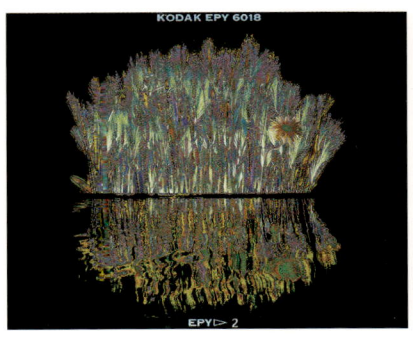

---

10. イメージメニューの色調補正からトーンカーブを選択。全体の明るさを調整するためにチャンネルをRGBにしてカーブの中心あたりで、入力:120、出力:135に設定し、シャドウ側で入力:8、出力:0に設定する。

10. Choose Curves from Adjust under the Image menu. To adjust the overall brightness set the Channel to RGB, indicating Input: 120 and Output: 135 for the middle periphery, and Input: 8 and Output: 0 for the shadows.

11. 次に赤味を除くためにチャンネルを緑（G）にしてカーブの中心あたりで、入力:114、出力:182に設定し、シャドウ側で入力:32、出力:79に設定してOKする。

11. In the same way set the Channel to Green, with Curves at Input: 114, Output: 182. Then set the Shadow point at Input: 32, Output: 79. Click OK.

12. トーンカーブの左下、鉛筆アイコンをクリックするとカスタムマップオプションに切り替わる。フリーハンドでカーブを自由に設定できるので、よりクリエイティブな作業が可能になる

12. On the lower left of Curves, click the Pencil icon, switching to the Arbitrary Map option. You can set the curves freehand, opening up creative possibilities.

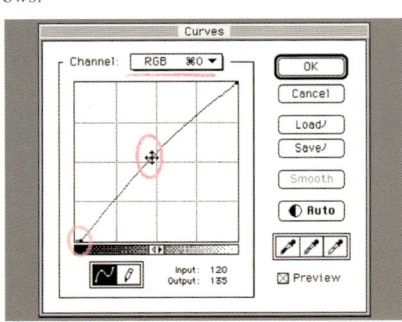

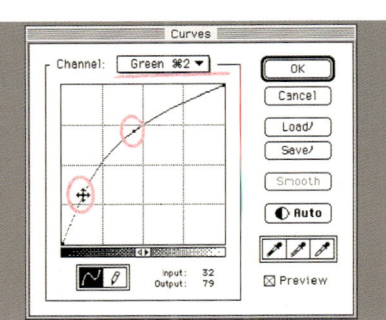

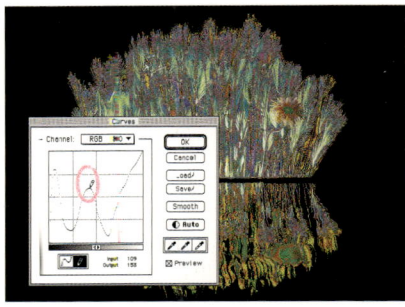

スキャニング画像の補正に便利なレベル補正コマンド

Correcting scanned images with the convenient Levels command.

Wrong FileのNo.1画像、全体に暗くかなり青い。タングステンタイプのフィルムを使って室内自然光でフィルター補正不足で撮影したようだ。そのうえ乳剤面に大きなスクラッチがある。これが使えるようになるのだろうか。

The image in Wrong File No. 1 is dark and tinted blue overall. It's like a photo taken indoors with tungsten film, natural lighting and an inadequate filter. On top, there's a large scratch on the surface. Can an image like this be used?

レベル調整コマンドはスキャニング画像の最初のカラーコレクションに都合が良い。ハイライト、シャドウ、中間トーンの3点を全体的にも各色別にも自由に調整できる。ダイナミックレンジを広げたりコントラストをつけたり、自動ツールを使っても**スポイトツール**を使っても、手作業でも自由自在だ。ただしカラーバランスが崩れるのでカラー画像に自動ツールを使うのはやめておいたほうが良い。**カラーバランス**は**トーンカーブ**ほど細かく調整できないが、各色別にマニュアル調整でこの作例程度の事は不自由しない。

イメージメニューの**色調補正**からレベル補正を選択、青味を除くため**チャンネル**を**青(B)**にしグレースライダを右にスライドして0.61に、黒のスライダを46に設定する。明度を上げコントラストをつけるため**チャンネル**を**RGB**にしてグレースライダを1.66に、黒スライダを6に、白スライダを250に設定。赤味を少し上げるため**チャンネル**を**赤(R)**にしグレースライダを1.05に設定してOKする。（添付ディスクのトーンカーブフォルダからGlass-Levelファイルを読み込みすると、上記の設定を自動的に処理する）。

Choose *Levels* under *Adjust* on the *Image* menu. To remove the blue, choose the *Blue Channel*, moving the gray slider to 0.61, and the black slider to 1.66. To raise contrast set the *Channel* to *RGB* and move the gray slider to 1.66, the black slider to 6, and the white slider to 250. To bring out the red slightly set the *Channel* to *Red*, move the slider to 1.05, and click OK. (If you *Load* the Glass-Level file from the *Curves* folder on the disk the same adjustments are performed automatically.)

The *Levels* command is particularly good for making initial corrections to scanned images. You can freely make adjustments to overall highlights, shadows and middle tones. You can expand the dynamic range or add contrast using either the automatic tool or the spot tool. But take care. The automatic tool will disrupt balance in a color image, and should not be used. *Curves* is better equipped for making fine corrections to color images, but the manual tool can also very effective.

---

13. イメージメニューの**色調補正**から**レベル補正**を選択する。青味を除くために**チャンネル**を**青(B)**にしグレースライダを右にスライドして0.61に、黒のスライダを46に設定する。

14. 同様に明度を上げコントラストをつけるため**チャンネル**を**RGB**にしグレースライダを左にスライドして1.66に、黒スライダを6に、白スライダを250に設定する。

15. 赤味を少し上げるため**チャンネル**を**赤(R)**にしグレースライダを左にスライドして1.05に設定、OKする。カラーコレクションの完了である。

13. Select *Levels* under *Adjust* on the *Image* menu. To remove blue, set the *Channel* to *Blue* and move the slider to 0.6. Move the black slider to 46.

14. In the same way, raise contrast by switching the *Channel* to *RGB* and moving the gray slider left, to 1.66, the black slider to 6, and the white slider to 250.

15. To raise the red tint slightly, set *Channel* to *Red*, and move the gray slider left to 1.05, and click OK. The color correction is finished.

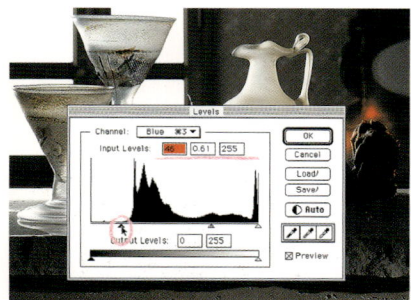

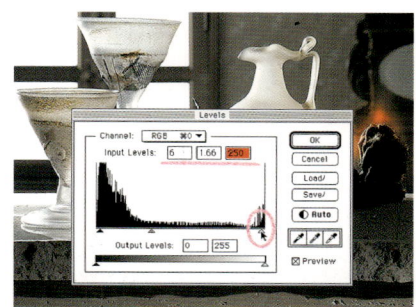

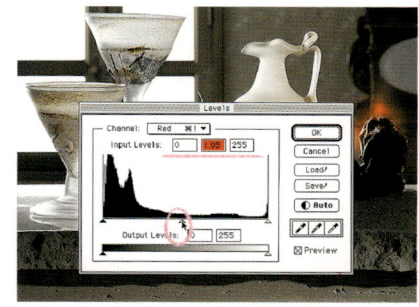

ラバースタンプツールの上手な使い方

Using the Rubber Stamp tool effectively.

スタンプツールはフォトショップのもっとも便利なツールの1つだ。傷やゴミの修整はもちろん合成や色変換、不用物消去、移植、着色、なじませ、透かし、その他あらゆる場面に活躍する万能ツールである。写真の処理ではブラシやエアーブラシに替ってほとんどが**スタンプツール**の出番だ。**スタンプツール**オプションの設定はほとんど**コピー(調整あり)**で行なわれるが、**コピー(調整なし)**も広い面積を同じテクスチャーで埋める場合などに便利だ。

The **Rubber Stamp tool** is one of the most useful tools in Photoshop. Naturally it is effective in repair work, but it has a myriad of other applications as well, from integrating and altering colors to erasing, moving objects, adding color, grading and adding transparency. In photography, where one would retouch using the brush and airbrush, the **Rubber Stamp tool** is the natural substitute.The **Rubber Stamp** options setting of **Clone (aligned)** is correct for most work, but **Clone (non-aligned)** can be useful for broad, one-texture images. **Snapshot**, an new addition to Ver. 2.5, is easy-to-use. It offers about the same functions as **From Saved**, but parts are selected and altered individually, so it is much faster.

いよいよスクラッチのレタッチだ。スタンプツールを使って上から下へ周囲のサンプリング画像で埋めていく。(オプションキーを押してクリックしたところがブラシサイズでサンプリングされる)。こまめにサンプリングする場所を変えながらレタッチしていく。シャープなところにボケ足のブラシを使うとそこだけシャープネスが失われるのでボケ足のないブラシを使うようにする。ボケ足のないブラシはブラシの形がはっきり出るので、小さめのブラシで細かくレタッチする。広い場所は大きく、細かい場所は小さく細かく使い分けるのがコツだ。

Soon we will take a look at a scratch retouch. Moving the **Rubber Stamp tool** from top to bottom, covering the entire sample area. (By holding down the **Option key** and clicking you can sample various brush sizes.) Carefully delineate the sampled area and do your retouch. In sharp spots don't use a brush with blurred lines or you will lose the sharpness. A sharp brush without blur will appear as a clear outline; use a small brush for the fine retouching. Use a bigger brush with big strokes in open areas, and a small brush with fine movements for detailing. That's the trick.

レタッチが完了した画像。これでほとんど撮影前に予想していた仕上がりどうりになった。

A finished retouch. This is about what the photographer expected when he took the shot.

---

16. スタンプツールオプションでコピー(調整あり)を選択。スタンプツールによるレタッチはほとんどこのオプションによることが多い。同じテクスチャーで広い面積を埋めるときはコピー(調整なし)が便利だ。

16. Select **Clone (aligned)** under **Rubber Stamp** options. Most retouching with the **Rubber Stamp tool** is done at this setting. The **Clone (non-aligned)** setting is useful for broad surfaces.

17. ブラシパレットでモードは通常、不透明度:100%でレタッチする場所に最適なブラシサイズを選んでおく。ブラシサイズの選択は重要である。作業中こまめにもち替えるようにする。

17. Under the **Brush Palette** set mode to **Normal** and **Opacity** to 100%. Use the correct size brush for the area you will retouching. Change brush sizes whenever required.

18. レタッチする場所毎に画像の流れにそって、サンプリングする箇所と方向を変える。いっぺんにやろうとせず、方向を変えて周囲から細かくせめて行くのがコツだ。

18. When retouching, consider the flow of the surrounding image. Don't try to finish everything at once. Change you direction. Attack carefully from various directions. This is the key.

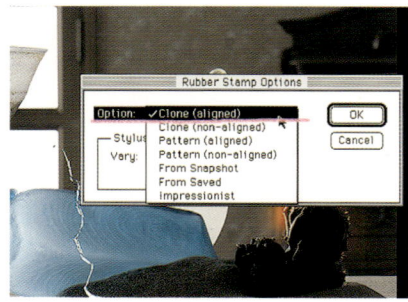

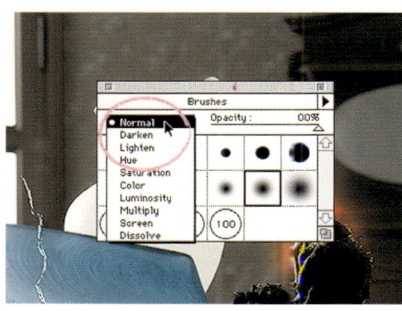

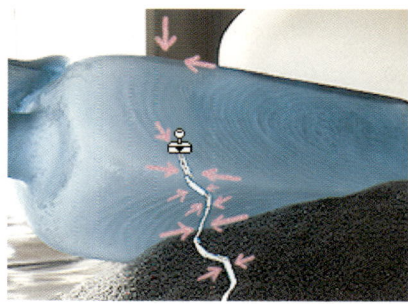

色変換テクニック

Color alteration techniques

なげなわツールで色変換したい部分を選択する。解像度に合せて境界のぼかし幅を調整する。（低解像度なら０ピクセル、高解像度なら１〜３ピクセル）。自動選択ツールでも選択できるがなげなわツールで直接選択したほうが精度が高く速い場合が多い。

Select the area of color you wish to change with the **Lasso Tool**. Set the **Feather Radius** to the correct resolution. (If low resolution, 0 pixels, high resolution, 1-3 pixels.) You can select with the **Magic Wand**, but selecting directly with the **Lasso Tool** is faster and more accurate.

色変換の基本は**色相・彩度**コマンドだ。**色相**を変化させることによって、デジタル画像ならではの劇的な変化を簡単に行なうことができる。しかし無彩色画像には効果がない。無彩色画像は**色相・彩度**内の**色彩の統一**をチェックすることで有彩色化してから**色相**を使って色変換する。**彩度**が100%で強すぎるので少し押さえたほうが良い場合が多い。真っ黒と真っ白は**色彩の統一**でも黒と白なので**明度(L)**でグレイトーンに変えて色をつける。おおよその色変換ができたら**トーンカーブ**コマンドで微調整をして希望の色、コントラストに仕上げる。

イメージメニューの色調補正から**色相・彩度**コマンドを実行。**色彩の統一**をチェックして**明度(L)**を-30、**彩度(S)**を80に設定してOKする。イメージメニューの色調補正から**トーンカーブ**コマンドを実行してトーンの微調整をする。

Initiate the **Hue/Saturation** command from **Adjust** under the **Image** menu. Check Color Size, setting **Lightness** at -30 and **Saturation** at 80. Click OK. From **Adjust** under the **Image** menu initiate the **Curves** command.

The key to color replacement is the **Hue/Saturation** Command. By changing the **Hue**, a digital image is instantly and dramatically altered.
But there is no effect at all on an image that has no color. Instead, to add and then change colors on a colorless image, check Colorize under **Hue/Saturation**. 100% **saturation** is usually too strong, so drop the level a bit. Pure white or black will remain under Colorize, so change them to gray tones under **Lightness**. When you have achieved approximately the coloring you desire use **Curves** to adjust coloring and contrast.

---

19. なげなわツールで境界のぼかし幅：１ピクセル、アンチエイリアシング：Onに設定。色変換をするすりガラスの水差し部分を選択する。

19. Under **Lasso Tool** set **Feather Radius** to 1 pixel, with **Anti-aliased:** On. Select the frosted glass pitcher.

20. イメージメニューの色調補正から**色相・彩度**コマンドを実行。**色彩の統一**をチェックして**明度(L)**を-30、**彩度(L)**を80に設定してOKする。色味を変えたい場合は色相を動かす。

20. Do the **Hue/Saturation** command under **Adjust** on the **Image** menu. Check **Colorize**, setting **Lightness** at -30, and **Saturation** at 80. Click OK. Use **Hue** to adjust the coloring in the area you want to change.

21. イメージメニューの色調補正から**トーンカーブ**コマンドでトーンの微調整をする。**RGBチャンネル**でコントラストの調整、**青(B)チャンネル**でハイライト側に青みを加える。

21. Use **Curves** form **Adjust** under the **Image** menu to make fine adjsutments to tone. **Adjust** contrast on the **RGB Channel**, adding blue to the highlighted side under the **Blue Channel**.

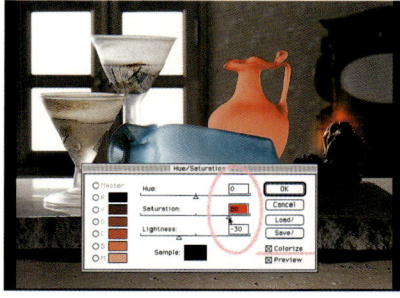

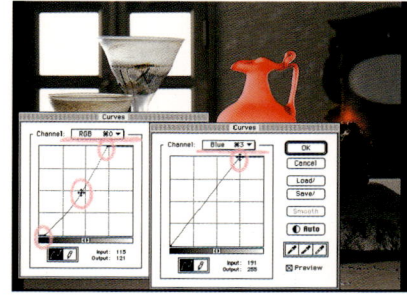

人工着色テクニック

Artificial coloration techniques.

人工着色テクニックは古くからある技術だが、コンピューター処理になって簡単かつ精度が高くなった。

白黒写真にモードを**色相と彩度**にした**ブラシ**で好みの色を着色することで、ほとんどカラー写真のようにすることが簡単にできる。いまさら人着写真などお呼びでない人にもこのテクニックは重要だ。無彩色の画像に好みの色を写真レベルでつけられるという事は、どんな色変換にでも対応できるという事だ。前ページの色変換テクニックにプラスしてマスターされたい。

Artificial coloration techniques have been around for a long time, but with the computer they have become much faster and more accurate. A black and white photo can be colored in any way by setting Mode to *Color* and using the *Brush*. You can easily make it look very much like a color photo.

Now even people who don't call themselves color retouch artists are placing great emphasis on this technique, adding whatever colors they prefer to any type of image. The techniques are widely applicable, and should certainly be mastered.

白黒画像を着色してカラーフォト化する。部分的に筆のタッチを生かしながらレタッチしていけば、絵画的なにおいの濃い画像になるし、作例のように全体的なレタッチをすると写真らしい仕上がりになる。

Adding color to a black and white image to make a color photo. By retouching only some parts the effect is like an oil painting; by retouching the entire image, the result is similar to a color photo.

トーンカーブコマンドを使って全体をセピアトーンに着色する。好きな色味にすれば良いが作例は、被写体の色にほぼ忠実にしてある。

Use the *Curves* command to give a sepia tone to the overall image. You can add any color you like, but here the coloring is made as much like the natural subject as possible.

石で作った果物を1つずつ着色する。ブラシパレットのモードを**色相と彩度**にしておくと、明度は変化せずにカラーだけが変わるので、大胆に着色してから、細かく色を変えながら整えていく。色をはみ出させないためにはあらかじめ選択しておくと良い。

Adding color to the stone fruits, one by one. If you set the *Brush Palette* mode to *Color*, only the color will change, with no alteration of the contrast. This results in bold coloring, which can be followed up with detailed adjustments. Use this setting when you don't want to crowd your colors.

---

22. 着色に使う色をあらかじめ**カラーパレット**に登録しておくと能率が良い。必要な色を**描画色**に表示、カラーパレットの下側空きスペースにカーソルをもっていってクリックするだけで登録できる。

22. It is more efficient to pre-record your colors on the *Color Palette*. Make the required color *Foreground color*, moving the cursor to the bottom of the *Color Pallette* and clicking to record your choice.

23. まず全体にセピアトーンにする。モードをグレースケールからRGBカラー変換してイメージメニューの色調補正から**トーンカーブ**コマンドを実行。チャンネルを**赤(R)**にして**入力:90、出力:155**に、チャンネルを**青(B)**にして**入力:64、出力:0**に設定し**OK**する。

23. First, add a sepia tone to the entire image. The mode on the *Image* menu will be changed from Grayscale to RGB. Execute the *Curves* command under *Adjust* on the *Image* menu. Set the *Red Channel* to *Input:* 90, *Output:* 155, the *Blue Channel* to *Input:* 64, *Output:* 0. Click *OK*.

24. ブラシパレットのモードを**色相と彩度**にして、適当なサイズのブラシとカラーを選択して着色する。場所によっては鉛筆ツールやエアブラシツールを利用する。

24. Set the *Brush Pallette* mode to *Color*, and use an appropriately sized *Brush* to *Add Color*. In places, the *Pencil* or air *Brush* tools are preferable.

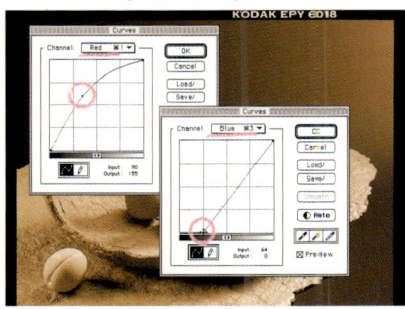

第3章　セレクションテクニック

Chapter 3　Selection Techniques

正確な選択範囲の作成が第一歩

Accurate selection is the first step

フォトショップに限らずほとんどの画像処理ソフトにおいて最初の作業は加工を加えたい部分を選択することである。必要に応じてボケ足を加えたりアンチエイリアシング処理をしたりするにせよ、正確にすばやく目的の場所を選択することが、もっとも重要な作業でありベテランとビギナーの差が顕著に現れる部分でもある。

マウスやタブレットの使い方に習熟するだけでなく、日頃からもっとも能率的かつ正確な選択方法を工夫して身に付けることが上達への近道だ。そのための選択ツールも各種揃っているので、状況に合わせて最適なツールを最適な利用法で使うようにしよう。

不定形の範囲選択

なげなわツールか**自動選択ツール**を使う。**なげなわツール**はマウスを使ったフリーハンドでの正確なトレースは難しいので、オプションキーを押しながらポイントをクリックしていくラバーバンドモードでの使用をお薦めする。オプションキーを押していても細かいところはそのままドラッグすればフリーハンドで選択することもできる。

自動選択ツールは選択する色の範囲の設定をこまめに行なえばかなりの精度で自動選択可能だが、いそがばまわれで**なげなわツール**で丁寧に選択するほうが結果がきれいで速い場合が多い。

ペンツールも使い慣れると形のはっきりした選択範囲を作るためには便利なツールである。もちろんトレース後**選択範囲の作成**コマンドで選択範囲に変換する必要はあるが。

定形の範囲選択

四角形の選択は**長方形選択ツール**、楕円形の選択は**楕円選択ツール**を使用する。シフトキーを押しながら選択することで正方形や正円形が選択できる。オプションで**縦横比を固定する**の設定や、**大きさを固定する**の設定もできる。さらに**なげなわツール**と同じ様に**境界のぼかし**の設定も可能だ。

コマンド+A キーもしくは**選択範囲**メニューの**全画面の選択**コマンドで全画面の選択、**コマンド+D** キーもしくは**選択範囲の解除**コマンドで選択範囲の取り消しができる。

マスク描画モードの利用

ツールボックスの**マスク描画モード**を選択するとフィルムへのマスキングワークと同じように、加工用画像を見ながらペインティングツールを使ってマスクを描くことができる。ブラシのサイズとボケ足を選ぶことで精度の高いマスクを迅速に作ることが可能だ。（選択ツールの加工スピードよりペインティングツールの加工スピードの方が圧倒的に速い）。描いたマスクは自動的にマスクチャンネルとして記録されているので**選択範囲**メニューの**選択範囲の選択**コマンドで選択範囲として呼び出すことができる。

選択範囲の加工処理

選択範囲メニューの各コマンドで選択範囲に対して様々な加工処理を加えることができる。**フロート／フロート解除**は選択範囲を画像から切り離すか一体化させるかを切り替える。**選択範囲の拡張**は選択範囲を拡張する。**近似色の選択**は選択範囲の近似色を選択する。**境界上の領域を選択**は選択範囲の境界を選択する。**境界をぼかす**は境界をぼかす。**フリンジ削除**は貼り込んだ選択範囲などフローティング状態の選択範囲から境界上のフリンジを除去する。

Not only in Photoshop, but with all image handling software, the first step in processing an image is selection of the area to be manipulated. In some cases one will need to add shadowing, or use anti-aliasing, and for this accurate selection is the key.

A remarkable difference can be seen between veterans and beginners in this most important aspect of image work.

What is required in order to gain expertise is not only practice with a mouse or tablet, but rather an effort to find your own preferred method of efficiently and accurately making a selection. This is the road to improvement.

A variety of tools are offered for making selections; learn to use the appropriate tool for any situation.

Selecting an amorphous shape

Use the **Lasso Tool** or the **Magic Wand Tool**. It is difficult to trace accurately using the **Lasso Tool** and mouse freehand. Instead, it is recommended that you depress the **Option key**, clicking at points and taking advantage of the Rubber Band mode. Even when the **Option key** is depressed you can drag/select finer areas when needed.

One can also make fairly accurate freehand selections by carefully setting the **Tolerance** and using the **Magic Wand Tool**, but in most cases the **Lasso** is faster and more efficient.

Once one has mastered its use, the **Pen Tool** can also be used to make a very clear selection. Of course, one must convert the selected area with **Make Selection** after the tracing is completed.

Selecting a geometrical shape

For a square shape use the **Rectangular Marquee Tool**, for an ovoid, the **Elliptical Marquee Tool**. One can select a square or circular shape by depressing the **Shift key**. One can also set the **Aspect Ratio** or **Fixed Size** with the option. Like the **Lasso Tool**, the **Feather Radius** can also be set.

One can select the entire screen with **Command+A** or All on the **Select** menu; one can cancel a selection with **Comman+D** or the **None** command.

Using Quick Mask mode

By choosing **Quick Mask mode** under the **Toolbox** one can achieve effects like film masking. The mask is drawn over the desired object with the painting tool. By adjusting the brush size and shadow one can speedily create a very precise mask. (The processing speed of the selection tool is far exceeded by that of the painting tool.) A mask created with the painting tool is automatically recorded as a channel; by choosing **Load Selection** from the **Select** menu one can call up the selected area.

Processing the selected area

One can process selected areas in various ways with the different commands on the **Select** menu.

The **Float/Defloat** command separate or imbeds an object from the surrounding image.

Grow enarges the selected area. **Similar** captures areas of the same color as the selected area.

Border selects the border area of the selected area. **Feather** shades the border.

Defringe takes pasted areas and other selections in a floating mode and removes their fringe.

セレクションテクニック........選択ツール利用法

Wrong FileのNo.3画像を*開く*。全体に彩度が不足しているので*イメージメニュー*の*色調補正*から*色相・彩度コマンド*で彩度を＋40までアップして*OK*する。気持ちの良いグリーンとスカイブルーに色補正するためには、全体的な補正では不可能なのでグリーンとブルーを別々に補正する。

Open the No. 3 Wrong File. The overall coloring of the image is lacking, so choose the *Hue/Saturation* command under the *Adjust* and increase *Saturation* +40. Click *OK*. In order to achieve eye-pleasing green and sky blue coloring do each color separately.

まずグリーン部分のみ選択する。これだけ濃度差のある絵柄は*自動選択ツール*ではかえって手間がかかる。グリーン部分を*境界のぼかし幅（半径）:1pixels*、アンチエイリアシング:オンに設定した*なげなわツール*でオプションキーを押して（ラバーバンドモード）細かくポイントをクリックしながら選択する。細部はそのままドラッグしてフリーハンドで選択することもできる。

In order to supplement the green coloring, first select the green area. In an image with this much difference in intensity the *Magic Wand Tool* will require too much time. Use the *Lasso Tool* instead. Set to *Feather Radius: 1 pixels, Anti-aliased: On,* depressing the *Option key* to put the *Lasso* in rubber band mode. Select by clicking along the fine points. When you release the *Option key* or mouse button, the area of points is confirmed as the selected area.

選択ツールとしてもっとも多用されるのが*なげなわツール*である。便利な*自動選択ツール*も濃度差の少ない単純な絵柄には便利だが、濃度差の激しい細かい絵柄には向いていない。*なげなわツール*もフリーハンドでドラッグしての選択では細かい部分的な選択には良いが大面積には対応しにくい。

*オプションキー*を押しながら選択境界のポイントポイントをクリックしていく*なげなわツール*のラバーバンドモードが最も使いやすく便利である。*オプションキー*とマウスボタンから指を離すとその時点で選択範囲が確定されるので、選択途中で席を離れられないのが欠点だが。　　　＊＊＊P.39に簡単な解決方法を掲載

The *Lasso Tool* is the most useful tool for making selections. The *Magic Wand Tool* is also convenient for simple pictures where coloring is not too diverse, but where coloring is very thick or finely detailed it is insufficient. The *Lasso Tool* is effective for freehand drag-selecting, but difficult to use over a large area. The Rubber Band mode of the *Lasso Tool*, which works by setting points, is the easiest and most convenient. However, because the selection is confirmed whenever the key or mouse button is released, the operation cannot be interrupted.

１．全体に彩度を上げるために*イメージメニュー*の*色調補正*から*色相・彩度コマンド*で彩度を+40に設定して*OK*する。

1. In order to raise overall coloring choose *Hue/Saturation* command under *Adjust* on the *Image* menu, set *Saturation* to +40, and click *OK*.

２．グリーン部分を選択するために*なげなわツール*オプションで*境界のぼかし幅（半径）:1pixels*,アンチエイリアシング:オンに設定して*OK*し、*なげなわツール*をオプションキーを押しながら（ラバーバンドモード）細かくポイントをクリックしてグリーン部分を選択する。

2. To select the green area, open the *Lasso Tool Option* and set to *Feather Radius: 1 Pixels, Anti-aliased: On,* and click *OK*. Depressing the *Option key* (for Rubber Band mode) click on fine points.

３．*イメージメニュー*の*色調補正*から*トーンカーブ*コマンドでチャンネルを*RGB*にしてハイライト部分を*入力:172,出力:255*、シャドウ部分を*入力:17,出力:0*に、*緑(G)チャンネル*で中間部分を*入力:118,出力:134*に設定して*OK*する。

3. Under *Adjust* on the *Image* menu choose the *Curves* command, setting *RGB*. Highlight to *Input*: 172, *Output*:255, and Shadow to *Input*: 17, *Output*: 0. Set the *Green channel* to middle area of *Input*: 118, *Output*: 134. Click *OK*.

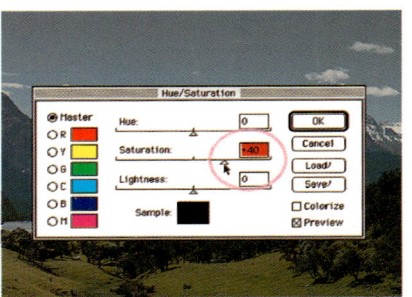

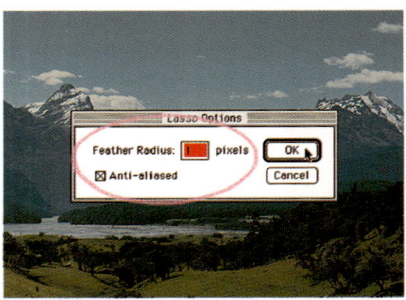

Selection Techniques ....Selection Tool uses and methods

　選択範囲を移動するには選択ツールでドラッグするか、**コマンドキー**を押しながら他のツールでドラッグする。選択範囲の境界だけを移動するには**コマンド＋オプションキー**＋選択ツールでドラッグする。

　選択したい複雑な部分の外側が単純な場合直接選択するよりも単純な外側を**自動選択ツール**で選択して**選択範囲**メニューの**選択範囲の反転**コマンドで反転したほうが簡単で便利だ。

　選択範囲メニューの**近似色の選択**コマンドは現在選択されている範囲の近似色を**自動選択ツール**ダイアログボックスでの設定にしたがって全て選択してくれるので利用範囲が広い。**選択範囲の拡張**コマンドは選択範囲を同様の基準で拡張する。

To move a selected object either drag it with the selection tool, or use the **Command key** + any other tool to drag it. To move only the border of a selected area, use **Command + Option** + selection tool, and drag. When the area to be selected is complex, but surrounded by a fairly simple outline, it is easiest to select the outside with the **Magic Wand Tool**, then use **Inverse** from the **Select** menu to switch the selection. There are many uses for the **Similar** command, which is found under the Select Menu, and selects areas of a specified color based on the setting in the dialogue box of the **Magic Wand Tool**. The **Grow** command works the same way to enlarge a selection.

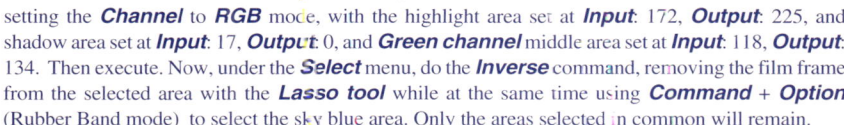

グリーン部分の色補正をする為に、**イメージ**メニューの**色調補正**から**トーンカーブ**コマンドで**チャンネル**を**RGB**にしてハイライト部分を**入力**:172,**出力**:255、シャドウ部分を**入力**:17,**出力**:0に、**緑(G)チャンネル**で中間部分を**入力**:118,**出力**:134に設定して実行する。**選択範囲**メニューから**選択範囲の反転**コマンドを実行、フィルムフレーム部分を選択範囲から除外するため**なげなわツール**でシフトキーとコマンドキーとオプションキー（ラバーバンドモード）を同時に押しながらスカイブルー部分を選択すると共通選択部分だけが残る。

To supplement green coloring, choose the **Curves** command from the **Adjust** menu, setting the **Channel** to **RGB** mode, with the highlight area set at **Input**: 172, **Output**: 225, and shadow area set at **Input**: 17, **Output**: 0, and **Green channel** middle area set at **Input**: 118, **Output**: 134. Then execute. Now, under the **Select** menu, do the **Inverse** command, removing the film frame from the selected area with the **Lasso tool** while at the same time using **Command + Option** (Rubber Band mode) to select the sky blue area. Only the areas selected in common will remain.

6図の要領で**トーンカーブ**コマンドを使ってスカイブルー部分の色補正を実行する。（添付ディスク内のCurvesフォルダーからPasture-Blue-Curveを**読み込む**と**トーンカーブ**の設定を自動的に行なう。Pasture-Green-Curveもグリーン部分に対して同様に効果がある）。

Use the **Curves** command to add color to the sky blue section of the image. (If you open the Curves Folder in the accompanying disk and **Load** Pasture-Blue-Curve the setting will be made automatically. The same holds true for the Pasture-Green-Curve and the green area.)

４．スカイブルー部分を選択するために**選択範囲**メニューから**選択範囲の反転**コマンドを実行する。

4. To select the sky blue area use the **Inverse** command under the **Select** menu.

５．フィルムフレーム部分を選択範囲から除外するために**なげなわツール**でシフトキーと**コマンドキー**とオプションキーを同時に押しながら下図の要領でスカイブルー部分を選択すると共通に選択された部分だけが残る。

5. To remove the film frame portion from the selected area use the **Lasso Tool**, simultaneously depressing the **Shift, Command** and **Option keys** to leave only the area of sky blue and other commonly selected parts.

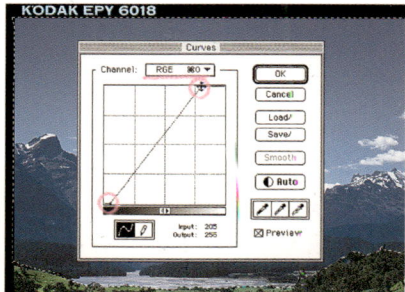

６．**イメージ**メニューの**色調補正**から**トーンカーブ**コマンドで**チャンネル**を**RGB**にしてハイライト部分を**入力**:205,**出力**:255、シャドウ部分を**入力**:12,**出力**:0に、**緑(G)チャンネル**で中間部分を**入力**:134,**出力**:121に設定してOKする。

6. From **Adjust** under the **Image** menu select the **Curves** command, setting the **RGB channel** to Highlight **Input**: 205, **Output**: 225, Shadow **Input**: 12, **Output**: 0. Set the **Green Channel** middle section to **Input**: 134, **Output**: 121, and click **OK**.

選択範囲の拡張と縮小 ....自動選択ツールを使う

Wrong Fileの No.4画像を第2章でカラー補正して保存しておいたファイルを開く。まずバックの色を変えてみよう。自動選択ツールのオプション設定を選択する色の範囲:32,アンチエイリアシング:オンにして、バックの中間辺りを選択する。クリックする場所によって選択される範囲が変化するのでちょうど良いところをクリックする。

Open the No. 4 Wrong File, which was supplemented with color in Chapter 2 and saved. First, let's change the background color. Set the **Magic Wand Tool** options to **Tolerance:** 32**, Anti-aliased:** On, then select the middle area of the background. Dependig upon where you click various areas will be selected, so choose the best place.

自動選択ツールで正確な選択範囲を作るのは思いのほか難しい。ここで紹介するようなテクニックを組み合わせて少しでも能率的な選択方法を身に付けることだ。

選択ツールとシフトキーとの組み合わせは選択範囲の拡張、コマンドキーとの組み合わせは選択範囲の縮小除外、コマンド+シフトキーとの組み合わせは選択された共通領域の選択になる。

コマンドキーと文字ツールの組み合わせはフローティング領域から選択範囲を切り離して画像の一部として確定させる機能を持っている。ほかの選択ツールでは選択範囲の内容が削除されてしまう。

バックの未選択部分をシフトキーを押しながらクリックして選択領域を拡張していく。この作例では4回クリックしてバック全部が選択できた。

Now select the unselected background area by depressing the **Shift key** and expanding the selected area. With this method the entire background can be selected in four clicks.

Selecting a precise area with the **Magic Wand** is much harder than one would expect. Here we will work with various methods; try to learn as much as possible about the different tools. The Selection tool and the **Shift key** expands the selected area, while the Selection tool and the **Command key** shrinks it. **Command + Shift** + Selection tool selects common areas. **Command key + Type Tool** selects a portion of a floating selection and fixes it to the image. Other selection tools will erase selected areas.

7．自動選択ツールの設定を選択する色の範囲:32,アンチエイリアシング:オンに設定してバックの中間辺りを選択する。

7. Set the **Magic Wand Options** to **Tolerance:** 32, **Anti-aliased**:ON, and select the middle area.

8．続けてバックの未選択部分をシフトキーを押しながら選択して選択領域を拡張していく。

8. Now depress the **Shift key** and expand the selected area over the unselected part of the background.

9．なげなわツールで大雑把に花の部分を選択する。自動選択ツールで直接花を選択しても良いが、思ったよりもてこずるはずだ。バックの方が単純なのでバックを自動選択ツールで選択除外したほうが早道だ。

9. Select the flower portion roughly with the **Lasso tool**. It's fine to select the flower directly with the **Magic Wand**, but it is more difficult than it seems. It is faster to simply select and delete the background.

Shrinking and Enlarging Selections

Using the automatic selection tool

Drag/Copy について　About Drag/Copying

選択範囲を**オプションキー**を押しながら選択ツールでドラッグすると、移動先に選択範囲のコピーができる。クリップボードを使わないので、スピードも速く、クリップボード内の画像と組み合わる場合に重宝する。今後この本の中では正規の**コピー＆ペースト**と区別して**ドラッグ／コピー**と言うコマンド名で登場するので記憶しておいて欲しい。

なげなわツールをラバーバンドモードで使う時の選択範囲の拡張縮少は、選択範囲外からスタートする場合は良いが、選択範囲内でスタートする時は、**オプションキー**を離しフリーハンドで何ピクセルか選択後、もう一度**オプションキー**を押してラバーバンドモードに入るとうまくいく。

If you depress the **Option key** and drag a selected area with the selection tool you can copy the selection before moving it. Since it isn't saved to the clipboard this method is fast, and because it can be used in conjunction with an image on the clipboard, extremely valuable. Later in this book the **Drag/copy** function will be used frequently, as opposed to **Copy&Paste**. Remember it.

There is no problem clicking outside a selected area when using the **Lasso Tool** in rubber band mode. However, when clicking inside the selected area, it is better to first release the **Option key,** go over some pixels with freehand, then depress the **Option key** again to enter the rubber band mode.

バックの色を変えるために為に、イメージメニューの色調補正から色相・彩度コマンドで色相を+153に設定して**OK**する。次に花の色を変えてみる。まず**なげなわツール**で大雑把に花を選択する。**コマンドキー**を押しながら**自動選択ツール**で選択除外したい部分をクリックしていく。除外しきれない部分は**なげなわツール**で同様に**コマンドキー**を押しながらドラッグして選択除外する。**選択範囲**メニューの**選択範囲の保存**で選択範囲を保存する。花芯の部分を**なげなわツール**で選択除外する。

In order to change the color of the background, select **Adjust** under the **Image** menu and choose the **Hue/Saturation** command, setting **Hue** to +153 and clicking **OK**. Next, change the color of the flowers. First, use the **Lasso Tool** to select a flower. Then, depressing the **Command key**, use the **Magic Wand** to click and delete the unnecessary areas. For areas that can't be selected cleanly this way employ the **Lasso Tool** to drag/select. Choose **Save Selection** on the **Select** menu save the selected area. Select the stamin with the **Lasso Tool** and **Command key** to de-select it.

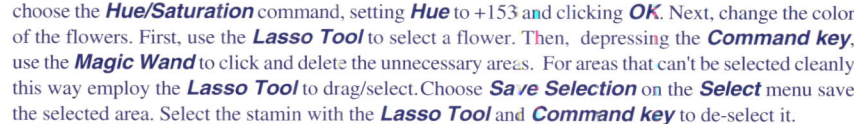

12図の要領で花の部分を色変換後、**選択範囲**メニューの**選択範囲の選択**コマンドを実行して花全体を選択する。オプションキーを押しながら選択ツールでドラッグすると選択された花のコピーが移動先に作られる。

After changing the color of the flower in Picture 12, choose the **Load Selection** command to select the entire flower. By depressing the **Option key** and **Drag/Copying** with the Selection tool the selected flower can be copied to the new position.

10．　自動選択ツールで不用なバック部分を**コマンドキー**を押しながらクリックして選択除外する。自動選択ツールで除外しきれない部分は**なげなわツール**を利用する。

11．　花芯の部分は色変換させないので**なげなわツール**で**コマンドキー**を押しながらドラッグして選択除外する。

12．　色変換するためにイメージメニューの色調補正から**色相・彩度**コマンドで**色彩の統一**をチェック、**明度(L)**を-13、**彩度(S)**を+80、**色相(H)**を-86に設定して**OK**する。

10. With the **Command key** depressed, click the **Magic Wand Tool** on the unnecessary portion of the background, removing it. Use the **Lasso Tool** to remove areas that cannot be handled with the **Magic Wand Tool**.

11. The stamin color will not be altered. so use the **Lasso Tool** and **Command key** to drag and de-select it.

12. To change the color go to the **Image** menu and select **Hue/Saturation** command under **Adjust**. Check **Colorize**, setting **Lightness** to -13, **Saturation** at +80, and **Hue** to -86. Click **OK**.

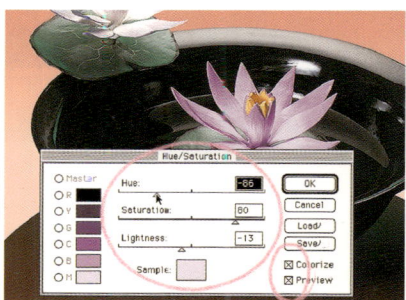

便利なマスクの使い方 ....使いやすいマスク描画モード

Wrong FileのNo.1画像を第2章でカラー補正とレタッチそして色変換して保存しておいたファイルをまたまた実習に利用する。今回は窓外に35頁で色補正実習に利用したNO.3画像（牧場の風景）を合成する。作業は単純で窓ガラス部分を選択して風景を選択範囲内へペーストするだけだ。ただしガラス部分を選択するのに選択ツールを使わずマスク描画モードでブラシを使って選択してみる。

The No. 1 Wrong File image was retouched and recolored, and finally saved, in Chapter 2. But it still has many uses. This time we will combine the glasses with the outdoor pasture image (No. 3) on page 35. It's an easy job. One simply selects the glasses and *Pastes Into* the pasture image. But instead of using the Selection tool we will select the glasses with the Brush in *Quick Mask mode*.

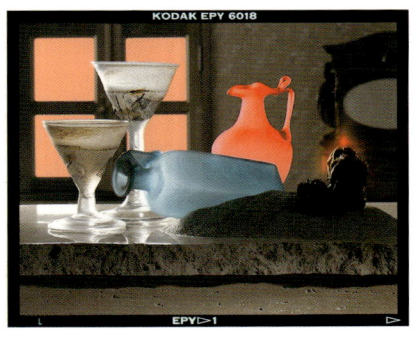

ツールボックス下部のマスク描画モードアイコンをクリックしてマスク描画モードに入る。ボケ足のある最小ブラシサイズに設定したノーマルブラシでシフトキーを押しながらガラスの境界をクリックして直線を引いていく。内部も塗りつぶし15区の要領でマスクを保存する。

At the bottom of the *Toolbox* click the *Quick Mask mode* icon. In *Quick Mask mode*, set to the smallest brush size, then use normal brush with *Shift key* depressed to click and select a straight line along the border of the glass. Select the inner area at fill for Picture 15 and Save as a *Mask*.

Ver.2.5になって最も便利な機能の1つにマスク描画モードがある。従来のアナログ合成やフィルムレタッチには不可欠だったマスクのハンドレタッチがシュミレーションされて、ほとんど同じ感覚でさらに精度高く実行できる。選択ツールを使って作ったマスクも細部は手を入れないと完全ではないので、元画像を見ながらマスクを加工できるのはなんと言っても有難い。

高解像度のファイルを扱う時、作業毎に書き換えられる選択ツールでの作業より、作業部分だけが書き換えられるペインティングツールでの作業（マスクモード）の方がはるかに速い。

In Ver. 2.5 one of the most convenient new features is the mask painting mode. Now you can retouch and mask almost exactly as you would in analog and photography, and with a very high degree of precision, too.

Simply using the Selection tool one cannot capture the finer areas, but neither can one hope to create an accurate mask separately without much difficulty.

When using a high resolution image file it is far better not to use the Selection tool, which must be redrawn each time. Instead, use the Painting tool (Mask mode), which only requires you to rewrite the portion you are working on.

13．ツールボックスからクイック描画モードを選択する。チャンネルパレットを見ると#4チャンネルにマスクが表示される。マスキングする部分に色をつけるかマスキングしない部分に色をつけるか、透明度と色相も含めてマスクの設定で設定できる。

13. Choose the *Quick Mask mode* from the *Toolbox*. If you look at the *Channels Palette* you will see that *Channel #4* is a *Mask*. Decide whether you will add color to the mask or the unmasked area, and what level of transparency and pigmentation you will use, and set these beforehand.

14．選択する場所によって最適なペインティングツールを選ばなければならないが、作例はボケ足のある最小サイズのブラシを使って、シフトキーを押しながらポイントをクリックする直線引きのテクニックを使っている。

14. Depending on the area to be selected it is important to choose the right painting tool, but this example was created with the smallest shading brush, using clicks to draw straight lines from point to point.

15．縁取りをしたら内部も塗りつぶしセレクトメニューの選択範囲の選択コマンドを実行。選択範囲の反転コマンドを実行して窓ガラス内を選択状態にし、#チャンネルに最終マスクとして選択範囲の記録（上書き）する。

15. After removing the frame select the inner fill and do *Load Selection*. Execute the *Inverse* command, then select the inner area of the glass and *Save Selection* (Write Over) as a mask to *Channel #4*.

Convenient Use of Masking ....*The easy Quick Mask mode*

作業上、マスクは選択範囲となんら変わることはない。選択範囲を保存したものがマスクである。保存されたマスクを呼び出せば画像上の選択範囲として利用できる。

マスクでなければできないことは、マスクチャンネル上でペインティングツールを使って作成加工できる自由さと、単独で保存できること、グレースケールのファイルはすべてマスクとして応用できることであろうか。

高解像度のファイルを扱う時、選択範囲を表示したまま、選択範囲内に加工を加えるより**コマンド+Hキー**で**境界線の消去**コマンドを実行しておいて加工するほうが処理スピードが速い。

While working on an image you can save a selected area that hasn't been altered in any particular way and recall it later as a mask for the selected area.

What you cannot do with anything but a true mask is create freely with the painting tool on a mask channel, save separately, and use grayscale files.

When using high resolution image files you can increase the speed of your processing by leaving selected areas highlighted and hitting **Command+H**, then executing the **Hide Edges** command.

完成保存されたマスクチャンネル。窓ガラス以外は完全にマスキングされている。このマスクにフィルターメニューのぼかしコマンドで適当なボケを加えることもできるし、ペインティングツールでさらに修整加工することも、グラデーションをかけることも可能である。複雑な合成作業をマスクを使わずに済ますことは難しい。このような簡単なマスクでも選択ツールで作るより精度の高いきれいなものをすばやく作ることができる。

A finished and saved mask channel. Except for the Window all other areas are masked out. Here the **Bluer** command on the **Filter** menu can be used to add an appropriate degree of shading, or the painting tool to further retouch or add gradation. It is difficult to create a complex composite without using masks. Even this simple mask can be created quickly, cleanly and precisely without using the Selection tool.

17図の要領で牧場の風景を窓外に合成する。ペーストした時にフローティング領域のコンディションをコントロールするのが合成のコントロールだが非常に便利なので使い込んで習熟されたい。作例は彩度を若干落とすために**不透明度**を90%に設定している。

In Picture 17 the pasture image is combined in the principal image area. When **pasting** a floating area the conditions can be controlled very accurately with **Composite Controls**. One should learn to use them well. In the example the coloring was reduced by bringing **Opacity** to 90%. The calculations can be selected easily in **Mode**, making the process of overlaying an object quite easy.

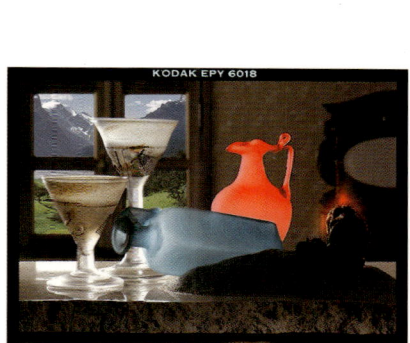

16. 左側の**マスク描画モード**からチャンネルパレットで一番上の**RGBチャンネル**をクリック（もしくは**コマンドキー+0キー**）、コンポジットモード（作画モード）に戻る。**選択範囲**メニューから**選択範囲の選択**を実行する。

16. From **Quick Mask mode** on the left side click on the **RGB channel** (or use **Command + 0 key**), and return to Composite mode (Picture mode) .Then from the **Select** menu choose the **Load Selection** command.

17. 35頁で保存しておいたNo.3画像（牧場の風景）を開き、合成したい部分を選択してコピー後閉じてから**編集**メニューの**選択範囲内へペースト**コマンドを実行する。ガラス面に室内側の映り込みなどがあれば**合成のコントロール**で調整する。

17. Open the No. 3 image (Pasture Photo) saved on page 35. Select the area you wish to superimpose, **Copy** and **Close**. Then from the **Edit** menu choose the **Paste Into** command. If there is interior reflection on the glass use the **Composite Controls** to touch up.

18. 34頁の解決策。海釣り用の大型の重り（鉛製）から削りだしたL型のウエイト。安くて簡単で想像以上に便利なので特にビギナーにお薦めする。これで作業途中にトイレにもいけるし電話にも出られる。

18. The finishing policy on page 34. Used here is a large fishing sinker from an ocean rig. It's made of lead, cheap, and very useful, especially for beginners. Use it while you're working. Then go to the toilet, or answer your phone.

Shift+Option Key   Command+Option Key

*Pen Tool*の効果的な利用法

第2章、人工着色テクニック実習で保存しておいたファイルを利用する。パスパレットからペンツールを選択して各果物を個別にトレースする。ペンツールになじめない人はペンツールをダブルクリックしてペンツールオプションでラバーバンド表示をチェックしておくと引かれていくラインが見えるので分かりやすい。

Here we will use the file created for artificial coloring purposes and saved in Chapter 2. Select the **Pen tool** from the **Paths Palette** and individually trace each piece of fruit. You can click points and trace, but for those who aren't good with the **Pen tool**, the **Pen tool options** can be opened and the **Rubber Band** checked to give the **Pen tool** the same Rubber Band mode as one finds in the Lasso tool.

Ver.2.5になって最も便利なもう1つの機能が大幅に機能アップした**ペンツール**だ。**ツールボックス**やメニューから全ての**パス**機能が**パスパレット**に移動して選択ツールとは無関係に独立して使えるようになったので、大きく利用範囲が広がった。ここでは基本的な使用法として、選択ツールの替わりに**パス**特有の滑らかな選択範囲を作って、直接色を加えてみる。もちろん**選択範囲の作成**コマンドを実行すれば選択範囲に変換できるが、新機能として**パス**のままで**パスの塗りつぶし**コマンドも**パス**の境界線を描くコマンドも実行できるようになったのだ。また**パス**をレイアウト用のアタリとして利用することも作業効率を高めるために有効なテクニックだ。

ペンツールでクリックしてドラッグすると曲線を描くスムーズポイントになりドラッグしないとコーナーポイントになる。描画後に変えたい場合はパスパレットから**方向点の切り替え**ツールを選択して変更したいポイントをクリックするとコーナーポイントに、ドラッグすると**スムーズポイント**に切り替わる。

If you click the **Pen tool** and drag a smooth, curved line is drawn. A **Direction Line** is shown beginning at the **anchor point**. If you don't drag, a **corner point** without a **Direction Line** will be created. If you want to change your drawing later, you can select the **Corner tool** from the **Paths Palette**, and click on the point you wish to change to create a **corner point**, or drag on the point to create a **smooth point**.

Another excellent tool in Ver. 2.5 is the upgraded **Pen Tool**. Now all the functions of the Paths have been moved from the **Toolbox** to the **Paths Palette**, and thus can be used without relation to the selection tools. This makes them much more useful. Here, as a basic method, we will make special **paths** instead of using selection tools to add colors to a selected area. Of course you can still switch the selected area with the **Make Selection** command, but new functions of **Paths** are the ability to use the **Fill** and **Stroke** commands. Also, **Paths** are a very effective means of efficiently creating layouts.

---

19. 果物を1つトレースする度にパスを保存する。パスパレットのメニューからパスの記録コマンドを実行、名前をつけて保存する。次の果物をトレースする前にパスパレットのパス名のチェックをクリックしてパスを非表示にしておく。

19. One of the fruits is traced, and saved as a **Path**. Do the **Save Paths** command under the **Paths Palette**, giving the selection a name. Before tracing the next fruit click the **Paths** name on the **Paths** Palette to hide the **Path**.

20. トレースした後でアンカーポイントを移動したり方向ポイントをドラッグすることで細かく調整することができる。

20. After tracing you can move the **Anchor points** or drag the **Direction points** to fine tune your outline.

21. 両側の**方向ポイント**を別々に調整したい場合は**コントロールキー**を押したまま**パス選択ツール**でドラッグする。そのまま反対側を調整するときは**コントロールキー**を押さずにドラッグしないと連動モードに戻ってしまう。

21. When you wish to adjust **Direction Points** on either side separately, hold down the **Control key** and drag with the **Selection pointer**. If you go to the opposite side to adjust and don't press **Control key** when you drag you will return to continuous mode.

Easy & Effective Ways of Using the Pen Tool

作成したパスはパスパレットのメニューでパスの記録コマンドを実行しておけばいくつでもレイヤーを変えて持つことができる。マスクチャンネルと違ってほとんどメモリーを喰わないのでマスク代りに気軽に利用できる。

マスクでなければできないこと以外はパスとして選択範囲を持つほうが作業効率は良いかもしれない。

パスを「イラストレーター」の書類として書き出すこともできる。EPSフォーマットで保存する場合、パスパレットのメニューでクリッピングパスを実行しておけば「イラストレーター」やレイアウトソフトに貼り込むときに切り抜きマスク付きの画像として使うこともできる。

If you save the Paths you produce with **Save Paths** on the **Palette** menu you can create a number of layers. Unlike **Masks**, **Paths** do not require a great deal of memory, and can thus be used freely. It's probably safe to say that anything that can be done with **Paths** rather than **Masks** is more efficiently achieved with the former. **Paths** can also be written and read in Illustrator. If you set the **Paths** Palette to **Clipping Path** and save in **EPS** format you can use masks as relief images in Illustrator and other software.

作成したパスを1つずつ表示しながらパスパレットのメニューからパスの塗りつぶしコマンドを使って22図の要領で好みの色をつける。ぼかしの半径を250Pixelsまでつけられるのでかなり変化をつけることができる。作例に不透明度:75%,ぼかしの半径:0 pixels,アンチエイリアシング:オンで描画モード:色相と彩度(明度はそのまま色だけ変える)で実行している。

Bringing up **Paths** one by one, use the **Fill Path** command to add the color of your choice to Picture 22. The **Feather Radius** can be set to 250 pixels, so a fair degree of variety can be achieved. The example was done with **Feather Radius:** 0, **Opacity:** 75%, **Anti-aliased**: On and **Mode: color**. (Brightness is unchanged; only Color was altered.)

23図の要領で器の縁に、にじんたラインを入れる。ブラシパレットでの設定がそのまま生かされるのであらかじめペイントツールとブラシパレットの設定をしておく。にじんだ感じを強調するためにブラシのサイズを変えながら3回に分けてパスの境界線を描くを実行している。

In Picture 23 a blurred line is added to the edge of the vessel. The settings of the **Brushes Palette** will be used, so adjust settings to the **Paint Tool** and **Brushes Palette** beforehand. In order to strengthen the blur of the line you can change the size of the **Brush** three times, each time executing **Stroke Path**.

22. 描画色に好みの色を表示しておいてパスパレットのメニューからパスの塗りつぶしを実行する。不透明度:75%,描画モード:色相と彩度,ぼかしの半径:0pixels,アンチエイリアシング:オンでOKする。

22. Choose the color of your choice for the **Foreground Color**, then do **Fill Paths** on the **Palette** menu. Set to **Opacity:** 75%, **Mode: Color**, **Feather Radius:** 0 Pixels, **Anti-aliased**: On, and click **OK**.

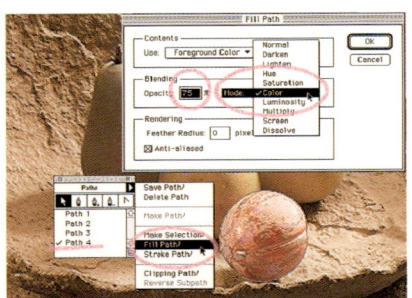

23. 描画色に好みの色を表示してエアーブラシツールを選択、ブラシサイズ29pixelsボケ足ありペイントの間隔:20%にしてパスパレットのメニューからパスの境界を描くコマンドを実行する。さらブラシサイズを小さくしながらパスの境界を描くコマンドを2回実行する。

23. Display the color of your choice for the **Foreground**, then select the **Airbrush tool**, setting the **Brush** size to 29 Pixels with shadowing, **Pressure** 20%, then execute **Stroke Paths** under the **Paths Palette**. Reduce size of the brush and do two more **Stroke Paths**.

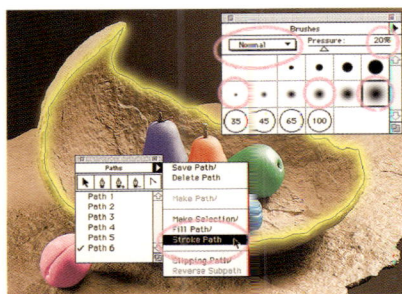

24. パスパレットのメニューからクリッピングパスを実行する。パス名を表示してワインディング規則を選択OKする。EPSフォーマットで保存すると他のソフトで切り抜きマスク付きの画像データとして利用できる。

24. Execute **Clipping Path** under the **Paths Palette**. Display the **Path** name and click **OK** for **Non-Zero Winding Fill Rule**. If you save in **EPS** mode you can use the path as a relief mask or image in other software.

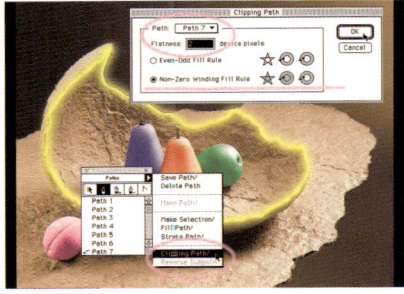

 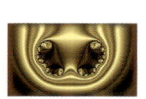   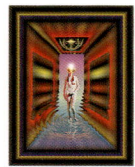

第4章 グラデーションテクニック

Chapter 4　Gradient Techniques

グラデーションテクニック *Gradient Techniques*

グラデーションを制するものはデジタルフォトを制す

写真とイラストの大きな差のひとつにグラデーションの違いがある。

写真は被写体に当たった光の反射光をフィルムに記録したものだ。理想的な平均照明を行わないかぎり必ず光の強弱がつき、それが写真の階調を作り上げている。ベタ塗りのイラストや白一色の石膏像であってもフィルムに写し取られた映像は照明光によって階調が表現されている。

つまり階調＝グラデーションが映像を作っているのだ。モノクロ写真の引き伸ばし処理を自分で行ったことのある人にとっては自明のことである。

デジタル処理で作られた映像と最大の差が、複雑で微妙な階調表現の有無にあるといってよい。デジタル映像のリアリティを増すためには複雑で微妙なグラデーションを取り入れることが早道だ。

基本的には単純なグラデーションであっても描くよりはスキャニングした写真データを利用するほうがリアリティは保証される。しかしそれでは芸がないので、この章では、フォトショップのグラデーション機能を最大限に引き出して複雑微妙な階調表現＝グラデーションテクニックを実習する。

By mastering gradients you have mastered digital photography

One of the great differences between photography and illustration is gradients.

In photography, the light reflected from the subject is captured on film. Except in ideal lighting, there is always stronger and weaker lighting, with the result that photos always have sharp gradations. Even photos of painted illustrations or pure white sculptures will exhibit gradations.

In other words, gradation is what creates a picture image. Anyone who has worked in a darkroom enlarging monochrome film will attest to this.

One of the cheif differences among digital images is the lack, or existence of, complex and subtle gradations. The fastest way to increase the reality of a digital image is to add such complex and subtle gradations.

Even with simple gradations, photography and scanning is a surer method than illustration for acheiving the desired effect. But this method lacks art, and this chapter is therefore devoted to the creation of gradations with the gradient techniques found in Photoshop.

マルチグラデーションの薦め

ご存知の通りマッキントッシュの1677万色を使用できるフルカラー環境においても階調数は256ステップである。どんなに広いスペースであろうとも狭いスペースと同じ階調数しか確保することはできない。広い面積にグラデーションをかけると階調のとび（バンディング）が目立つのは良く経験することである。スキャニングした自然画ではまず問題になることはないのに、『イラストレーター』で作成したイラストや、フォトショップ上で描いた絵や背景用のグラデーションでは気になることが多い。**フィルタメニューのノイズからノイズを加える**を選び適度のノイズを各チャンネルごとにかけるとバンディングを目立たなくするのに効果がある。また単色のグラデーションは別にして、後述の例のように何段階かに分けて連続したマルチグラデーションをかける工夫で、階調のとび（バンディング）の目立たないきれいなバックを作ることが可能だ。

W:450×H:86ピクセルで**新規**ファイルを作成し、**長方形選択ツール**で上半分を選択、グラデーションツールで茶色のグラデーションを作る。選択範囲を下半分 **ドラック／コピー**、イメージメニューの**鏡像（垂直方向）**を実行すると、茶色の対称型マルチグラデーションができる。

Create a **New** file of W:450xH:86 pixels and use the **Rectanglar marquee Tool** to select the upper half. Then use the **Gradient Tool** to create a brown gradient. Now **Drag/Copy** the gradient to the bottom half, and select **Flip (Vertical)** from the **Image** menu to create a symmetrical "multi-gradation."

同様に**新規**ファイルを作成、上半分弱を選択し赤のグラデーションを作る。次に残りの部分を選択しグラデーションツールで反対方向のグラデーションを作る。非対称型のマルチグラデーションができあがる。

Now create a second **New** file, selceting a bit less than the whole upper half and creating a red gradient. Now select the remaining area and use the **Gradient Tool** to produce the reverse gradient. Here you have another symmetrical multi-gradation.

4分割型のマルチグラデーションである。**長方形選択ツール**で上から順番にグラデーションをかける範囲を選択しながらグラデーションツールでグラデーションを下に向けてかけていく。ハイライトが2本入った複雑なマルチグラデーションができあがる。

A four-part multi-gradation. Using the **Rectangular Marquee Tool,** select the gradient area; use the **Gradient Tool** to create a downward gradation. Now you have a complex multi-gradation with two highlights.

A recommendation for multi-gradation

As you know, Macintosh is a full color environment with some 16,770,000 potential colors. However, there are exactly 256 tonal gradations. No matter how wide or narrow the image space, these are the only gradations available. When the working space is broad one often notices the "banding" of the gradients. There is no real problem with scanned, natural photographs, but with images done on "Illustrator," and pictures and backgrounds created in Photoshop, numerous problems arise. One can achieve an effective reduction in banding by choosing **Add Noise** from **Noise** under the **Filter** menu and using it to add an appropriate degree of noise to each channel. Or, with the exception of one-color gradations, one can use the method described in this chapter to separate bands into numerous sections and implement continuous multi-gradations to reduce banding and achieve a very clean effect.

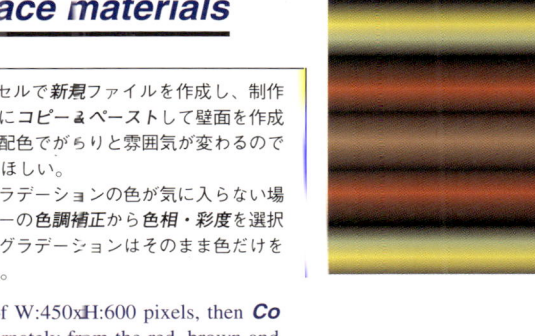

壁面用素材を創る *Creating surface materials*

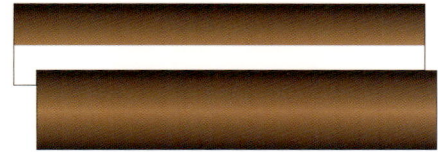

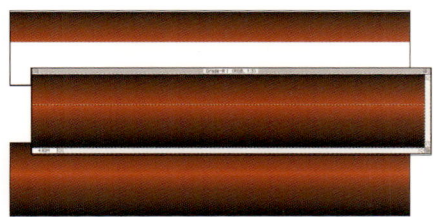

W:450×H:600ピクセルで新規ファイルを作成し、制作済みの壁素材を交互にコピー＆ペーストして壁面を作成する。組み合わせる配色でがらりと雰囲気が変わるのでじっくり取り組んでほしい。
もしできあがったグラデーションの色が気に入らない場合はイメージメニューの色調補正から色相・彩度を選択し色相を調整すればグラデーションはそのまま色だけを変えることができる。

Create a new file of W:450xH:600 pixels, then *Copy* and *Paste* alternately from the red, brown and green files to create the wall. Depending on the mix of colors the atmosphere will differ greatly, so apply them carefully. The greatest advantage of the computer is the ability to use simulation. If you don't like the finished gradation select *Hue/Saturation* from *Adjust* under the *Image* menu. You can adjust the *Hue* without changing the gradation.

長方形選択ツールを使ってW:212×H:362ピクセルの選択範囲を画像の中心部に作る。パスパレットのメニューからパスの作成を実行してレイアウト用のパスに変換する。
パスは表示しておいてもパスとは無関係に他のコマンドを実行できるのでアタリ用に便利だ。

Using the *Rectangular Marquee Tool* create an area of W:212xH:362 pixels in the center of the image. Using *Make Path* under the a *Path Palettes* menu, revert to a Path for the layout. When using a Path you can still employ other commands, which makes this command convenient for layouts.

---

1. ファイルメニューの新規でW:450×H:600ピクセルの新規ファイルを作成する。

2. グラデーションの設定はグラデーションツールオプションで色の変化:通常、種類:ライン状、中間位置:50%にする。

3. パスパレットのメニューからパスの作成を実行後、同じメニューのパスの記録コマンドでパスを保存する。

1. With *New* under the *File* menu create a *New* file of W:450xH:600 pixels.

2. The gradient setting is done with the *Gradient Tool* option, here set to: *Style: Normal*, *Type : Linear*, *Midpoint Skew :* 50%.

3. Under menu select *Paths Palettes*, then click *Make Paths*. Then choose *Save Path* from the menu.

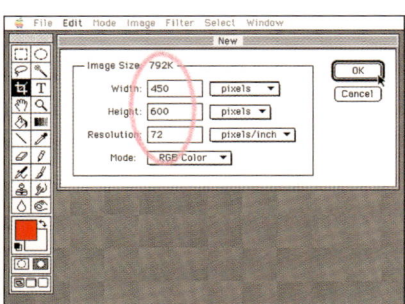

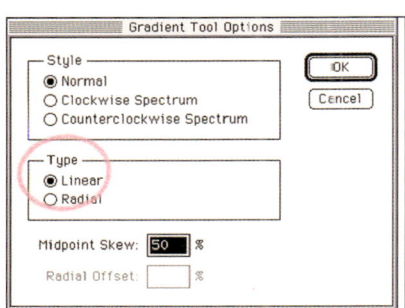

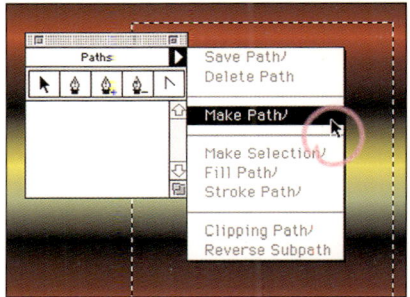

額縁型グラデーションマスクの作成

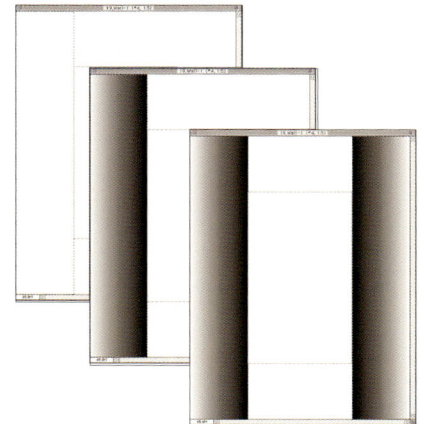

壁面に額縁型の赤いグラデーションをつけるためのグラデーションマスクを作る。
前頁で作ったパスを表示しておいてチャンネルパレットのメニューから**チャンネルの追加**を実行し、パスの左側を上から下まで**長方形選択ツール**で選択する。
グラデーションツールを使って選択範囲内の左から右端へ白から黒のグラデーションを作る。
そのままドラッグ／コピーしてパスの右側へ配置して、**イメージ**メニューの**鏡像**から**水平方向**を選択する。

For the red gradient wall frame create a gradation mask. As explained on the previous page, choose **New Channels** undermenu and **Channels Palette**, then use the **Rectangular Tool** to select the left side of the path, moving from top to bottom. Then use the **Gradient Tool** to create a white-to-black gradient from left to right in the selected area.

選択範囲を**ドラック／コピー**して**イメージ**メニューの**回転**から**90度反時計回り**を実行して**編集**メニューから**カット**を実行する。

Drag/Copy the selected area, then do a **90° CCW** with **Rotate** under the **Image** menu. Then use **Cut** under the **Edit** menu.

なげなわツールでパスの上側を逆台形状に選択し、**編集**メニューから**選択範囲内へペースト**する。

Select the upper part of the Path with the **Lasso Tool** and create the opposing frame piece. The choose **Paste Into** from the **Edit** menu.

なげなわツールでパスの下側を台形状に選択し、**編集**メニューから**選択範囲内へペースト**する。**イメージ**メニューの**鏡像**から**垂直方向**を選択する。

Now use the **Lasso Tool** to select the bottom frame piece, and **Paste Into**. Then choose **Vertical** under **Flip** in the **Image** menu.

完成したグラデーションマスク。このまま保存すると逆マスクになるので、**イメージ**メニューの**階調補正**から**階調の反転**を実行して白黒反転してから**保存**する。

The finished gradation mask. If you Save now the mask will be reversed, so use **Invert** under **Map** on the **Image** menu to create a black and white reverse. Now **Save**.

4．チャンネルパレットのメニューからチャンネルの追加を実行。チャンネルオプションはそのままOKする。#4の代わりにわかりやすい名前をつけるのも便利である。

4. Select **New Channels** under **Channels Palette** on the menu. Leave **Channel** options as is. Use an easy-to-remember name for convenience.

5．イメージメニューの回転から90度反時計回りを実行する。選択範囲が直角に反時計回転する。

5. Do a **90° CCW** with **Rotate** under the **Image** menu. **Rotate** counter-clockwise to a right angle.

6．イメージメニューの鏡像から垂直方向を実行する。選択範囲が上下反転する。

6. Do **Vertical** with **Flip** under the **Image** menu. The selected area will be turned upside down.

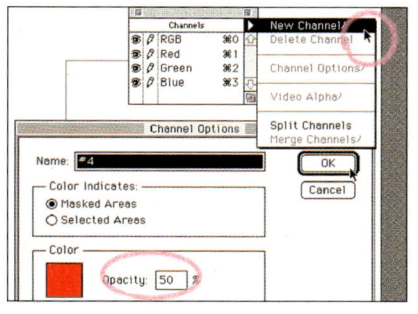

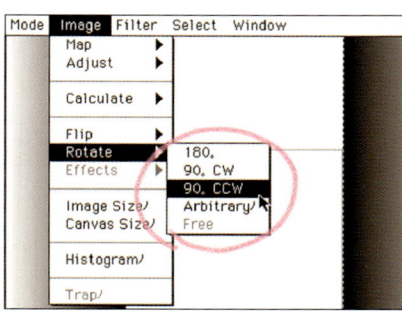

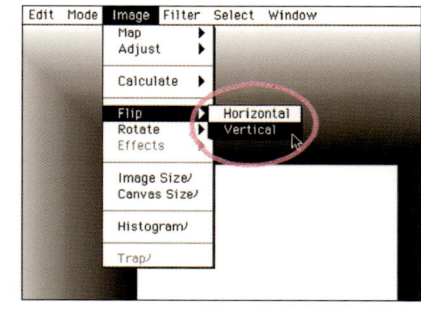

Making a framed gradation mask

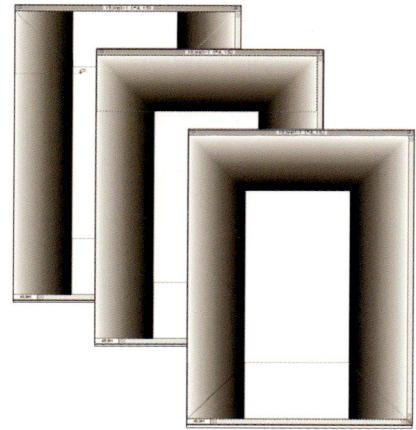

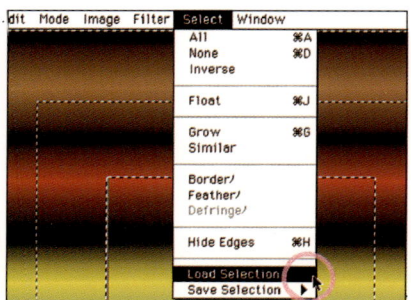

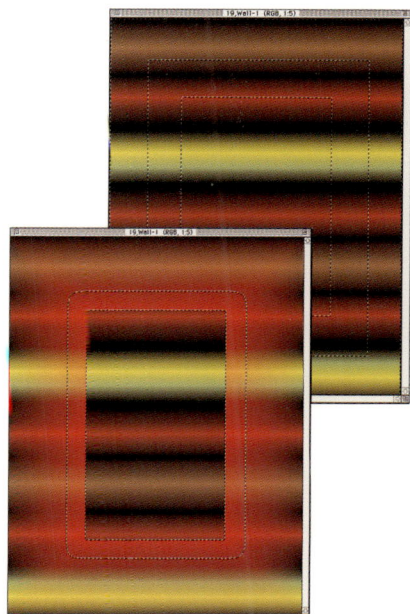

描画色を赤色に設定、選択範囲メニューの選択範囲の選択を実行してグラデーションマスクの選択範囲を表示する。

After making the **Foreground color** red, choose **Load Selection** under the **Select** menu. This will show a red gradient mask in the selected area.

編集メニューの塗りつぶしオプションを不透明度：50％、描画モード：通常で実行。1回目のグラデーションをかける。長方形選択ツールの境界のぼかし：20ピクセルに設定コマンド＋シフトキー押しながら2度目のグラデーションをかける部分を選択する。

Set the **Fill** option (under **Edit** menu) at **Opacity:**50%, **Mode :Normal**. The first gradation is set. Set the **Father Radius** (under **Rectangular Marquee** option) at 20 pixels. Then, holding down the **Command + Shift keys**, do the second gradation.

編集メニューの塗りつぶしオプションを不透明度：50％、描画モード：通常で実行すると2回目のグラデーションがフレーム内側選択部分のみにかかる。パースペクティブをかけるためのアタリをパスパレットのペンツールを使って描き、パスの記録して「壁素材」として保存する。

With the **Fill** option (under **Edit** menu) set at **Opacity** 50% and **Mode Normal**, do the second gradation only in the selected area of the frame. Use the **Pen Tool** to draw the area where the perspective will fit, then use **Save Paths** under **Path Palettes** menu and **Save** as Wall Materials.

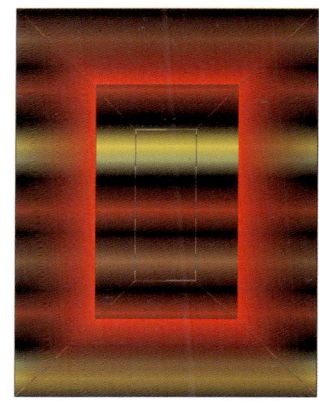

7．選択範囲メニューから選択範囲の選択を実行する。マスクチャンネルで設定した選択範囲が表示される。

7. **Load Selection** under **Edit** menu. The are selected under mask channel 2will be shown.

8．編集メニューから塗りつぶしを実行。塗りつぶしオプションを 使用内容：前景、不透明度：50％、描画モード：通常に設定してOKする。赤色が50％の透明度で選択範囲内に上塗りされる。

8. Use **Fill** under the **Image** menu. Set **Fill** option at **Contents: Foreground**, **Blending Opacity :** 50%, **Mode : Normal**. The red area will fill the selected area at 50% transparency.

9．長方形選択ツールをダブルクリックして長方形選択ツールオプションを設定する。選択範囲：通常、境界のぼかし：20ピクセルでOKボタンをクリック。

9. Double-click the **Rectangular Marquee Tool** to set **Rectangular Marquee Tool** options. Click OK button for **Normal** and **Feather Radius** 20 pixels.

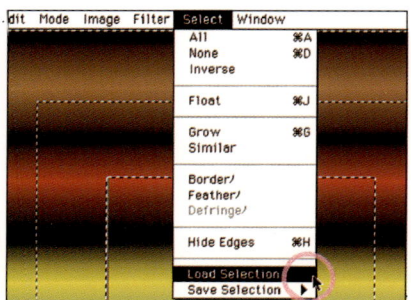

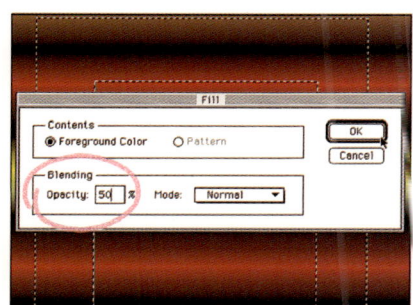

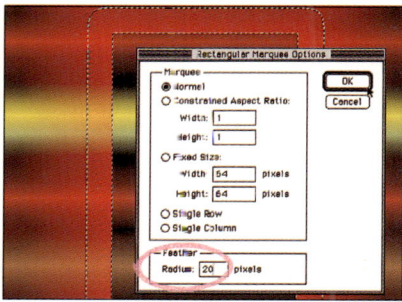

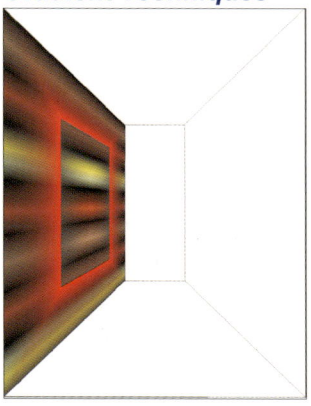

壁面にパースをつける

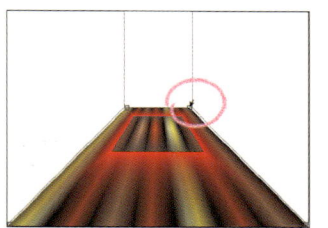

完成した「壁素材」ファイルを開く。パスパレットでチェックしてレイアウト用に作成保存しておいたパスを表示し、イメージメニューの変形から台形を実行、パスの形に変形後「壁素材左」として別名で保存する。

Open the Wall Materials file, which you completed on the previous page. Bring up the path you prepared for layout under *Paths Palette*, then do *Perspective* under *Effects* in the *Image* menu. After the path shape has changed, *Save As* "Left Wall Materials."

「壁素材」ファイルを開く。パスパレットでパスを表示し、オプション＋シフトキーを押しながらすべてのパスをクリック、カットしておいてイメージメニューの回転から90度時計回りする。イメージメニューの画像解像度で幅：450ピクセルにリサイズ、カットしておいたパスをペースト。パスの底辺を壁面の底辺に合わせ「壁素材横」という名前で別名で保存する。

Open the Wall Materials file. Bring up the path which you checked and prepared for layout, then, holding down the *Option Key + Shift* at the same time, click-select all paths and *Cut*. Set *Rotate* (under *Image* menu) at *90°CW*. *Resize* with *Image Size* (under *Image* menu) to 450 pixels, then *Paste* to the previously *Cut* path. Align the bottom of the path with the bottom of the Frame and *Save As* "Side Wall Materials."

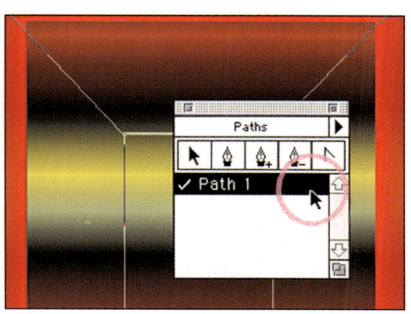

イメージメニューの変形から台形を実行。パスのレイアウトラインよりやや小さめに変形してから「壁素材下」として別名で保存する。

Use *Perspective* under *Effects* on the *Image* menu. After reshaping to somewhat smaller dimensions than the layout, save the path as "Bottom Wall Materials," using the *Save As* command.

ガイドラインとしてパスを利用する

　壁面を立体的に構成するため、壁にパースをつけて組み合わせる。その素材作りがこの見開きページでの作業内容である。

　素材を変形するためのガイドラインとしてパスを有効に利用している。パスは目安として使うだけだが、レイアウト用にパスを表示したまますべてのコマンドがパスとは無関係に実行可能なので、形も自由自在なガイドラインとしてこれほど便利なものはない。

　あらかじめレイアウトが決まっている場合レイアウト用紙をスキャナーで取り込んでパスに置き換えておけば正確なレイアウトをなんの造作もなく行うことができる。

Using Paths a guidelines

In order to make a surface appear three-dimensional, one adds perspective to it. The creation of such materials is shown on these pages. Paths are convenient for use in changing the shape of materials. They are only used as approximations, but as paths have absolutely no effect upon the execution of commands they are extremely convenient. When a layout has been decided beforehand it can be scanned and converted into paths for extremely accurate layout work with very little waste of computer memory.

---

10. パスパレットでパス1をクリックしてレイアウト用のパスを表示する。パスパレットのホワイトスペースをクリックするとパスを非表示にできる。

10. Bring up the path prepared for the layout by clicking path 1 under *Path Palettes*.

11. イメージメニューの画像解像度でファイルサイズを変更。変更後のファイルサイズの幅を450ピクセル、縦横比を固定をチェック、ファイルサイズを固定のチェック外しで高さは自動的に338ピクセルになる。

11. Change the file size with *Image Size* under the *Image* menu. Set *New Size* at *Width* :450 pixels and check *Proportions*. If File Size is left unchecked *Height* will default to 338 pixels.

12. イメージメニューの変形から台形を選択して壁素材を変形する。

12. Choose *Perspectives* under *Effects* on the *Image* menu, and change the shape of the Wall Materials.

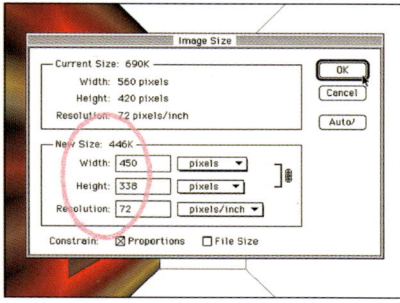

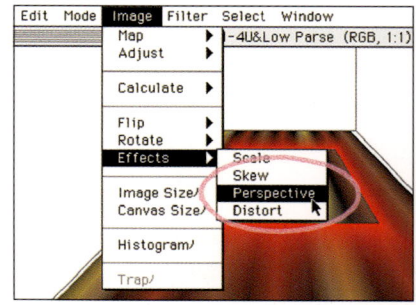

Adding perspective to the wall

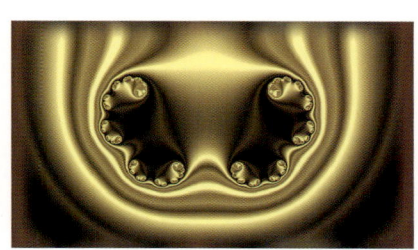

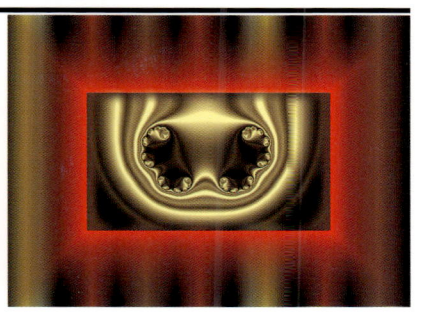

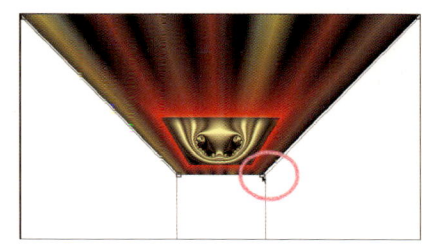

天井部分に変化と雰囲気をつけるための素材。

Materials for altering and changing the mood of the ceiling.

「壁素材横」ファイルを開く。イメージメニューの鏡像から垂直方向を選択する。長方形選択ツールで赤いグラデーションの内側を選択し左のゴールド素材を選択範囲内へペーストする。

Open the "Wall Materials" file. Select the inner area of the red gradient with the **Rectangular Marquee Tool**, then **Paste Into** with the gold materials on the left.

パスパレットでチェックしてレイアウト用に作成保存しておいたパスを表示し、イメージメニューの変形から台形を実行、パスの形よりやや小さめに変形後「壁素材上」として別名で保存する。

Bring up the path which was checked and saved for layout. Do **Perspective**, from **Effects** (under the **Image** menu). **Save As** "Wall Materials" in a somewhat smaller size than the path.

マルチグラデーションテクニックのキーポイントは1段目の最後と2段目の最初を同色に保つことだ。そのためには**描画色**と**背景色**に交互に新色を表示しながらグラデーションをかける方向を連動して変えるとよい。

Ver.2.5からは**ツールパレット**のカラー表示部分右肩の**描画・背景色切り替え**で描画色と背景色の切り替えが簡単にできる。描画色に次の色を表示してから**描画・背景色切り替え**で背景色と描画色を切り替えてグラデーションをかけるようにすればすべて同一方向に統一できる。

The key in multi-gradations is to keep the color the same between the end of step 1 and the beginning of step 2. To do this it is good to alternate the adding of new colors between the **Foreground Color** and **Background Color**, changing the direction of gradation. On the right shoulder of Color, under **Tools Palette**, is a **Switch Colors** command which makes changing between **Foreground** and **Background** a simple operation. When setting the second color for **Foreground Color** use **Switch Colors** to shift from **Foreground** to **Background**, unifying the gradation operation into one direction for all .

13. 編集メニューから**選択範囲内へペースト**を選択する。選択範囲内にデータがペーストされる。**選択範囲の後ろへペースト**コマンドは選択範囲の背後側にデータがペーストされる。

14. 台形コマンドを実行中はカーソルの形が変化する。選択範囲外では左側の◎形でそのままクリックすると変形作業を中止する。選択範囲内では右側のハンマー形でクリックすると変形が確定する。

15. ツールパレットの描画・背景色切り替えをクリックすると描画色と背景色を交互に切り替えることができる。Ver.2.5からの便利な新機能である。

13. Choose **Paste Into** from the **Edit** menu. Data will be **Paste** the selected area. With **Paste Behind** the selected data will be **Pasted** as background.

14. While executing the **Perspective** command the cursor can be moved outside and clicked, stopping the change operation. Inside the selected area, the cursor becomes a hammer. It is clicked on the right to set the change.

15. You can switch from **Foreground** to **Background** by clicking **Switch Colors** under the **Tool Palette**. This is a convenient new feature in version 2.5.

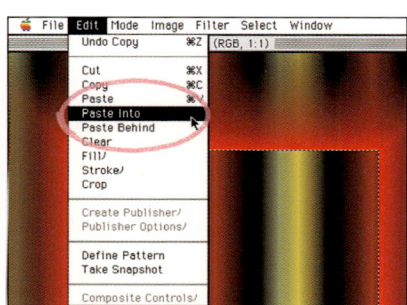

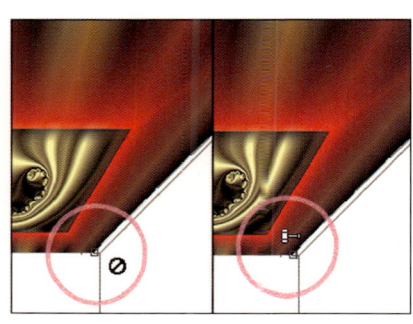

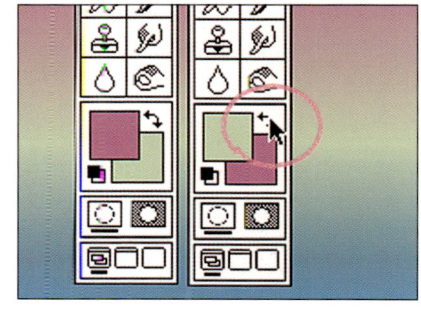

水面と空を作る Creating water and sky surfaces

W:450×H:600ピクセルで新規ファイルを作り不思議な色合いの空と水面を6段階に分けたマルチグラデーションテクニックで創造する。上部6分の1強を長方形選択ツールで選択しグラデーションツールで濃紺から紫までのグラデーションを作る。その下側6分の1弱を長方形選択ツールで選択しグラデーションツールで紫からマゼンタまでのグラデーションを作る。同様にその下にマゼンタからグリーンまでのグラデーションを作る。

Create a new file of W:450xH:600 to make six-step multi-gradation sky and water surfaces of unique coloring. Select more than 1/6 of the upper portion with the **Rectangular Marquee Tool** and make a dark blue to purple gradient. Under this, use the **Rectangular Marquee Tool** to create a gradient of purple to magenta over an area just under 1/6 of file size. Under this, make another gradient of magenta to green.

下側に向かってグリーンから水色、水色から明るい水色、明るい水色からブルーのグラデーションを作る。カラーパレットに組み合わせる色を登録しておくと便利だ。中間部の色の選択をいろいろ変えてみるのもよい。

Again, below this draw downward green to aqua, then aqua to light blue gradients. If you preset the colors under the **Colors Palette** this work will proceed more smoothly. By playing with the middle colors you can achieve even more daring effects.

完成したバックの上に「壁素材左」ファイルの壁面部分だけを選択してコピー&ペーストし位置を左端にそろえる。選択範囲をドラック/コピーして右側に移動、イメージメニューの鏡像から水平方向を実行する。

Above the finished background select the "Left Wall Materials" and use **Copy & Paste** to align it with left edge. **Drag/Copy** the selected area to the right, then use **Horizontal** under **Flip** on the **Image** menu.

「壁素材上」ファイルの壁面部分のみ選択してコピー&ペーストし位置を上端に合わせ、広がりを感じさせるために左右の壁との間を少しあけて隙間を作る。

Select only the upper portion of the "Upper Wall Materials" file and **Copy & Paste** to the upper edge. In order to give a sense of expanding space, leave a gap between the edge and the left wall.

「壁素材下」ファイルの壁面部分だけを選択してオプションキーを押しながらコピー&ペーストし合成のコントロールで不透明度：50%にする。左右の壁との間を少しあけて下端に配置する。

Select only the lower portion of the "Lower Wall Materials" and hold down the **Option Key** while **Copy&Pasting**. Then with **Composite Controls** set **Opacity** : 50%. Leave a bit of space between the left and right walls, positioning the addition along the lower edge.

16. フォトショップVer.2.01ではツールパレットに描画・背景色切り替え機能がないので描画色と背景色に交互に次の色を表示し、グラデーションをかける上下方向も交互に変えながら作っていく。

16. In Photoshop Ver. 2.01 there is no **Switch Colors** in the **Palette Tool**. Therefore **Foreground color** and **Background color** gradation will be created alternately in an upward direction.

17. あらかじめ使用する色をカラーパレットに登録しておくと便利だ。描画色に色を表示しパレットの空きスペースにカーソルをもっていってペンキ缶になってからクリックするとその色が登録される。

17. It is convenient to record the colors in the **Color Palette** beforehand. By moving the cursor to an empty space on the Palette it becomes a paint can;you canrecord the **Foreground** color by clicking.

18. 合成のコントロールオプションの設定画面。不透明度：50%、描画モード:通常で実行。合成のコントロールはペーストの際、非常に役立つコマンドなのでぜひマスターしてほしい。

18. The **Composite Controls** Setting menu. Settings are **Opacity** :50%, **Mode** : Normal. By all means learn to **Paste** with **Composite Controls**, as it is a highly useful command.

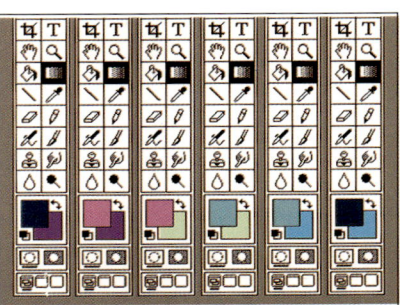

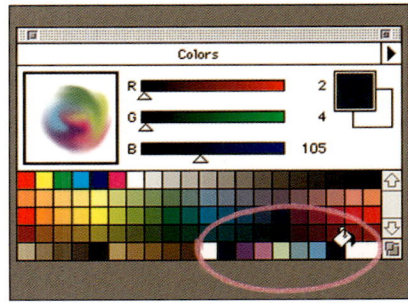

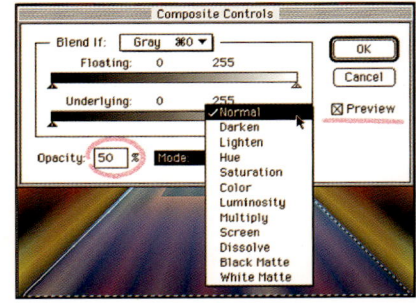

背景の合成作業

Background composite work

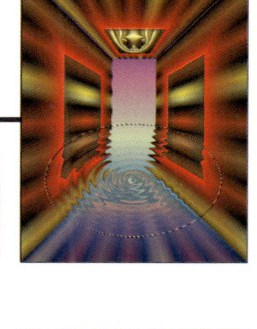

楕円選択ツールを使ってセンターより下側に波紋を作るための楕円領域を選択する。フィルタメニューの変形からジグザグを選択し大きさ：20、折り返し：10、左上、右下方向で実行する。

Using the *Elliptical Marquee Tool* select a downward facing ellipse for the ripples. Then select *Zigzag* under *Distort* from the *Filter* menu and execute at *Amount* :20, *Ridges* :10, *Pond Ripples*.

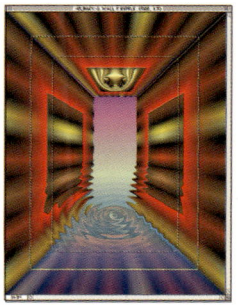

次頁の額縁をつけるガイドラインとして額縁の内側を長方形選択ツールで選択しパスパレットのメニューからパスの作成でパスに変換後パスの記録をしておく。再度パスにそって選択し長方形選択オプションで境界線をぼかす：10ピクセルにしてコマンドキーを押しながら選択範囲の内側を選択除外する。

As a guideline for the green frame on the next page use the *Marquee Tool* to select the inner area of the frame. Save it as a path with *Make Path* under the *Path Palette* menu. Then, select above the path and use the *Rectangular Marquee* option to set a *Feather Radius* of ten pixels. Pushing the *Command key*, select the inside of the area for exclusion from the command.

塗りつぶしコマンドで不透明度：2%にて白色を選択範囲内に塗り重ね、ハロー効果を作る。さらに長方形選択オプションで境界のぼかし：5ピクセルにてコマンドキーを押しながら選択範囲の内側を選択除外し塗りつぶしコマンドの不透明度：2%で白色を残った選択範囲内に塗り重ねハローを強調する。

Select *Fill* from the *Edit* menu and set *Opacity* : 2%. Select white and paint inside the selected area to achieve the feathered effect. Next, using the *Rectangular Marquee* option, set *Feather Radius* : 5 pixels, and holding down the *Command Key* exclude the inner portion while painting the rest of the selected area with:2% white, emphasizing the feathered effect

---

19. フィルタメニューの変形からジグザグを選択、設定を大きさ：20、折り返し：10、左上、右下方向で実行する。石を水面に投じたような波紋効果を得ることができる。

19. Select *Zigzag* under *Distort* on the *Filter* menu, setting variables at *Amount* : 20, *Ridges* : 10, *Pond of Ripples*. This creates ripples like those caused by stones thrown into water.

20. 長方形選択ツールをダブルクリックして長方形選択オプションの設定をする。選択範囲は通常、境界のぼかしを10ピクセルでOKボタンをクリック。

20. Double-click on the *Rectangular Marquee Tool* to bring up *Rectangular Marquee* Options. Set at Normal, with *Feather Radius* of 10 pixels. Click OK.

21. 編集メニューから塗りつぶしコマンドを選択。使用内容を前景、不透明度：2%、描画モード：通常で実行する。同メニューの境界線を描くコマンドは線分のみに作用する。設定できる内容は塗りつぶしと同じである。

21. Select the *Fill* Command from the *Edit* menu. Set to *Foreground Color*, *Opacity*: 2%, *Mode*: Normal. *Stroke* Command on the same menu is used only to control lines. Settings are the same as for *Fill*.

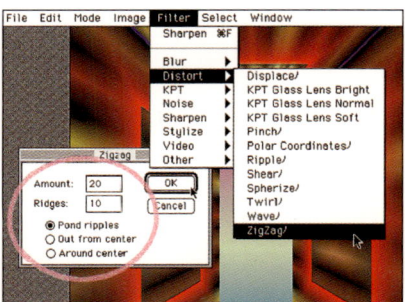

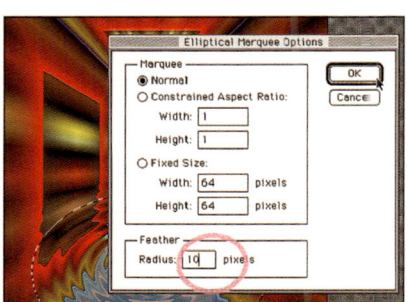

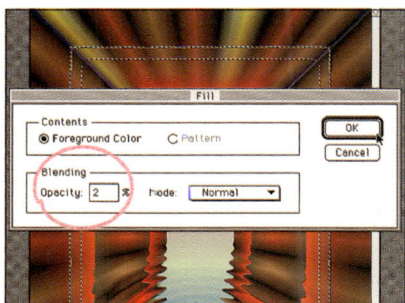

額縁を作る

長方形選択オプションで境界線をぼかす：5ピクセルにしてコマンドキーを押しながら選択範囲の内側を選択除外して細い幅の選択範囲をシャドウ用に作る。

After setting **Feather Radius** : 5 pixels (under the **Rectangular Marquee** options) hold down **Command Key** to exclude the inner portion of selected area while selecting the narrow area for shadowing.

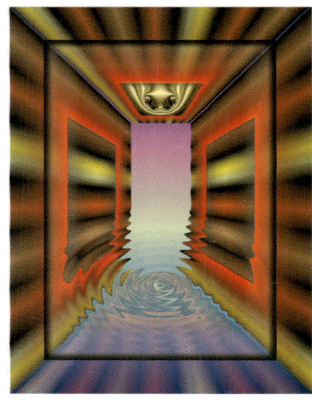

編集メニューの塗りつぶしを選択し**不透明度**：100%で黒色を選択範囲内に塗り重ね、シャドウを作る。「背景」という名前で**別名で保存す**る。

Select **Fill** under the **Edit** menu, creating a shadow in the selected area with black paint at **Opacity** :100%. Save under the name "Background."

まずフレーム素材の作業。**新規ファイル**をW:56×H:600ピクセルで作る。まず**カラーパレット**に使う組み合わせの配色を登録しておく。登録の方法は描画色に登録したい色を配置してパレットの空きスペースへカーソルをもっていきクリックするだけでよい。**長方形選択ツール**で幅12ピクセル縦600ピクセルを選択、**描画色**にグレー、**背景色**に濃いグレーを配色し**グラデーションツール**でグラデーションを作る。その右隣を幅8ピクセルで選択し濃いグレーから赤みのある黒、次を18ピクセルで赤みのある黒から山吹色のグラデーションを作る。同様に12ピクセルで紫から青、6ピクセルで青から黒のグラデーションを作ればフレーム素材のできあがりである。

Making frame materials

To make materials for a frame open a new file of W:56xH:600 pixels. Pre-record the colors you wish to combine under the **Color Palette**. To record the color you wish to use in the **Foreground**, bring it up and move the cursor to an empty place on the Palette, and click. Then use the **Rectangular Marquee Palette** to select a W:12 xH:600 pixel area. Make the **Foreground** gray, the **Background** dark gray, then use the **Gradient Tool** to create a gradation. Next to this, on the right side, select an 8 pixel area to grade from grey to rust , then an 18 pixel area next to this to grade from reddish black to copper. Likewise, create 12 pixel purple to blue and 6 pixel blue to black areas , and your frame is finished.

---

22. あらかじめ使用する色を**カラーパレット**に登録しておくと便利だ。**描画色**に色を表示しパレットの空きスペースにカーソルをもっていってペンキ缶になってからクリックするとその色が登録される。

22. It is convenient to enter colors you wish to use in the **Color Palette**. Show the color for the **Foreground**, then move the cursor to an empty place in the palate. When it becomes a paint can, click to record the color.

23. グラデーションの設定は**グラデーションツール**をダブルクリック、**グラデーションツールオプション**で**色の変化：通常**、**種類：ライン状**、**中間位置：50%**にする。

23. To set the gradient, either double-click the **Gradient Tool** or use **Option Key + Click**; this will bring up the **Gradient Tool** option dialogue. Set it to **Style**: Normal, **Type**: Linear, **Mid-point Skew**: 50%.

24. 反対側のフレームを作るために**イメージ**メニューの**鏡像**から**水平方向**を実行する。選択範囲が左右反転して左側のフレームから右側のフレームに形を変える。

24. To make the opposite side frame select **Horizontal** from **Flip** under the **Image** menu. By moving selection from left to right the left-side frame becomes the right-side frame.

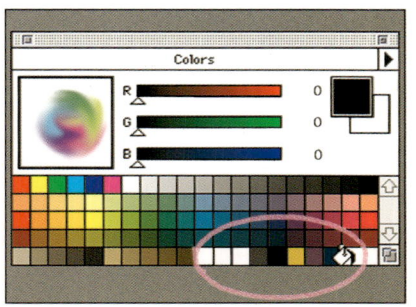

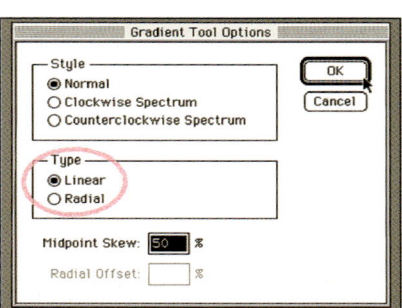

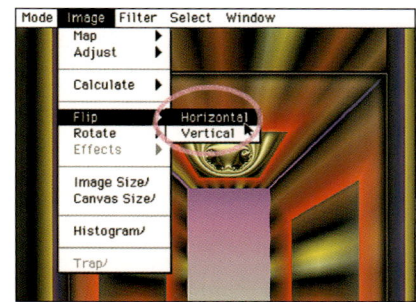

Making a frame

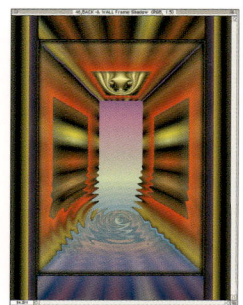

「背景」ファイルを開いてパスパレットのパス1をクリックしてガイドライン用のパスを表示する。
「フレーム素材」をコピー＆ペーストしてガイドラインにそって左端に配置する。選択範囲をドラック／コピーして右端に配置しイメージメニューの鏡像から水平方向を実行する。

Open the "Background" file and click on path 1 under the **Path Palette** to show the guideline path. **Copy** & **Paste** "Frame Materials," placing them in line with the guidelines. **Drag/Copy** the selected to the right edge, then do **Horizontal** under **Flip** on the **Image** menu.

完成した背景

Completed background

なげなわツールとオプションキーの併用でラバーバンドツールとして使い上部を逆台形に選択する。
ガイドラインの角と画像の角をポイントに結ぶだけでよい。

Use the **Lasso Tool** and **Option Key** to bring up the **Rubber Band Tool**, then use it to select the upper portion as an inverted pedestal. Then just bring the point of the image together with the corner of the guideline

「フレーム素材」を選択範囲内へペースト、イメージメニューの回転から90度時計回りを実行する。
同様に下部を選択して「フレーム素材」を選択範囲内へペースト、90度反時計回りすると右上の状態になる。 *

Use **Paste Into** to insert "Frame Materials," and **Rotate 90° CW** (under the **Image** menu). Likewise, select the bottom section and paste in "Frame Materials."

---

25. イメージメニューの回転から90度反時計回りを実行する。選択範囲が直角に反時計回転して下側のフレームになる。

26. 次頁のオブジェクト素材のマスクを作る作業である。自動選択ツールをダブルクリックしてオプションダイアログで選択する色の範囲：32アンチエイリアシングをオンに設定してバックを選択する。

27. チャンネルパレットで#4チャンネルを選択、RGBの左端の欄をクリックすると下図のマスク描画モードになる。下絵が見えるのでマスクの修整加工に便利だ。セレクションツールで修整するより作業スピードも速い。

25. Execute a **90° CCW Rotate** on the **Image** menu. The selected area will rotate at a right angle to become the bottom of the frame.

26. To make the mask for the subject on the next page double-click on the **Magic Wand Tool**; the Options dialogue will appear. Set it to **Tolerance** :32, **Anti-aliased**: ON. Then select the background.

27. Select channel #4 under the **Channels Palettes**. Click on the far left column to bring up the **Mask Mode**, shown below. You can see the picture underneath, which is convenient. This is faster than correcting with the Selection Tool.

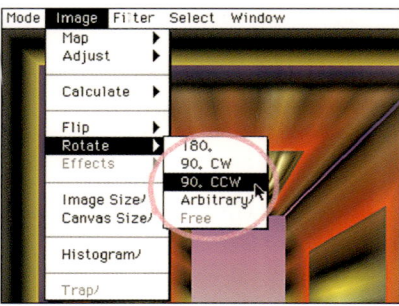

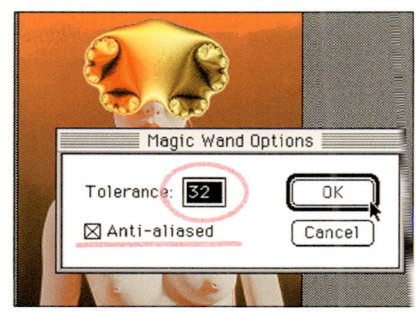

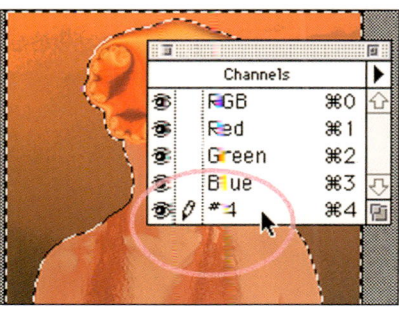

背景とオブジェクトの合成作業.......水面に映り込みを加える

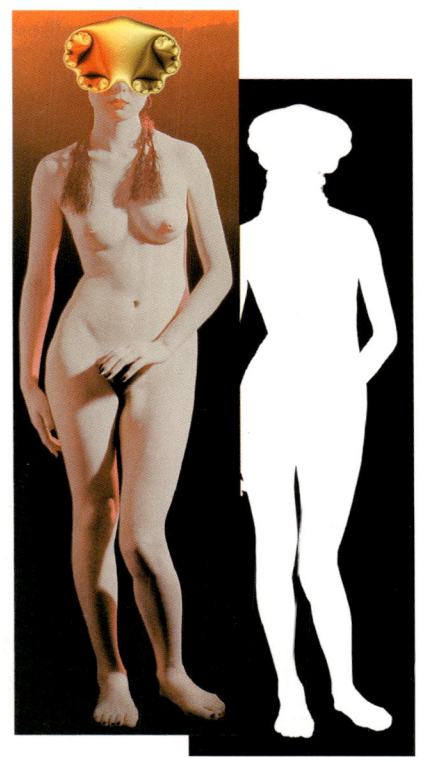

オブジェクト素材、バックおよびサイドから赤の強い光があたった仮面をつけたヌード。
切り抜き用のマスクを作る作業である。**自動選択ツールオプション**で**選択する色の範囲：32**、アンチエイリアシングをオンに設定した自動選択ツールでシフトキーを押しながらバック全体を選択し**選択範囲の記録**をする。チャンネルパレットの#4チャンネルを選択し**RGBチャンネル**の左端をクリックしてマスクモードにする。コマンド＋Dキーで選択範囲を解除して細部をブラシツールで修正する。
選択範囲で**選択範囲の選択**後 **選択範囲の反転**してオブジェクトのみを選択状態にしてから再度#4チャンネルに**選択範囲の記録**をしてマスクの完成である。添付ファイルは126ピクセル×417ピクセルあるので最後に**イメージメニューの画像解像度**で50%縮小して**保存**する。主要テーマが小さなサイズの場合、正確なマスクを作るためには倍サイズでスキャニングして作業後、50%縮小して実際の使用サイズにすると精度があがる。縮小後ピントが甘く感じられるようならフィルタメニューのシャープを1回かけるとシャープになる。
選択後すぐコピーし同じ作業を2度としないのであればマスクチャンネルを保存する必要はない。不要なαチャンネルを多数持つことはメモリーの浪費以外のなにものでもない。

The subject is a masked nude shown in reddish light cast from the side and background. Here the mask is created for the layout work. Set the **Magic Wand** Options to **Tolerance** 32, **Anti-aliased** ON. Then hold down the **Shift Key** and **Magic Wand** to select and save the background. Now Select channel #4 from the **Channels Palette**, and click on the left edge of the **RGB Channel** to select Mask Mode. Use **Command + D** to remove the selected area, then touch-up with the **Paintbrush Tool**. After Loading Selection on the **Select** menu use **Inverse** to select only the subject and again **Save** to channel #4. The Mask is complete.
The accompanying file is of 126x417 pixels, so reduce its size by 50% with **Image Size** on the **Image** menu, then Save. When the subject of the work is small, it should be scanned at double the size, then shrunk, in order to create an accurate mask, and a more precise image in actual size. If the image seems a bit out of focus after shrinking, use **Sharpen** under the **Filter** menu one time to improve definition.
After selecting the work **Copy**, and if you do not need to do the work twice you need not save the Mask Channel. Saving Channels unnecessarily will use up memory and serves no useful purpose.

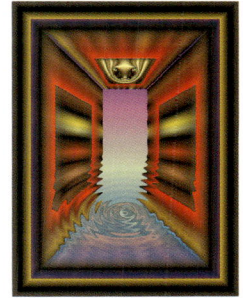

合成前の「背景」
Before combining

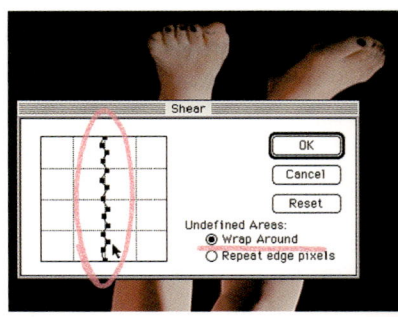

オブジェクト素材を**選択範囲の選択**で選択「背景」にコピー＆ペーストして波紋の真ん中に配置する。**選択範囲**メニューから**選択範囲の記録**するとマスクが#4チャンネルにできあがる。

Subject materials are selected with **Load Selection**. **Copy** & **Paste** to "Background," positioning the subject in the midst of the ripples. From the **Select** Menu click on **Save Selection**. This will bring up the mask on channel #4.

フィルタメニューの変形からシアーを選択したところ。線分をクリックしてドラッグすれば自由に画像をカーブさせることができる。

Choose the **Shear Filter** under **Distort** on the **Filter** menu. By clicking on the lined part and dragging you can freely alter the curvature of the image.

Combining the subject and background
....adding reflection to the water

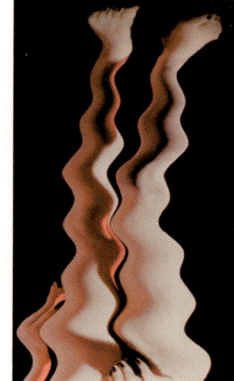

水面の映り込みを演出するためにオブジェクト素材をイメージメニューの鏡像の垂直方向で上下反転させ、フィルタメニューの変形からシアーを選択してから7回カーブを描いて実行する。水面に波紋をつける前に貼りこんでおけば、この作業は必要ない。ただしオブジェクト貼りこみ前ではオブジェクトとの調整が困難だ。

In order to create the reflection on the model **Flip/Vertical** is chosen under the **Image** menu. This turns the shape upside down. Then the image is given 7 curves with **Shear** under **Distort** (on the **Filter** menu.) If you have already laid ripples on the water this work is unnecessary. However, in that case adjusting the subject before pasting in will be quite difficult.

水面への映り込みに奥から手前にかけて調子をつけるためのマスクを作る。チャンネルパレットのメニューからチャンネルの追加を実行し#5チャンネルの下5分の1程のところから下にかけてグラデーションをかける。選択範囲メニューから選択範囲の選択で#4チャンネルの選択範囲を表示し編集メニューの塗りつぶしを使って黒色で塗りつぶす。不用な部分を黒色で塗りつぶしてマスクの完成である。

Now a mask is made to adjust the reflection from background to foreground. A **New Channel** is chosen under the **Channel** menu and a 5-step gradation is laid under Channel #5 from top to bottom. Show the selected area of channel #4 with with **Load Selection** under the **Select** menu and use **Fill** under the **Edit** menu to paint in black. The unnecessary area is painted in black and the mask is finished.

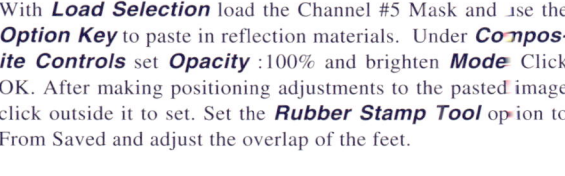

#5チャンネルのマスクを選択範囲の選択で表示してオブジェクトの映り込み用素材をオプションキーを押しながら選択範囲内へペーストする。合成のコントロールで不透明度:100%、描画モードを比較（明）にしてOK後、貼り込み済みのオブジェクトとの位置関係を調整してから選択範囲外をクリックして確定する。スタンプツールオプションを復帰して足元の重なり具合を修正する。

With **Load Selection** load the Channel #5 Mask and use the **Option Key** to paste in reflection materials. Under **Composite Controls** set **Opacity**:100% and brighten **Mode**. Click OK. After making positioning adjustments to the pasted image click outside it to set. Set the **Rubber Stamp Tool** option to From Saved and adjust the overlap of the feet.

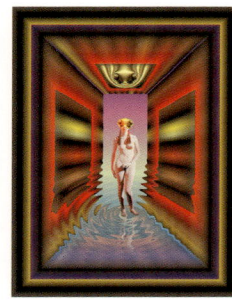

このままではいかにも切り抜き風なので、足の下側をバックになじませる。「背景」を同時に開いておく。スタンプツールオプションをコピー（調整あり）、ブラシパレットの不透明度：10%、描画モード：比較（明）にする。オプションキーを押しながら「背景」の足先に相当するポイントをクリックし、作業中のファイルの同じポイントをクリックして少しずつ下から上にかけてなじませていく。シャドウのみにバックの水面が透過、反映して一体化していく。

This image still appears much like a relief, so the feet are moved back somewhat. "Background" is left **Open**. Set **Rubber Stamp Tool** option to **Clone (aligned)**, and **Brushes Palette** to **Opacity:** 10%. **Mode: Lighten**. Holding down the **Option Key**, click at a point on the background about where the toes are positioned, then click on about the same point in your working file and gradually move it upwards. Only in the shadow is the background water reflective, so keep the reflection unified.

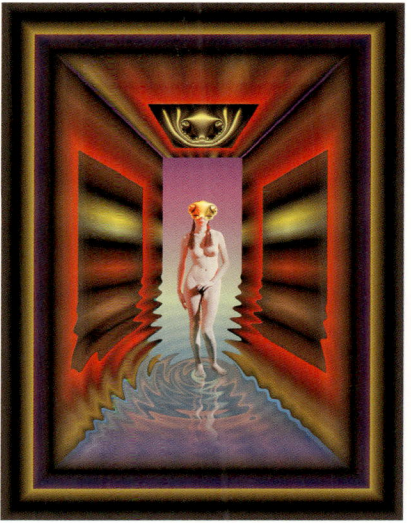

完成一歩手前のグラデーションワーク
フィルタメニューの表現手法から逆光を選択し明るさ：75%、レンズの種類：35mm で頭の上をセンターポイントに実行したものが冒頭の作例。

Lastly, choose **Lens Flare** under **Stylize** on the **Filter** menu and set to **Brightness:** 75%, **Lens Type:** 35mm Prime. Set the center point right above the head. The result is the image you see.

フィルタメニューの表現手法から逆光フィルタの設定をしているところ。

Setting the **Lens Flare Filter** on **Stylize** under the **Filter** menu.

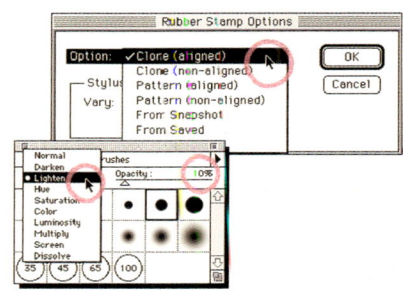

スタンプツールオプションとブラシパレットのオプション設定をしているところ。

Setting **Brush Palette** and **Rubber Stamp Tool** options.

第5章 モノクロフォト応用術

Chapter 5　Monochrome Techniques

モノクロフォトを素材として利用する

Using monochrome photo materials

バック用素材
Background material

オブジェクト用素材

Subject material

　写真家ならプロアマを問わず誰しも単独ではいまいち面白さに欠けるのでお蔵入りさせたネガフィルムの一つや二つお持ちのはず。古いコンタクトブックから引っぱり出したお蔵入り写真も意外性のある組み合わせで思わぬ傑作になる可能性も！フォトショップならそれが可能だ。

　両素材ともモノクロ35mmのネガフィルムから引き伸ばした8×10インチサイズのプリント。素材としてはライティング、コントラスト、粒状性、倍率などそろったものが望ましい。

　最終的に4×5インチサイズのポジフィルムに出力する予定なので、出力機の性能にあわせて最大4096ピクセル×3072ピクセル以内の近似値で、平面スキャナーを利用してコンピュータに取り込む。(作例はヒューレットパッカード社製のSCANJET II-Cを利用した)

　きれいなスキャニングのコツは、取り込み後サイズを変えないですむように、正確な使用サイズを計算することにつきる。

　濃度、色合いなどはフォトショップで調整できるが、まず直すことのできないのがドットの乱れで低下した画質である。

　中途半端なリサイズは画質を悪化させることはあってもよくすることはない (50%、25%など切りのよい縮小は例外として)。

Whether pro or amateur, all photographers probably have a few black and white prints that didn't meet with expectations and now languish in a drawer.

With Photoshop, old black and white prints can be resurrected and combined with other materials to produce surprisingly artistic works.

You'll need both the negative film and an 8x10 print. The material should be of good quality, i.e. well-lit, with good contrast, and not too grainy.

Eventually, the work will be turned out as a 4x5 slide, so you should utilize an appropriate flatbed scanner to read the data. One with maximum resolution of 4096x3072 pixels is best.

The example here was created with a scan made on Hewlitt-Packard ScanJet II-C. The key to beautiful scanning resides in not changing the size of the image after scanning. Calculate the image size and start with a photo of the proper dimensions.

You can alter color, density and other factors after scanning, but once you have changed the dots, it will be difficult to retrieve the original image quality.

Once the image has been altered with resizing it will be impossible to restore its original quality. (Well-cut %50 and %25 reductions are the exception.)

バック用素材のエフェクト処理 Handling background effects

空のグラデーション描くためにチャンネル#4に
マスクを作る。
なげなわツールを使って空を選択し選択範囲メ
ニューから選択範囲の記録を実行。

To draw the gradation of the sky create a
Mask on Channel 4.
With the **Lasso Tool** Select the sky, then
Save Selection under the **Select** menu.

フォトショップでレベル補正とスタンプ
ツールを使ったレタッチ、調整をして下処
理終了後のバック用素材。

A retouch made with **Levels** and the
Rubber Stamp Tool. The finished effect is on the right.

トーンカーブを使ってカラーフォト化したバッ
ク用素材。
鮮やかさを高めるためにイメージメニューの色
調補正から色相・彩度を選択して彩度を約50
％上げてある。
空の面積を増やすために全画面の選択後下方
に移動、天をあけておく。

Create color photo background materials
with **Curves**.Use the **Adjust** command
under the **Image** menu to contorol brightness. Here **Hue/Saturation** is raised 50%.
To enlarge the area of sky **Select All** and
pull downwards.

1．まず平面スキャナーの基本設定をチェック
する。取り込みモードは256グレイフォト、
シャープニングはノーマル、解像度はスク
リーン（72DPI）。

1. First check the basic settings on your scanner. The reading mode is 256 gray photo, sharp-
ening is normal, resolution at screen setting
(72DPI.)

2．バック用素材をスキャニングする。4x5
ポジ出力を予定しているので長辺を4082ピ
クセル短辺を2885ピクセルとし、自動露出
で取り込んでいる。

2. Scan the background photo. Presuming output of 4x5 inches, a length of 4082 pixels, and
width of 2885 pixels gives the proper automatic
exposure.

3．任意の名称をつけてファイルを保存する。
フォーマットはPICTを選択している。保存先
ディスクは十分に余裕のあるハードディスクを
指定すること。

3. Decide a file name and Save the file. Select
the **PICT** format. Remember to save to a hard
drive with plenty of open memory.

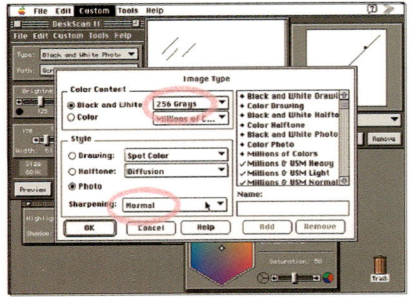

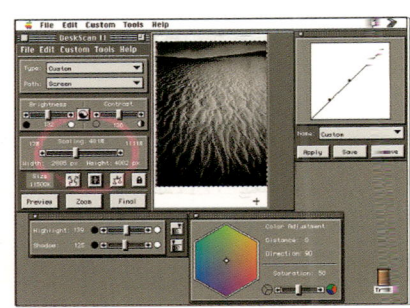

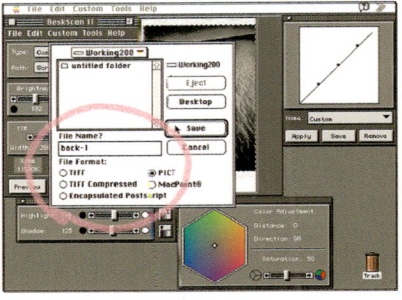

オブジェクト用素材のエフェクト処理

バックグラウンドの完成

選択範囲の選択を実行してグラデーションの始点色と終点色を描画色と背景色に指定する。グラデーションツールを選択して始点から終点までドラッグすると空のグラデーションができる。

The finished background

Use **Load Selection**, setting the beginning color and ending color as **Foreground Color** and **Background Color**. Then select the sky with the **Gradient Tool** and drag from beginning to end to achieve color.

フォトショップで**レベル補整**と**スタンプツール**を使ってレタッチをした下処理終了後のオブジェクト用素材。

Subject material after retouching using **Levels** and **Rubber Stamp**.

合成するためのマスクを作る。**自動選択ツール**を使ってバックの白い部分を選択してから**選択範囲**メニューの**選択範囲の反転**を実行、**選択範囲の記録**を実行する。

Creating a Mask to prepare the composite. Using the **Magic Wand**, select the white area, then use **Inverse** on the **Select** menu, and **Save Selection**.

4．同様にオブジェクト用素材をスキャニングする。切り抜きを前提にしているので不要な部分はカットして取り込む。合成するバックとの比率合わせは正確に決定する。

4. Scan the materials for the background in the same way. The piece will be pasted, so unnecessary portions should be cut before scanning. Background percentage of the composite should be accurately figured.

5．フォトショップで開いたファイルをまずイメージメニューの色調補正から**レベル補正**を選択して、ハイライトレベル、シャドーレベルを調整し、必要であればガンマ補正を実行。

5. After opening the file in Photoshop, select **Levels** from **Adjust** under the **Image** menu. Adjust the Highlight Level and Shadow Level; if necessary, use Gamma Adjustment.

6．モードを**RGB**に変換してイメージメニューの色調補正から**トーンカーブ**を選択し、レッドチャンネルのグラフを鉛筆で描き換える。滑らかにをクリックすると階調の急激な変化を押さえることができる。

6. Change the **Mode** to **RGB**, then select **Curves** from **Adjust** under the **Image** menu. Use the **Pencil** to draw with the red channel graph. By using **Smooth** you can even out the sharp gradations.

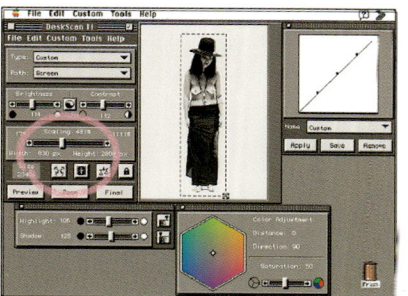

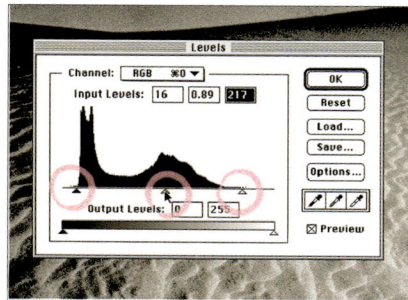

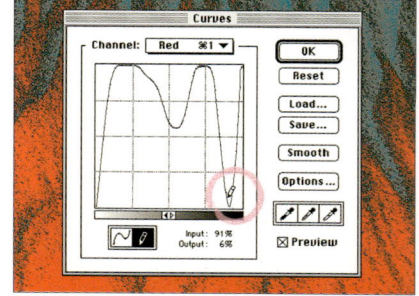

Handling subject effects

トーンカーブを使ってカラーフォト化したオブジェクト用素材。鮮やかさを高めるために**イメージメニュー**の**色調補正**から**色相・彩度**を選択して彩度を約50%上げてある。

The Subject recreated in color using *Curves*. To bring out brightness, the *Adjust* command under the *Image Menu* was used toraise *Hue/Saturation* by 50%.

一般用の平面スキャナーは製版用のスキャナーに比べて精度がかなり落ちる。レイアウトのアタリ用やテスト用に使う分には十分だが、印刷用途には性能不足だ。もしどうしても手持ちの平面スキャナーで印刷用にスキャニングしたい場合は、可能なかぎり大きく取り込んで使用サイズに縮小するとよい。また最終段階で**フィルタメニュー**の**シャープ**から**アンシャープマスク**を必ずかけること。設定はケースバイケースだが標準的なファイルを標準的に印刷する場合は**適用量**：100%、**半径**：2.0**ピクセル**、しきい**値**：3〜6くらいを目安にするとよい。

The average flatbed scanner is considerably less precise than an actual printing film scanner. Generally, they are fine for layout work and testing, but inadequate for printing. But if you really must use a flatbed scanner to create film, try using the largest material possible, and then shrinking it. Also, in the final stage, definitely lay an *Unsharp Mask* with *Sharpen*, found under the *Filter* menu. Settings will vary, but a standard file in a standard printing situation might be set at *Amount 100%*, *Radius 2.0 Pixels*, and *Threshold 3~6*, or thereabouts.

オブジェクト素材の完成

The finished subject material

７．バックグラウンド同様、**RGB**モードに変換して**トーンカーブ**でカラー化後、部分的に強調したい範囲を**なげなわツール**を使って選択する。

7. The process is the same as you used for the background. In *RGB* mode, use *Curves* to add color, then adjust specific intensity by selecting with the *Lasso Tool*.

８．**トーンカーブ**と**カラーバランス**を使って赤を強調する。単独で使用するよりもさらに強く効果を上げることができる。最後に全体の調子を**レベル補整**を使って調整しておく。

8. Brighten the red with *Curves* and *Color Balance*. They will give you a stronger effect when used together. Then use *Levels* to adjust overall color.

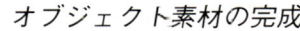

９．影を演出するために、**選択範囲の選択**をしておいて、オブジェクトを**イメージメニュー**の**変形**から**台形**を選んで先細りに変形。このとき右方向に変形のためのスペースを十分にとっておく。

9. To emphasize the shadow, *Load Selection*, then choose *Prespective* from *Effects*, under the *Image* menu. Use it to narrow the top. At this time, leave plenty of space on the right for further alterations.

合成作業 .... 長い影をつけて雰囲気を盛り上げる

最終オブジェクトの選択範囲を最終バックグラウンドにオプションキーを押しながらペーストして、合成のコントロールの不透明度を50%にして、影をつけるためのアタリを作る。

Paste the finalized object against the finished background by holding down the **Option key an**d pasting. Set **Opacity** (under **Composite Controls**) at 50%, then create a place to lay the shadow.

影用ファイルから影を**選択範囲**の選択後コピーしてからオプションキーを押しながらバックグラウンドにペースト、合成のコントロールで選択範囲内の画像のブラックレベルを255にしてOK後、影の位置を調整する。イメージメニューの色調補正から明るさ・コントラストで選択範囲を暗くしてバックに程よい濃度の影をつける。

Open the file and **Load Selection**, then **Copy**. Holding down the **Option key**, **Paste** the shadow against the background. Set the **Floating Black Level** (under **Composite Controls**) at 255. Click **OK**, then adjust the position of the shadow. Use **Brightness/Contrast** of **Adjust** under **Image** menu to darken the selection to an appropriate degree.

---

10. イメージメニューの変形から平行四辺形を選んで右方向に斜めにする。影の形を想定している。選択範囲メニューの境界をぼかすを20ピクセルで実行して**選択範囲の記録**後、影用ファイルとして**保存**する。

10. Choose **Skew** from **Effects** under the **Image** menu. Move the object diagonally to the right. Imagine the shadow that would begin at the model's feet. Set the **Feather** command under the **Selection** menu at 20 pixels. Execute, then **Save** the file.

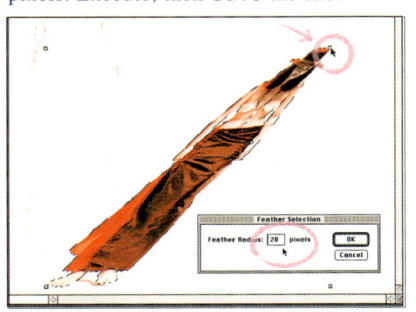

11 影用ファイルの選択範囲をコピー、アタリ付きの背景にオプションキーを押しながらペースト、合成のコントロールで**選択範囲内の画像**のブラックレベルを255にしてOKすると影の選択範囲のみがペーストされる。

11. After selecting and copying the file choose Acrylic Background by holding down the **Option Key** and Pasting. Set **Floating Black Level** at 255 under **Composite Controls**. Click OK to paste only the **Selection**.

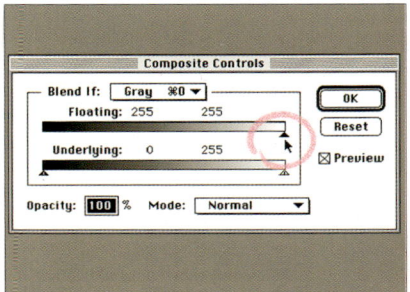

12. イメージメニューの色調補正から明るさ・コントラストで明るさを−60に設定、OKすると影ができる。さらに細部の影をなげなわツールオプションを10ピクセルで作って同様に濃度を上げて調整する。

12. On the **Adjust** bar under the **Image** menu set **Brightness/Adjust** at -60. Click OK and your shadow is created. **Lasso** the upper body and set at 10 pixels with option. In the same way increase darkness for the shadow effect.

Composite Work ...... with a long shadow

最終オブジェクトの選択範囲をペーストして、アタリ上に正確に重ねる。まず全体像を見ながらペーストして、拡大して細部の見当あわせをする。

Now **Paste** the finalized outline of the subject in the correct position. First lay it with an eye to the whole fiqure, then enlarge and correct by segment.

影用ファイルの**Mask**チャンネル

The shadow file on Mask Channel

　合成したオブジェクトの周囲に拡大して**鉛筆ツール**で修正。周りの色を**オプションキー**を押して拾いながらレタッチしていく。ある程度広い範囲は**スタンプツール**を使ったほうがきれいにいく。

　バックとなじませたほうがよい部分はぼかし.**シャープツール**を小さめのサイズにしてなじませる。大きめのサイズで大ざっぱにすると、なじむどころかえって目立ってしまう。

　フォトショップでは**ぼかしツール**や**指先ツール**の使用は必要最小限に抑えることが洗練されたテクニックといえる。

　プラグインフィルターの効果に寄りかかったり、稚拙なぼかしやにじませを多用した、いかにもくさい作品はすぐにあきがくる。

Enlarge the area around the composite image and retouch the background with the **Pencil Tool**. Hold down the **Option Key** to redo color. In the larger section use the **Rubber Stamp Tool** to achieve cleaner effects.

Use the **Blur Tool** in its small size to blend sections that need blending. By using the large size tool the blended area may end up sticking out. Using the **Blur Tool** and **Smudge Tool** as little as possible is a good rule when working in Photoshop.

Works produced with much use of the Plug-in Filter, or too much blur, tend to appear amateurish and are soon laid aside.

モノクロフォトを素材にしたカラーデジタルフォトの完成

A finished color digital photo made from monochrome materials

　合成作業は**イメージメニュー**の**演算**から**合成(マスク指定)**や**合成(%指定)**、**スクリーン**など計算方法を選んで最適な合成が自動的にできる。しかし同サイズのデータを2つ同時にオープンして計算させるため、大きなデータではかなりの計算時間がかかる。

　この程度の合成はオブジェクトを切り抜いて**コピー&ペースト**したほうが能率がよい。特にVer.2.5からは**合成のコントロール**で主要な**演算**コマンドをコントロールすることができるようになったのでなおさらだ。

You can achieve ideal composites by using **Screen, Composite** and **Blend** commands under the **Image** menu. These **Calculation methods** automatically determine the ideal composition. But trying to calculate two material files - a large amount of data - can take quite a lot of time. In a composition of this scale, it is more efficient to **Copy & Paste** the separate object, especially with Ver. 2.5, using **Calculate** Command under **Composite Controls**.

第6章 形を変える

Chapter 6　Distortion Techniques

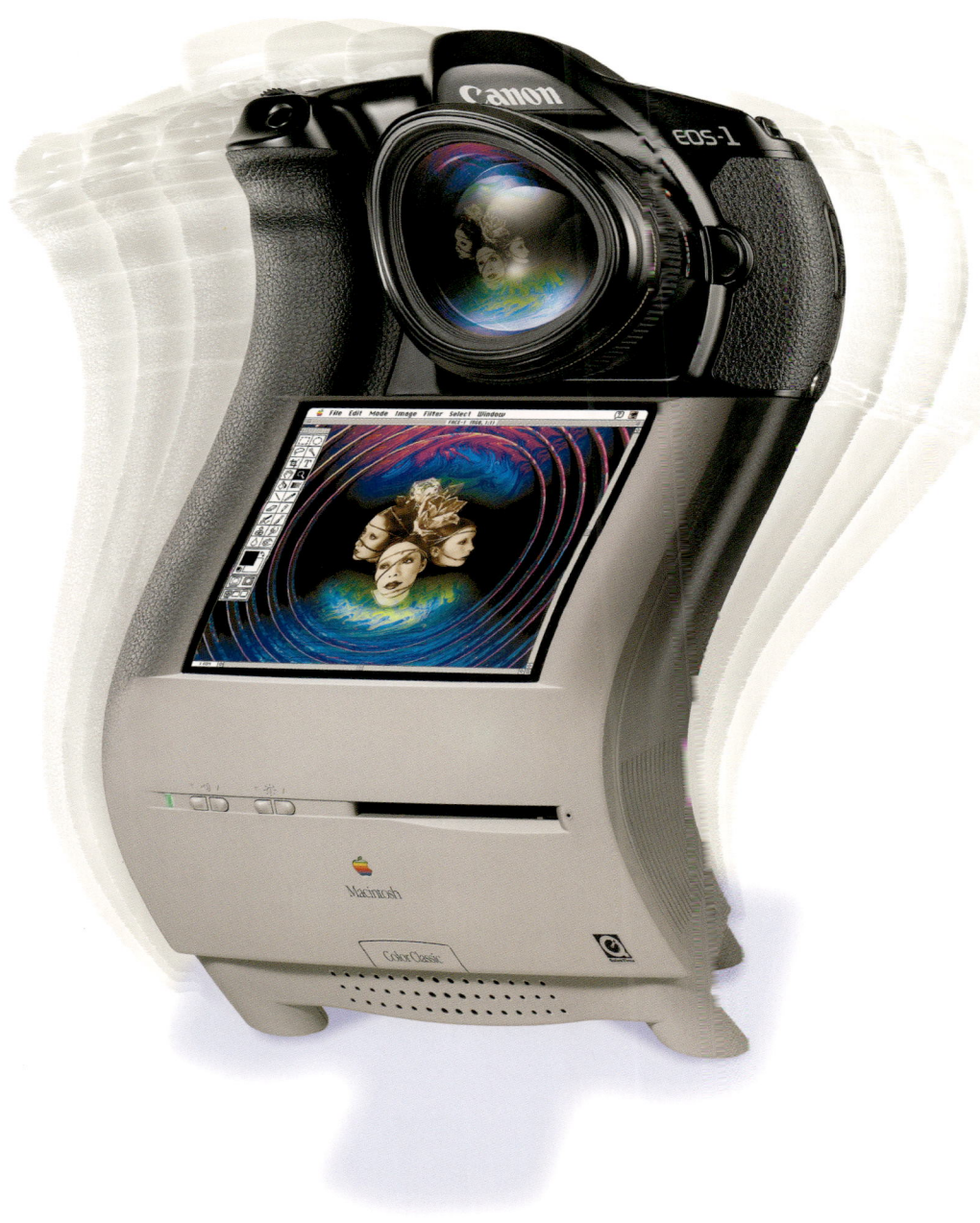

形を変える **Altering the shape**

素材を準備する

レンズ映り込み用素材   *Lens material*
黒バックで撮影した
シャボン玉

Jumbo eyeball shot against a black background.

合成用素材ー1   *Composite Materials-1*
デジタルフォトを象徴して一眼レフとカラークラシックの合成変形が、この章のテーマである。

This chapter uses a single-lens camera and a Mac Color Classic as elements of a distortion composite symbolizing digital photography.

レンズ表面を**なげなわツール**で選択してシャボン玉を**オプションキー**を押しながら**コピー**&**選択範囲内へペースト**、合成のコントロールで**描画モード**を**色相**に設定して**OK**。画像サイズでファイルサイズを拡大しておいて、ワインダー部分を**変形の拡大・縮小**を使って260%ほど縦方向に拡大、**スタンプツール**を使ってなじませる。次にマックと溶け込ませるために長いボケ足のマスクを作る。このマスクのでき具合によって合成の巧拙が決まる。

The surface of the lens is selected with the *Lasso Tool,* and the big eye is selected by holding down the *Option Key* to *Paste Into.* Set *Mode & Color* under the *Composite Controls.* The winder portion of the body is selected and stretched 260% with *Scale,* found under *Effects.* The *Rubber Stamp Tool* is used to blend.Next, in order to place it in the Mac, a long, blurred mask is made. The quality of this mask will mean the success or failure of the work.

写真を様々な形に変形するのはデジタルフォトの独壇場だ。

オリジナルのフォトショップはそれほど多彩な変形機能を持っているわけではないが、機能を組み合わせて使うことで作例程度の変形は容易である。

変形作業の場合、高解像度で作ることが前提で、低解像度のデータは何回か変形をかけるとドットが乱れて使いものにならない。1000ピクセル以下で作る場合はできるだけ少ない変形回数で済むように工夫する（作例は3000×4000ピクセル、添付ファイルは677×843ピクセル）。

きれいな画像を作るためには拡大変形をしないこと、変形作業を加えることによってできた画像がオリジナルより小さいか同寸になるようにすれば画像の乱れを抑えることができる。たとえばパースペクティブをかける場合、最大部分を固定し最小部分側に縮小する。

Ver.2.5にバージョンアップして**シアーフィルタ**が内蔵された。**波形**フィルタを使って苦労していた設定がスプライン曲線グラフで簡単に設定できる。

部分ごとに様々な変形効果を加えてフォトショップ上で合成することで、ほとんどの変形化要求に答えることが可能である。

1．合成のコントロールで描画モードを**色相**に設定する。ハイライトのトーンはそのままカラーがシャボン玉の色味に変化する。オプションキーを押しながらペーストすると合成のコントロールを呼び出すことができる。

1. Setting *Mode & Color* with *Composite Controls*. With *Highlight Tones* you can change the color of the jumbo eye. By holding down the *Option key* and selecting *Paste* you can call up the *Composite Controls*.

2．レンズ面に合成のコントロールで描画モードを**スクリーン**に不透明度を50%に設定して顔をペーストする。レンズのハイライトを損なわずに溶け込ませることができる。

2. From *Composite Controls* select *Mode, Screen,* and *Opacity,* setting the later at 50%. and *Paste* it to the face. You can pour the image without damaging the lens highlighting.

3．下方に引き延ばしたワインダー部分を**スタンプツール**を使って修整する。特に両サイドをシンプルにきれいにする。

3. The film winder on the bottom is repaired with the *Rubber Stamp Tool*. The sides are especially simple and clean.

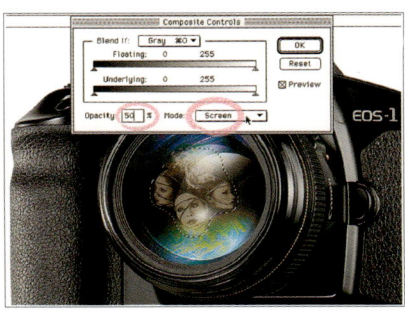

Preparing composite materials

The ability to alter a photo in various ways is a forte of digital photography.

Photoshop does not have a great number of alteration functions, but works of interest can be created by combining its functions in creative ways.

A high-resolution image is required in work that uses distortion. The dots in a low-resolution image will quickly mutate after a few alterations, and the image will be useless. In situations where images of less than 1,000 pixels must be used, try changing the shape a minimum number of times. (The example uses a 3000x4000 pixel image, with an attached file of 677x843 pixels.)

As a rule, to create a clear image one should avoid enlarging. Depending on the amount of distortion, try to work with the same measurements as the original, or smaller. This will limit disintegration of the dots. In something like a perspective, it is best to set your largest items, and then shrink them for use in the smallest places.

The Version 2.5 update contains the **Shear Filter**. Settings that were once painful to do on the **Wave Filter** are now shown on a curved graph for easy setting. With the latest 3-D software these filters could be used perfectly to freely control image distortion.

But with Photoshop alone a variety of shape alterations can be achieved, and with retouched and composite images, the possibilities are unlimited.

合成用素材－2
Preparation materials - 2

合成用の一眼レフとアングルを揃えて撮影したカラークラシック。フォトショップ上でパースペクティブやスケールは合わせられるがアングルを揃えることは難しい。

The single-lens camera and Color Classic photos both taken from the same angle. With Photoshop perspective and scale can be adjusted, but it is not easy to realign angles.

画面はめ込み用素材　*Materials for the screen*

レンズの映り込みに使ったシャボン玉を合成した作品。

The jumbo eye to be placed over the lens.

フォトショップの画面スナップショットはコマンド＋シフト＋3で撮ることができる。
一眼レフとの合成時に支障があるので、右後ろ上部をスタンプツールで描き加えてある。
合成作業のために**画像サイズ**を700×900ピクセルにして保存する。

You can take a snap shot of the screen with **Command+ Shift+3**. Part of the image was impaired in the lens composite. The upper right was repaired with the **Rubber Stamp Tool**. For purposes of combining elements the **Canvas Size** was set at 700x900 pixels.

4．フォトショップバージョン2.5の新しい機能マスクモードはこのような微妙なマスク作成にはうってつけだ。原画を見ながら**ブラシパレット**の**不透明度**、ブラシサイズを調整して精度の高い作業が可能だ。

4. **Mask Mode**, the new function in Ver. 2.5, enabling the laying of very precise masks. By adjusting the **Opacity** and **Brush Size** of the **Airbrush Tool** quality much finer than analog is possible.

5．マックのモニター画面にはめ込み用画像を開いておいてコマンド＋シフト＋3でスナップショットを撮る。カラークラシックの画面に合せて平行四辺形、自由な形に、拡大・縮小で変形してペーストする。

5. A picture of the image on the Mac screen can be taken with **Command+Shift+3**. The image is **Skewed, Distorted** and **Scaled** on the Color Classic monitor. Then it is **Pasted**.

6．イメージメニューの**画像サイズ**でファイルサイズを700×900ピクセルにする。今後の作業領域を確保するためだ。画面内のマックの位置も作業しやすい適当な場所に移動しておく。

6. The **Canvas Size** on the **Image** menu is set at 700x900 pixels. The positions of the screen marks are aligned for easy manipulation.

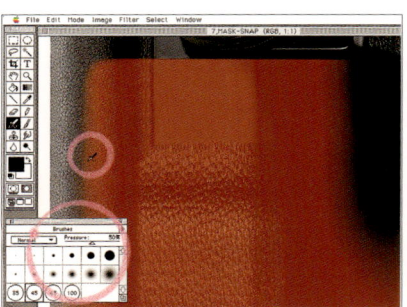

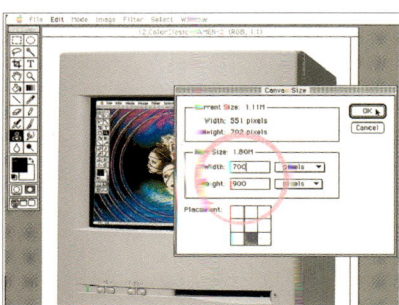

合成と変形作業

Combination & Alteration work

カラークラシックのマスクでカバーした画面外の選択範囲にあらかじめ選択コピーしておいた一眼レフを**選択範囲内**へペーストする。カメラをドラッグして調整しても重なり具合が思いどうりでなければ削除して前に戻って一眼レフの切り抜き用マスクを修正する。よければ**コマンド＋D**を押して確定してからツール類を使って細部の修正をする。

A Mask of the Color Classic's screen is made and laid over the screen. Then the whole image is **Pasted Into** the photo of the camera. If you cannot drag the camera to fit perfectly behind the Mac, **Delete** and start over. Correct the Mask of the camera. Use **Command+D** to set the image, then use Tools to finish the work.

フィルタメニューの変形からシアーを選んでグラフのカーブを変形したい形に曲げる。1回ではなかなか望みどうりにならないので何回か設定を変えて試みる。作例は3000×4000ピクセルとサイズが大きすぎるために変形せず同じカーブを2回かけて予定した形に近づけた。さらに細かく変形したい場合は**イメージメニュー**の変形から**自由な形に**を使う。フォトショップVer.2.5ではプレビュー状態で各々のポイントを動かして効果を確認できるので格段に使いやすい。最後に、つける影やブレの位置を考えて画像を移動配置してから切り抜き用のマスクチャンネルを作って保存しておく。

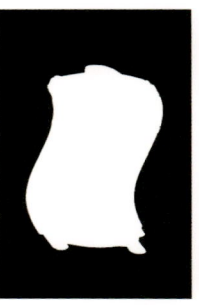

Select **Shear** from **Distort** under the **Filter** menu. Bend the graph's curve to create the shape you want. It's very difficult to get the right shape. Try resetting it until you get it right. The 3000x4000 pixel example started out large, and was based on projections of several curves, until a similar shape was achieved. When desiring to make fine alterations select **Distort** from **Effects** on the **Image** menu. With Photoshop Ver. 2.5 you can use **Preview** to adjust points at each stage of your work. Finally, think about the position of the shadow and blur, move it to the correct place, the create a relief mask channel and save it.

合成時に画面を保護するためのマスクを作る。まず画面を選択して**選択範囲の反転**をかけて**選択範囲の記録**で保存する。

To protect the composite a Mask is created. First select the screen, then use **Inverse**, then **Save Selection**.

７．選択範囲の選択して画面マスクを呼び出してからあらかじめ**コピー**しておいた一眼レフの選択範囲を**選択範囲内**へペーストする。選択ツールを使ってぴったりあうように調整する。

7. After opening with **Load Selection** call up the image Mask. The select the lens image you saved with **Copy** and **Paste Into**. Use the Selection Tool to fit it perfectly the screen.

８．フィルタメニューの**変形**から**シアー**を選択する。スプライン曲線に従ってイメージを曲げることができる。作業画面が狭い場合、はみ出た画像は**ラップアラウンド(巻き戻す)**にしておけば反対側に出てくるので合成可能だ。

8. Choose **Shear** under **Distort** from the **Filter** menu. You can bend the image based on the spline curve. When the work area is narrow you can preset it for **Wrap Around,** which automatically brings up the opposite side.

９．変形を細かくコントロールするには**イメージメニュー**の変形から**自由な形に**を使う。Ver.2.5からプレビュー機能が加わったのでよりきめの細かい変形が可能になった。

9. To fine-tune alterations use **Distort**, under **Effects** on the **Image** menu. Ver.2.5 offers **Preview**, which enables even more precise adjustments.

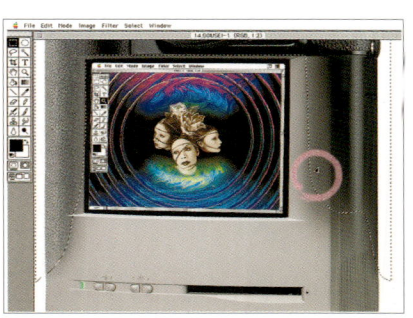

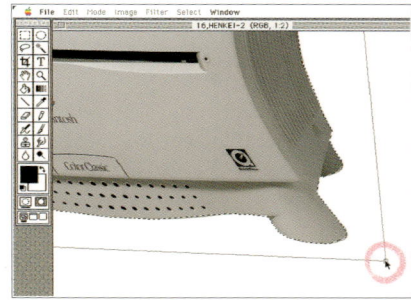

影をつける　*Adding the shadow*

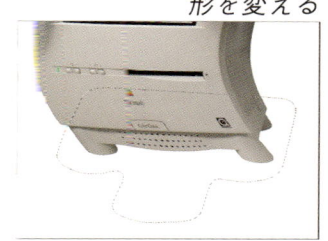

　影は写真にリアリティをつけ加えるために非常に重要な要素だ。とくに合成された写真がリアルに見えるか見えないかは影のつけ方の巧拙にあるといっても過言ではない。
　影のない写真には本能的に嘘臭さを感じるのが普通だ。
　写真の世界では演出された写真のリアリティを保つために「太陽は１つ」という言葉がおまじないのように使われている。太陽は１つだから影も１つであるべきだが、現実の世界は、反射光や様々な人工光のおかげで複雑な影ができていることが多い。
　また影のボケ足も光源の性質によって様々に変化する。太陽であればくっきりした影が、曇天になればぼんやりした影になり、蛍光燈ではブレたような影になる。
　状況によっては複数の影をつけることで、よりリアリティが増すこともあるので単純な見方には捕われないようにしよう。

Shadows add a very important element of reality to a photo. The reality of the shadows in a composite work will determine whether it appears artificial or realistic.
A photo without a shadow looks fishy. In photography, the words "there's only one sun" are an old saw. They mean there's only one sun, so there's only one shadow, but in fact in this world there are reflections, and man-made lighting, too.
The outline of a shadow will also appear differently depending upon the quality of the lighting. Strong sunlight creates a sharp shadow, a cloudy sky an unfocused shadow, a florescent light a blurred shadow. In some cases, several shadows will give an image it's most realistic appearance. Don't get caught in one way of thinking.

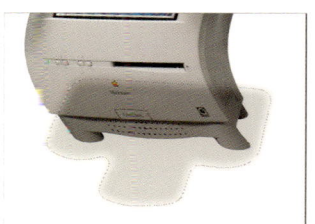

　選択範囲の選択でマスクを呼び出し選択範囲をコピー後、なげなわツールオプションで境界のぼかし幅(半径)を10ピクセルにして影の形を選択する。

When loading selection call up a *Mask* and *Copy* the outline. Then set *Feather Radius* (under *Lasso Options*) at 10 pixels and select the form of a shadow.

　イメージメニューの色調補正から明るさ・コントラストを選んで影の濃度を調節する。

Select *Brightness/Contrast* from *Adjust* under the *Image* menu and set the darkness of the shadow to the desired degree.

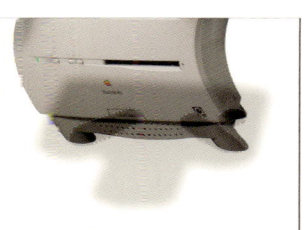

　さらに影のリアリティを増すために細部を境界のぼかし幅(半径)を5ピクセルにしたなげなわツールで選択して明るさ・コントラストで暗くする。

In order to further improve the reality set *Feather Radius* (under *Lasso Tool*) at 5 pixels, then darken the *Brightness/Contrast*.

　選択範囲の選択でマスクを呼び出し選択範囲内にクリップボードからペーストしてフリンジ削除する。(1ピクセル)

Call the *Mask* up from *Load Selection*, then *Paste* and *Defringe* on the Clipboard. (1 pixel)

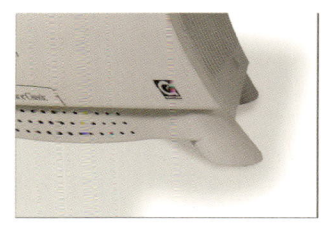

---

10. オプションキーを押しながらなげなわツールをクリックするとなげなわツールオプションの設定ができる。境界のぼかし幅(半径)を10ピクセル、アンチエイリアシングチェックで影をつける部分を選択する。

10. While holding down the *Option Key* click the *Lasso Tool*, which brings up the *Lasso* Options. Set *Feather Radius* at 10 pixels, and put *Anti-alias "On"*. Then select the position where the shadow is to be placed.

11. イメージメニューの色調補正から明るさ・コントラストを選んで明るさを－60にする。プレビューをチェックしておくと効果をそのまま確認できる。

11. Select *Brightness/Contrast* from *Adjust* under the *Image Menu*. Lower *Brightness* to -60. You can check the effect on *Preview*.

12. ブレの部分を作るためにサイドを選択してイメージメニューの回転から角度入力を選んで数値で回転をコントロールする。今回は5度ずつ左右に回転をそれぞれ3回行っている。

12. To create the unfocused portion select side, then go to *Arbitrary* under *Rotate* on the *Image* menu to control the rotation with number values. In this case the shadow was rotated left and right three times, each time by five degrees.

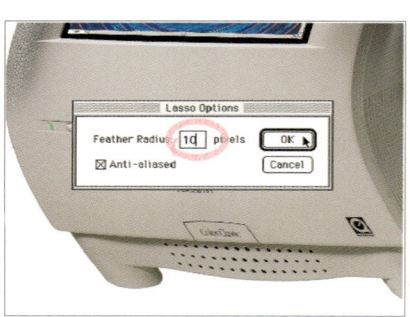
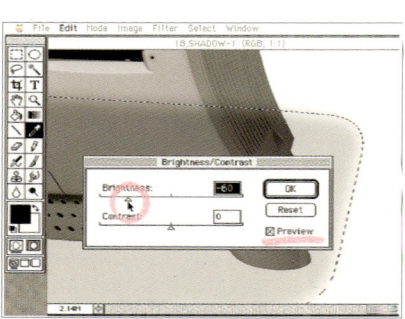
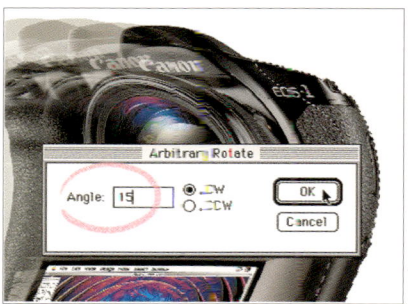

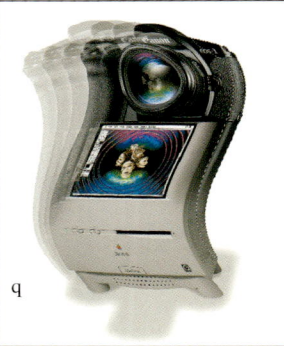

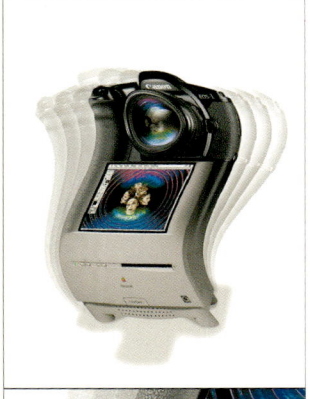

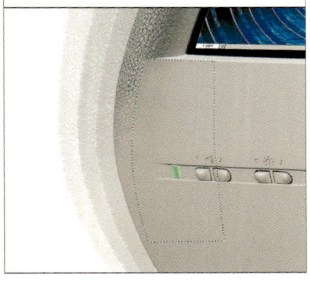

動きを表現する

Showing motion

選択範囲の選択 でイメージを選択状態にして クリップボードにコピーしておいてから画像の 左側部分のみ残すように なげなわツールオプ ションで境界のぼかし幅(半径)を30ピクセルに して コマンドキー を押しながら不用部分を除外 する。
オプションキーを押しながら選択部分をドラック /コピー、回転の角度入力で15度反時計回転し 適当な位置にドラックする。

Select the image with **Load Selection**, then **Copy** it to the **Clipboard**. Now, to leave just the left-hand portion, set the **Feather Radius** (under **Lasso** options) at 30 pixels, and push the **Command Key** to remove the unwanted area.Hold down the **Option Key** to **Drag/ Copy** the selected part. Set **Arbitrary** under **Rotate** at 15 degrees CCW and **Drag** to an appropriate place.

同じようにオプションキーを押しながらドラック /コピーして5度ずつ時計回転して内側に配置して いく。

In the same way, hold down the **Option Key** and **Drag/Copy** five CW rotational degrees to the inside.

右側についても同じように回転とドラック/コピ ーでブレ画像を作っていく。ブレを増やしていく ときに通常のコピー&ペーストは使わないこと。最 後にメイン画像をペーストできなくなる。

Do the same thing on the right side to create a shaking image. **Copy** & **Paste** are not normally used to increase blur, because pasting of the main image then becomes impossible.

最後に選択範囲の選択を実行してから選択範囲 内にクリップボードから保存していた原画をペー ストすると元どうりの場所にぴったりおさまって ほぼでき上がりである。影がブレと同色で冴えない ので、影をもう一度なげなわツールで選択しトーンカー ブ を使ってブルー系に色を変えたのが完成品であ る。

Finally, after **Load Selection** is completed, **Paste** the image you saved to the Clipboard over the selected area. It should fit perfectly. You are almost finished. It won't do to have the shadow the same color as the shaking image, so use the **Lasso** to select the shadow, and **Curves** to change its color to blue. Now you're finished.

スタンプツールで合成部分の最終調整をする。ス タンプがはみ出さないようにあらかじめなげなわ ツールで作業領域を限定しておくと便利だ。

Use the **Rubber Stamp** to put the finishing touches on the composite areas. Use the **Lasso** to limit the work area so that the **Rubber Stamp** work progresses easily.

動感を表現するためフォトショップには**ぼかし(移 動)、ぼかし(放射状)、風**といったフィルタがある。 うまく使うと効果的な表現が可能だ。**ぼかし(移動)** はアニメーションにスムーズな動感を表現するため には必須であるし、**ぼかし(放射状)**は回転とズー ムそれぞれ性格の違うブレを表現できる。

ただベストクオリティで大きなファイルサイズで 実行すると計算時間がものすごくかかる。小さなテ ストファイルで試行錯誤して狙いどうりの結果が出 たら、本番のファイルサイズをテストのファイルサ イズで割った数を、適用量の数字にかけて実行する と、ほぼ同じ結果に仕上がるので能率的だ。

テストファイルでの実行値はすべてメモしておい て本番時の参考にする。フィルターによってファイ ルサイズに関係なく効果が一定のものと、ファイル のピクセル数に比例して数値を増やさなければ効果 がはっきりしないものとがある。いろいろなデータ を頭とメモに蓄えることがベテランへの第一歩だ。

作例はブラす部分に色とトーンの変化が少ないた めかぼかしでは狙いどうりの効果が出なかったの で、上記のフィルタを使わずマルチ効果で動感を表 現してみた。これらの手法以外にも動きを表すため には様々な方法が考えられる。自分なりの表現を求 めていろいろこころみてほしい。

かつてはコンピュータで動感を表現できるなんて 考えもしなかったものだが、時代は変わった。3D ソフトでもぼけをレンダリングできるようになって きている。

Photoshop has **Motion Blur**, **Radial Blur** and **Wind Blur** filters, all of which impart the image of motion. By using them effectively you can achieve various effects. **Motion Blur** is essential for adding motion to animation, while **Radial Blur** has **Spin** and **Zoom** effects, each of which has a unique character.But for the best quality in a big file a very great deal of calculation time is required. If the desired results can be achieved on a small test file, recalculate figures for the actual file, enter them as the **Amount**, and start. The result will take only about the same amount of time, and be just as good. Write down the values used in the test, so you can use them in the real work. Some filters work without relation to file size, but others require you to raise values in proportion to the number of pixels. Accumulating data in your brain and notes is the first step towards becoming a veteran.

In this example, because there is little variation in color and tone in the blur, it didn't turn out quite right. Therefore, instead of filters I tried Multi-expression for the motion effects. Various other methods can be used to create motion effects. You want to try various methods to get the effect you want.

Once upon a time no one thought of getting motion effects on a computer, but times have changed. Blur can now be achieved with 3-D software, too.

完成したカメラクラシック
The finished camera/classic

変形作業は万能グラフィックソフトのフォトショップを
もってしても難しい作業の１つである。それだけにやりが
いのある興味のつきないテーマであるといえる。

　フォトショップの機能をフルに利用すれば大概の作業は
こなすことができる。

　フォトショップVer.2.5からライセンス契約を結んだサー
ドパーティ製アクセラレーターボードに対応するようにな
り、今まで時間がかかりすぎるので使用を諦めていたコマ
ンドも気軽に使えるようになった。

　68040CPUマシンにアクセラレーターボードの組み合わせ
で快適なマシンができ上がる。

　これでメッシュ変形とメッシュマッピングをプラグイン
でサポートすればできないことはなくなってしまう。

　「イラストレーター」や「ディメンションズ」を併用す
ることでドローイングツールとしての機能や３Ｄソフトの
機能の一部も利用することができる。

　フォトショップのプラグインツールは多くのグラフィッ
クソフトに取り入れられて業界標準に近くなった。

　従ってプラグインツールの開発も採算のとれる商売に
なったので、これからますます多種多様なツールが開発販
売されるようになる。

　第11章で現状の有益なツールについて解説してあるが、
フォトショップの機能をより高めるツールを積極的に取り
入れることがフォトショップ上達の近道であり貴重な時間
の節約になる。

Even with the powerful graphics of Photoshop shape alteration is not an easy operation. But to the same extent, it
offers a great deal of thematic potential.
By fully utilizing all the capabilities of Photoshop one can
create most kinds of works.
Now a licensed third-party makes an accelerator board for
Photoshop Ver. 2.5, allowing for freer use of commands
which would otherwise take a prohibitive amount of time.
With an accelerator board a 68040CPU becomes a comfort-
able machine. Mesh altering and Mesh Mapping can be
plugged in for almost unlimited power.
With Illustrator and Dimensions some drawing and 3-D
tools can be used in concert for a yet broader range of effects.
Many of the Plug-in tools supported by Photoshop are almost industry standards and are found in many graphic software programs.
It now pays to develop and market graphic tools, so many
more can be expected on the market in coming years.
There is a glossary of graphic tools found in Chapter 11 .
One should use these aggressively to improve the capabilities of Photoshop. Don't begrudge the time requires to master the use of new tools.

伝藤製薬イノセア ポスター下絵用作品
Stomach poster for Satoh Pharmaceutical Co.,Ltd.

シアー、台形、自由な形にを組
み合わせて使うことで変形でき
る。

Use **Shear**, **Perspective** and
Distort to alter shapes.

オリジナルフォト
Original photo

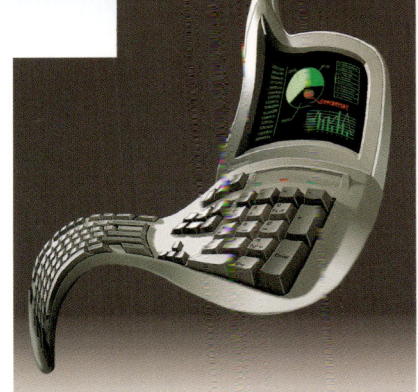

第7章 チャンネル利用法

Chapter 7   Channel Techniques

チャンネルの利用法 *Using channels effectively*

チャンネルの上手な使い方

フォトショップを使いはじめたビギナーにとってわかりにくい概念のひとつにチャンネルがある。その次に難かしいのが演算であろう。

この章ではその両方を同時にマスターすることを目標にしている。RGBカラーが赤、緑、青の加色法三原色で構成されていること、CMYKカラーがシアン、マゼンタ、イエロー、黒の減色法三原色プラス墨のプロセスカラー4色で構成されていることはご存知だと思う。

フォトショップではその各色に8ビット(256諧調)のチャンネルをひとつずつ割り当てRGBカラーが3チャンネル1セット、CMYKカラーが4チャンネル1セットで1枚の画像を構成している。

チャンネルパレットを使うとフルカラーでの表示状態(コンポジットカラー表示)と各チャンネル別の表示状態を切り替えて見ることも加工することもできる。

さらに特殊効果を加えたり、合成の際にマスクとして有効利用できるチャンネルを最大16チャンネル(画像データ分も含む)まで持つことができる。コンポジットカラー表示分を除く付加的なチャンネルをすべてαチャンネルと称する。RGBカラーでは#4チャンネル以降、CMYKカラーでは#5チャンネル以降がαチャンネルになる。このαチャンネルが通常ではできないことを可能にする魔法の玉手箱なのだ。

1. 二つの画像を合成する際のマスクとして利用する
2. ぼけ足の長い選択範囲を作るために利用する
3. 二つ以上の単純なマスクから複雑なマスクを作り上げる
その他工夫しだいで様々な利用法が考えられるだろう。

またチャンネルを分割して再統合する際に、各チャンネルを入れ替えることによって色分解フィルタを使った特殊撮影や、印刷時の版の入れ替えによる特殊技法と同じことが簡単にシミュレートできる。

Using channels effectively

One of the most difficult concepts for beginners in Photoshop is the use of channels. The next most difficult is probably the use of calculations.

The aim of this chapter is to master both of these concepts at the same time. As I believe you know, RGB stands for the three colors Red, Green and Blue, of the three-color mode, and CMYK for the four-color reduction process, which includes the three basic colors cyan, magenta and yellow, and the additional pigment, black. In Photoshop, each color represents an 8 bit (256 color) channel, meaning that RGB uses a set of three channels, and CMYK a set of four, to create a single image. With the **Channels Palette** one can work with the individual channels that compose a full color image, switching between them and executing processes. Moreover, one can use them to create special effects. In composite images, up to sixteen channels (including channels used for data) can be used for creating masks. Channels other than those containing the image data are referred to as alpha channels. In RGB situations all channels over #4 are alpha channels, and in CMYK all channels over #5 are alpha channels. These alpha channels are really the magic boxes which enable us to do what would otherwise be impossible.

1. They are used for masking when creating composite images.
2. They are used for creating areas where long, irregular shapes are placed.
3. They are used for creating complex masks out of two or more masks.
And other uses can be devised as one begins to master the skills.
Moreover, when separating channels for reforming of composites, each channel can be switched and used with color filters for special photographic effects. One can easily simulate the special techniques of color printing, as well.

チャンネルの演算による合成技法

チャンネルの演算は習うより慣れろでいろいろ試行錯誤してみれば、思ったより早くマスターできる。使い込むと非常に便利な機能である。後頁で各演算方法の特徴を写真技法にあてはめて解説してあるので、それを参考に様々な条件の画像で試してほしい。同じコマンドでも絵が違うとまったく別のコマンドを使ったようなる。慣れれば事前に予測がつくようになるのでデータをため込むことだ。ほかのコマンドに比べて最初のうちわかりにくいのは、演算させる二つのデータが縦横完全に同1サイズでなければならないこと、二つともオープンしていなければならないということだろう。どうしてもできないというビギナーの失敗を見ると、微妙にサイズの違うデータを開いていたり、まだ開いていないデータを演算させようと捜し回っていることが多い。同一サイズのデータを開いておいて演算すれば結果はどうあれ、できないということはありえない。

後頁では**演算**コマンドから、森とオブジェクトの演算を9通り紹介している。直接合成に関係のない残り二つのコマンドのうち**複写**コマンドは複写に使用する。画像の複製を作ったり、マスクのないデータに他のマスクをコピーしたり、マスクチャンネルだけを単独で取り出したりできる。**一定値**コマンドは指定した濃度でチャンネルをベタ塗りするためのコマンドである。

演算コマンドは**合成のコントロール**や**塗りつぶし**オプション、**境界線を描く**オプション、**ブラシオプション**からも一部のコマンドが使用可能だ。メモリーが少ない場合はそれらを利用するほうがスピードが速いし応用性が広い。合成作業はすべて**演算**コマンドを使うものだと思い込まないでほしい。実際のところ**演算**コマンドを使わなければ絶対できない作業など滅多にあるものではない。

Composite methods using channel calculations

Rather than trying to understand channel calculations it is better to experiment. You will find that you master the concepts rather quickly this way, and that they are extremely useful and convenient. In the following pages each method is explained and illustrated, and you will want to try them with images under various conditions. The same command will seem to produce entirely different effects from image to image. When you grow accustomed to the use of calculations you will begin to understand their effects, and thereby start to build your own database of experience. What makes the use of channel calculations more difficult than other methods is probably the requirement that two objects be of exactly parallel dimensions, and open at the same time. When trying to determine why beginners fail in the execution of caluculations one often finds that they are working with objects of slightly different dimensions, or are attempting to run calculations on data they haven't actually opened. If you open and run calculations on data of the same size, there is no way the command can fail to work. In the following pages nine **calculate** commands are introduced. The remaining two commands are not related to composite images, one of them being the **Duplicate** command, which makes a copy. You can use this when duplicating an image, or copying a mask to data which has no mask as yet, or simply calling up a single channel. The **Constant** command is used for painting over a channel with a stipulated color. Some **calculation** commands can be used under **Composite Controls** and **Fill** option, **Stroke** option, **Brush** option and others. When memory is low it is often faster and more applicable to use them through these avenues. But don't believe that **calculatie** commands can be used in all aspects of composite work.

オブジェクトを準備する　*Preparing subject material*

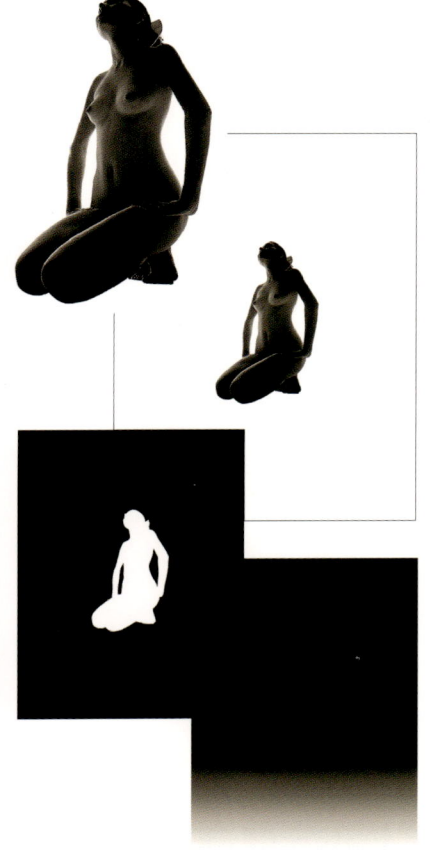

白バックで撮影したモノクロのヌードフォトのネガを大日本スクリーンのDTS-1015卓上型ドラムスキャナーでスキャニング後、イメージメニューの階調補正から階調の反転コマンドでポジにし、バックを明るくして調子を整え、484×640ピクセルの新規ファイルの真ん中にレイアウト（添付ファイルはこの状態で保存してある）RGBモードに変換する。バックの白スペースを自動選択で選択、シフトキーを押しながら両腕内側の白スペースをクリックして、すべてのバックスペースを選択してから選択範囲メニューの選択範囲に反転コマンドを実行して選択領域を反転、オブジェクトのマスクとして#4チャンネルに選択範囲の記録で保存する。

After scanning the negative of this black and white nude photo on a Dai Nippon Screen DTS Desktop Drum Scanner the image was put into positive with **Invert**, under **Map** on the **Image** menu. Then the back was pulled, and the subject placed in the center of a new 484x640 pixel file. (Here the accompanying file was saved in Grey Mode.) Change the **Mode** to **RGB**. The white space of the background was then selected with the **Magic Wand**, and the **Shift Key** held down while the white area inside the arms was clicked with the cursor. Next, with all the back space selected, **Inverse** was chosen from the **Image** menu to reverse the selected area. It was then saved as a mask for the subject on Channel #4, using **Save Selection**.

オブジェクトの選択範囲をコピーしてからコマンド＋Dキーで選択解除する。チャンネルパレットのメニューからチャンネルの追加を実行、#5チャンネルにグラデーションツールを使って影用のグラデーションマスクを作る。オブジェクトの膝下からファイルの下端までほどよいグラデーションをつける。実際のマスクは反転して使うので手間を省くためには白黒逆のグラデーションをかけたほうが速い。RGB表示に戻って選択範囲メニューから選択範囲の選択で#5チャンネルを表示、選択範囲の反転をしてマスクとして使える状態にする。

Now **Copy** and **Command+D key** are used to delete the selected area of the subject. A **New Channel** is created on the **Channels Palette** menu, and the **Gradient Tool** used to create a shadow gradation mask on Channel #5. The desired finished effect is considered for the area from the knees to the bottom of the frame as this gradation is created. The actual mask will be used in reverse, so in order to save time the black and white gradation can be done upside down, but this way it is easier to estimate the finished effect. **Revert** to RGB display and choose **Load Selection** from the **Select** menu, then **Inverse**, to prepare channel # 5 for use as a mask.

---

1. 自動選択ツールオプションの設定を選択する色の範囲：32、アンチエイリアシングにして、バックの白スペースだけを選択する。選択範囲の反転コマンドで反転しオブジェクトのみを選択状態にする。

1. Double-click the **Magic Wand Tool** to bring up **Magic Wand** options. Set to **Tolerance:** 32, **Anti-aliased:** ON. Select only the background white space. Now use **Inverse** command to reverse and select only the subject.

2. 選択範囲メニューの選択範囲の記録コマンドを実行して、#4チャンネルにマスクを保存する（チャンネルパレットの表示は選択範囲の記録実行後の表示）。

2. Execute the **Save Selection** command under the **Select** menu, saving as a Mask to **Channel #4** (After **Save Selection** the **Channels Palette** will be displayed.)

3. チャンネルパレットのメニューからチャンネルの追加を実行して#5チャンネルに新しいαチャンネルを作る（チャンネルパレットの表示は#5チャンネルができる前の表示）。

3. From the **Channels Palette** menu choose **New Channels** to create a new alpha channel under **Channel #5** (**Channels Palette** will appear before Channel # can be used).

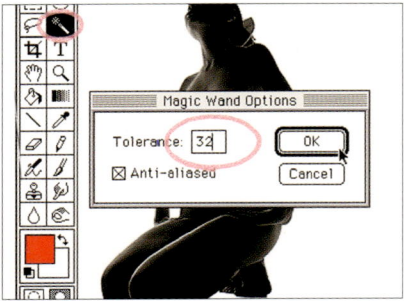

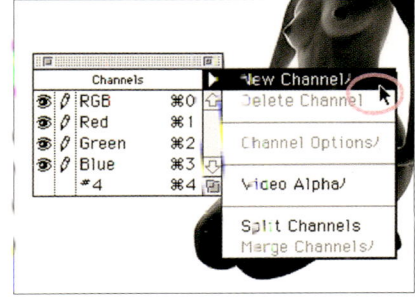

白黒写真のカラー化
Changing a monochrome photo to color

マスクの選択範囲に コピーしておいたオブジェクトを選択範囲内へペーストし、イメージ メニュー の鏡像から垂直方向を実行する。編集メニューの塗りつぶしコマンドで黒ベタに塗りつぶし、影として自然な位置に移動する。選択範囲メニューから択範囲の選択で#4チャンネルを表示してもう一度オブジェクトを選択範囲内へペーストする。影との接続部分をレタッチ後#5チャンネルを削除して保存する。

Use *Paste Into* to splice the pre-copied subject material to the Mask, then choose *Vertical*. under *Flip* on the *Image* menu. With the *Fill* command on the *Edit* menu paint over with black and move to the natural position of the shadow. Now from *Channel #4* of the *Select* menu use *Load Selection*, and once again *Paste Into* the subject. After retouching the areas of contact with the shadow, *Delete Channel* on *Channel #5* and *Save*.

選択範囲メニューから選択範囲の選択で#4チャンネルを表示、オブジェクトを選択し、イメージ メニューの色調補正からトーンカーブを選んで赤のトーンカーブを調整しセピアトーンに色調を変換する。

From *Select* menu use *Load Selection* on *Channel #4* and select the subject. Now choose *Curves* under *Adjust* on the *Image* menu. *Adjust* the Red *Curve* to make a sepia color.

　　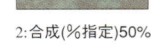

1:加算　　　　2:合成(%指定)50%

1:Add　　　　2:Blend50%

いよいよ演算コマンド使った実習である。最初は取っつきにくいが慣れてしまえばなんということはない。基本は各チャンネルどうしの対応するピクセルごとに計算させるので、ファイルは同一サイズでなければならないことと、必ず開いていなければならないことである。

Now it is nearly time to execute the calculation command. If you've learned the difficult beginning moves the rest is easy. Basically, pixels will be calculated for each subject channel, so files must be of the same size, and they must be *Opened*.

---

4. イメージ メニューの鏡像から垂直方向を選択して実行する。選択範囲が上下反転して表示される。

5. イメージ メニューの色調補正からトーンカーブコマンドを選択して、チャンネルを赤(R)に切り換え、カーブをドラッグして色調を変える。

6. イメージ メニューの演算から合成(%指定)を選択。アクティブな画面が画像1に現れる。比率(%)で画像1、画像2どちらをより主体的に表現するか調整することができ、50%で半々に表現される。

4. Select *Vertical* under *Flip* on the *Image* menu. The selected area will be inverted.

5. Select the *Curves* command under *Adjust* on the *Image* menu. Switch the channel to *Red* and drag to adjust the color.

6. Select *Blend* from *Calculate* on the *Image* menu. The active screen will be the *Source*. With *Weight* the main image can be determined, with 50% treating both images equally.

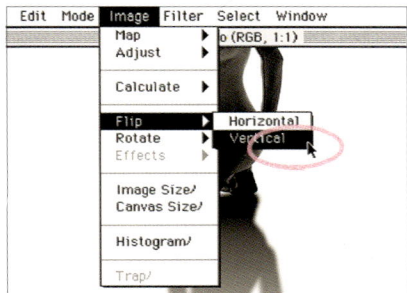

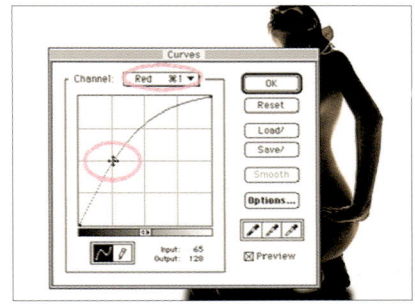

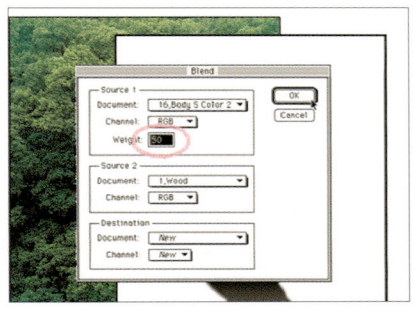

演算コマンドの実際　Executing calculation commands

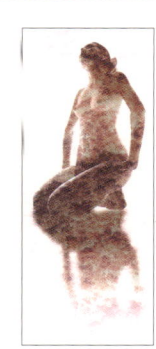

3:合成(%指定)+α	4:合成(マスク指定)	5:比較(暗)	6:差の絶対値	7:比較(明)	8:乗算	9:スクリーン	10:減算
3:Blend50% +α	4:Composite	5:Darker	6:Difference	7:Lighter	8:Multiply	9:Screen	10:Subtract

1：加算は写真の二重露光と同じ効果を表現。スケール：1で標準的、スケール：2でレベルを平均化、合成(%指定)50%と同じ結果。オフセットは±255レベルで濃度を変えることができる(作例はスケール：1、オフセット:0)。

1: **Add** gives the picture double the exposure. **Scale**:1 gives standard double exposure, **Scale**:2 averages the level, giving the same effect as **Blend** 50%. **Offset** can be altered +/-255 to change density. (Ex: **Scale**:1,**Offset**:0)

2：合成(%指定)は比率を決めて画像をブレンドする。

2: **Blend** will blend the image at a set percentage.

3：は合成(%指定)後明るさ／コントラストコマンドで明るさ：70、コントラスト：60を実行したもの。

3: **Blend** shows an image after blending and setting **Brightness/Contrast** (under **Adjust** ,on the **Image** menu) to **Brightness**: 70, **Contrast**: 60.

4：合成(マスク指定)は指定したマスクによる合成ができる。

4: **Composite** allows the combining o two source masks.

5：比較(暗)は二つの画像の暗いピクセルだけを表示する。

5: **Darker** shows two images in dark pixels only.

6：差の絶対値は二つの画像のピクセルの差を画像として表示する。

6: **Difference** shows the difference between the pixels of two images as an image.

7：比較(明)は二つの画像の明るいピクセルだけを表示する。

7: **Lighter** shows only the lighter pixels of two images.

8：乗算は2枚のポジを重ね合わせて見たような効果を表現する。

8: **Multiply** gives the effect of overlaying two different positives.

9：スクリーンは2枚のネガを重ね合わせてプリントしたような効果を表現する。

9: **Screen** gives the effect of overlaying and blending two negative images.

10：減算は画像1から画像2のレベルを差し引いた映像を作り出す。画像1と画像2を入れ替えるとネガポジ状態が逆転する(作例はスケール：1、オフセット:128)。

10: **Subtract** creates an image by subtracting the level of **source #2** from **source #1**. By switching **source #1** and **source #2** the nega-posi situation is reversed.

---

7. 合成(マスク指定)はαチャンネルや他の256グレーモードのファイルをマスクとして画像1のファイルを画像2のファイル内に合成する。マスクの形にしたいものを画像1に配置、背景を画像2に配置する。

7. **Composite** takes alpha channel and other **256 Grey Scale Mode** files and combines them as **source #1** with **source #2**. When masking, make **source #1** the shape, and **source #2** the background.

8. 差の絶対値は画像1の画像のピクセルと画像2の画像のピクセルの差を画像として表示する。同じ画像を演算すると差が0になるので真黒な画像ができる。ネガポジを演算すると面白い表現効果が得られる。

8. **Difference** shows the difference in the pixel images of **source #1** and **source #2** as an image. Calculating the same images with a difference of zero will produce a black and white image. Calculating posi-negative images produces interesting effects.

9. 減算は加算の逆で写真的には実現不可能な演算方法である。画像1の画像から画像2の画像のレベルを差し引いた画像を創りだす。スケール1で標準、スケール2で平均化。オフセットは画像の濃度を変える。

9. **Subtract** is the opposite of **Add**, and affords an effect impossible in photography. The level of **source #2** is subtracted from source #1 and expressed as an image. **Scale #1** is Standard, **Scale# 2** is Average. **Offset** adjusts the density of the image.

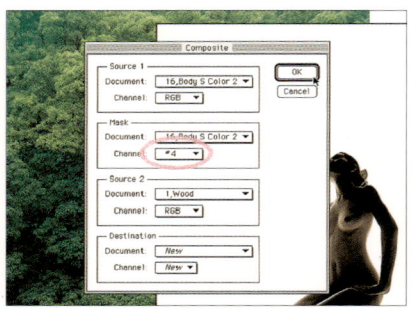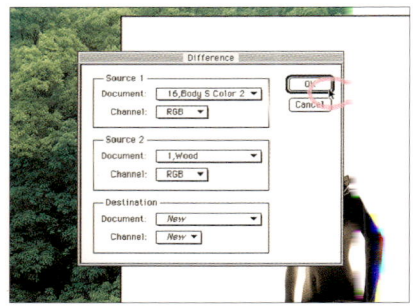

演算コマンドを使って合成する

Using calculation commands in composites

前頁のテストの結果演算は加算コマンドを使うことにする。背景の森の写真に演算の複写コマンドを使ってオブジェクトの#4チャンネルをコピーする。選択範囲の選択してパスパレットのメニューからパスの作成を実行。パスをガイドラインにして仕上がりを想像しながら葉の重なり具合をスタンプツールで調整する。

The result of the test on the previous page is achieved with the **Add** command. A forest photo is used as background. The **Duplicate** Calculation command is used and the Subject copied to channel #4. After doing **Load Selection**, **Make Path** is executed under the **Palette** menu. Using the path as a guideline, try to imagine the finished product while overlaying and adjusting the leaves with **Rubber Stamp Tool**.

背景の森とオブジェクトのファイルを両方とも開いておいてイメージメニューの演算から加算を選択しスケール:1、オフセット:0で実行する。そのさい、両方のファイルが同一サイズであることをオプションキーを押しながらウインドウの左下端をクリックして確認しておく。

With both the forest image file and the subject file **Open** select **Add** under **Calculate** on the **Image** menu. Set to **Scale**:1, **Offset**: 0 and execute. At this time, confirm that both files are of the same size by holding down the **Option Key** and clicking the left-hand bottom corner of the window.

スタンプツールや覆い焼き・焼き込みツールを使って調子を整え立体感を強調する。特に膝下と影の境目を自然な感じで分離するようにトーンをつけ、マスクを継続するためにオブジェクトのファイルから#4チャンネルを複写して別名で保存する。

Using the **Rubber Stamp Tool** and **Dodge/Burn Tool** accentuate the three-dimensionality of the image. Take care to add tone to the shadow below the knees in order to give a sense of separation. In order to keep the mask, choose **Channel #4** for the subject file and **Duplicate/Save As**.

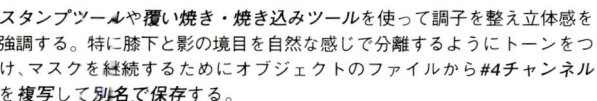

---

10. 演算合成をする前に森の写真の細部を調整する。オブジェクトに合成される部分をマークするためにパスを利用する。
パスパレットのメニューからパスの作成を実行してガイドラインにする。

10. Before executing the composite calculation make adjustments to the forest photo. Use a path to mark the area to be combined. From the **Paths Palette** menu create guidelines with **Make Path**.

11. オブジェクトと森の写真を開いておいてイメージメニューの演算から加算コマンドを選択、スケール:1、オフセット:0で実行する。

11. With the subject and forest files **Open** choose **Add** under **Calculate** on the **Image** menu. Set to **Scale:** 1, **Offset:** 0, and execute.

12. 合成する二つのファイルはサイズが同じでなければならない。オプションキーを押しながらウィンドの左下角をクリックするとサイズ情報を確認することができる。

12. The two files which are to be combined must be of the same size. By holding down the **Option Key** and clicking on the lower left and corner of the window you can check size information.

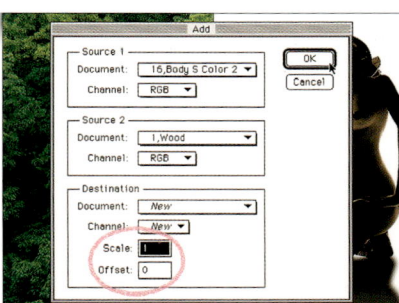

空をマスク合成する　*Creating a sky mask*

合成したオブジェクトファイルに空を合成するためのグラデーションマスクを作る。#5チャンネルにグラデーションツールで黒から白のグラデーションをかける。全画面の選択で全体を選択しておいてコマンドキーを押しながら長方形選択ツールで中心部をW：268×H：321ピクセル選択解除する。残った周囲の選択範囲内を黒色塗りつぶし100％で塗りつぶす。選択範囲の選択を実行してオブジェクトの選択領域を呼び出し黒色塗りつぶし100％で塗りつぶして保存する。

In order to add a sky to the composite subject file create a gradation mask. With the **Gradient Tool** lay a black to white gradation in **Channel #5**. With **Select All** choose the entire area, then hold down the **Command Key** while using the **Rectangualr Marquee Tool** to create an area of W: 268xH:321 pixels, and delete it. Now use **Fill** to paint in the remaining area 100% in black. Now with **Load Selection** call up the sbject in the **Open** area and **Save** the file with an all-black background.

空の写真をイメージメニューの色調補正から色相．彩度を選択して彩度：-25，明るさ：+25で実行する。
オブジェクトファイルの#5チャンネルを選択範囲の選択して空の写真を選択範囲内へペーストする。

With **Hue/Saturation** (under **Adjust**, on the **Image** menu) set the picture of the sky to **Saturation: -25**, **Lightness:** +25, and execute.
Do **Load Selection** with **Channel #5** of the Subject, and **Paste Into** with the sky image.

細部を修整する。
Touching up the fine lines.

---

13. 確認してファイルサイズが違っていた場合イメージメニューの**画像解像度**コマンドで調整することができる。縦横のプロポーションを変える場合は**縦横比を固定**とファイルサイズを固定、両方のチェックをはずしておくこと。

13. Check the file size. If the size is different, you can change it with the **Image Size** command on the **Image** menu. When altering the vertical and horizontal proportions check with both **Proportions** and **File Size**.

14. **編集**メニューから塗りつぶしコマンドを実行する。ツールパレットの塗りつぶしツールを使うより処理時間が速くて、いろいろなオプションが使えるので便利だ。

14. Execute the **Fill** command on the **Edit** menu. This is faster than using the **Paint Bucket Tool** under the **Palette** menu. Many Options can be used, as well.

15 オレンジ色の背景と組み合わせたときに空のブルーが強すぎるので彩度を下げ明度を上げる。**色相・彩度**コマンドは全体でもR,Y,G,C,B,M,個別でも色相と彩度と明度を調整することができる。

15. When the orange image is combined with the blue sky the colors are too strong. Color is lowered and Brightness is raised. With **Hue/Saturation** command the entire image or individual colors - R,Y,G,C,B,M - can be adjusted.

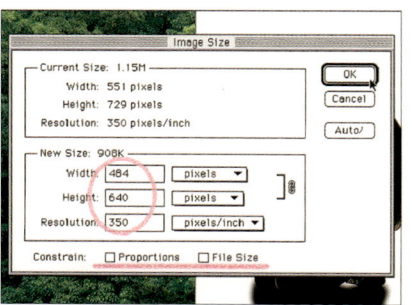

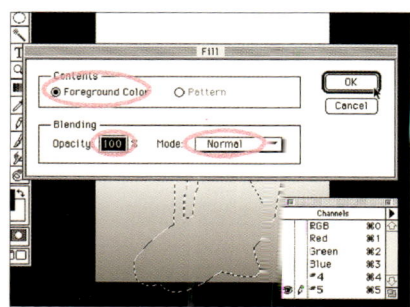

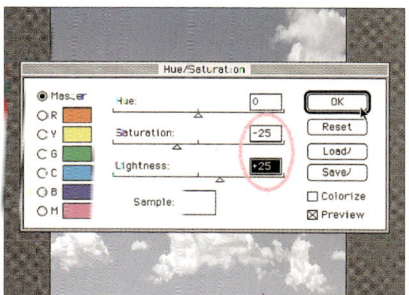

チャンネルの入れ替え技法......... バックを作る

Channel switching methods....Creating the background

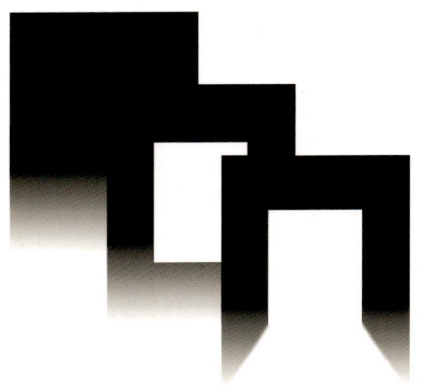

森の写真を開く。チャンネルパレットのメニューからチャンネルの追加を実行、#4チャンネルを表示する。上端から400ピクセルを起点として下端までグラデーションツールを使って黒から白へのグラデーションをかける。情報パレットのポインタの位置を見ながらx:120、y:152ピクセルのポイントを起点にして長方形選択ツールでW:240×H:320ピクセルを選択して消去する。なげなわツールの境界のぼかし幅(半径)を5ピクセルにして下部を台形に選択して消去する。RGB表示に戻って選択範囲の選択後選択領域を消去する。マスクチャンネルはこれで不用になるので、チャンネルパレットで#4チャンネルをクリックしてメニューからチャンネルの削除を実行して保存する。

After checking that the foreground is black and the background is white, **Open** the forest photo. From the **Channels Palette** menu execute **New Channel** ; **Channel #4** will appear. From the 400 pixel point of the upper part of the image use the **Gradient Tool** to draw a gradation to the bottom of the image. Watching the **Position of Pointer** on the **Information Palette**, position the **Rectangual Marquee Tool** on x:120, y:152 and select an area of W:240XH:320 pixels to **Clear**. With the **Feather Radius** of the **Lasso Tool** set at 5 pixels: select a pedestal at the bottom, and **Clear**. Return to the **RGB Mode**. **Load Selection**, then **Clear** selected area. The mask channel is now unnecessary, so click **Channel # 4** under **Channels Palette** and **Delete Channel**.

RGBモードは赤、緑、青、3色のチャンネルで構成され、CMYKモードはシアン、マゼンタ、イエロー、黒、4色のチャンネルによって構成されている。両モードにおいてチャンネルを入れ替えると印刷工程の版の入れ替えと同様の、面白いカラー効果が得られる。ここでは背景の森を紅葉の状態にするために利用している。RGBモードでも、CMYKモードでも実行可能だが結果はそれなりに異なるので目的によって選択する。RGB、CMYKモードは自由に相互通行できるが、変換のたびに元の情報が変化していくので変換は必要最少限にする。

As you know, **RGB Mode** is composed of three color channels: Red, Green and Blue, while **CMYK Mode** is composed of four channels: Cyan, Magenta, Yellow and Black. In either mode, the channels can be switched, much as they can be in color printing, and interesting effects can be achieved in this way. Here, this method is used to change the green forest to autumn colors. Either **RGB or CMYK modes** may be used, but the effects are different, and the choice is therefore determined by the desired result. In Photo shop, one can switch freely between RGB and CMYK, but when switching between the two the basic information is altered, so this should be avoided except when necessary.

---

16. グラデーションツールオプションの設定は通常、色の変化:通常、種類:ライン状、中間位置:50%でよい。円形のグラデーションをかけたい場合は種類を放射状にする。

17. チャンネルパレットのメニューからチャンネルの分割を実行する。コンポジットファイルの各チャンネルが各々8ビットのグレイモードファイルに分割する。

18. バックの墨っぽさを除くために黒チャンネルのシャドウ部を明るくする。イメージメニューの色調補正からレベル補正を選択、出力レベルのシャドウを0から60に変更する。

16. Double-click the **Gradient Tool** under the **Tool Palette** to set **Gradient Tool** options. **Normally Style: Normal**, **Type: Linear**, **Midpoint Skew:** 50% is best. When wishing to create a radial gradation set to **Type** and **Radial**.

17. Execute **Split Channels** under the **Channels Palette** menu. Each channel of the composite file will be separated into one 8 bit grey mode file.

18. To delete the darkness in the background lighten the shadowed part of the **Black Channel**. Choose **Levels** from **Adjust** under the **Image** menu, resetting the **Output Level** of the shadow from 0 to 60.

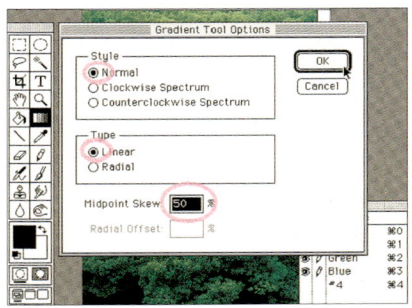

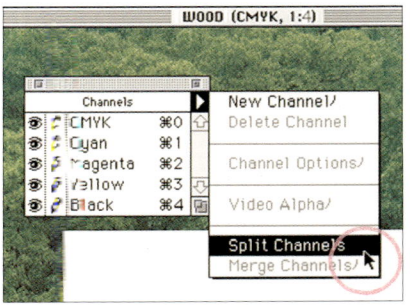

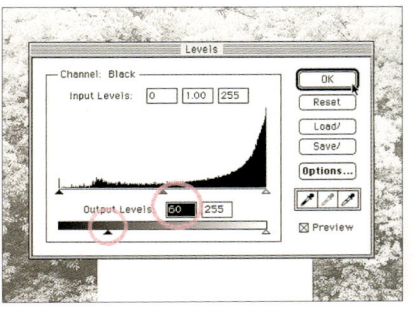

チャンネルを分離する

Separating channels

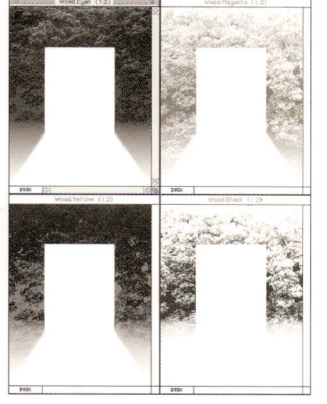

モードメニューでCMYKカラーモードに変換する。チャンネルパレットのメニューからチャンネルの分解を実行するとシアン、マゼンダ、イエロー、黒の4ファイルに分かれる。

黒チャンネルをアクティブにしてイメージメニューの色調補正からレベル補正を選択、出力レベルのシャドウを0から60に変更してシャドウ部分を明るくする。

イエローチャンネルをアクティブにして、フィルタメニューのその他からスクロールを選択して、設定を水平方向:7ピクセル 垂直方向:7ピクセル 端のピクセルを繰り返して埋めるで実行、全体に7ピクセル右下に移動する。

マゼンダチャンネルをアクティブにしてフィルタメニューのその他からスクロールを選択して設定を、水平方向:0ピクセル、垂直方向:-7ピクセル、選択範囲外からスクロールさせるで実行、全体に7ピクセル上に移動する。

シアンチャンネルをアクティブにしてフィルタメニューのその他からスクロールを選択して、設定を水平方向:-7ピクセル、垂直方向:0ピクセル、ラップアラウンド(巻き戻す)で実行、全体に7ピクセル左に移動する。

スクロールで各チャンネルを意識的にずらすことによって重ね合わせたときにブレたような動きと不思議な色彩効果を演出。森の量感と遠近感もオリジナルより強調されている。

In **Mode** menu, change to **CMYK Color** mode. From the **Channels Palette** menu execute **Split Channels** to separate into four channels, **Cyan**, **Magenta**, **Yellow** and **Black**.

Make the **Black Channel** active, selecting **Levels** from **Adjust** under the **Image** menu and altering **Output Level** from 0 to 60, brightening the shadowed area.

Make the **Yellow Channel** active, selecting **Offset** from **Other** under the **Filter** menu and setting it to **Horizontal:** 0 pixels, **Vertical:** -7 pixels. Then use **Repeat Edge Pixels** to move the entire image up by 7 pixels.

Make the **Magenta Channel** active, choosing **Offset** from **Other** under the **Filter** menu and setting it to **Horizontal:** 0 pixels, **Vertical:** -7 pixels. Execute **Set to Background** to move the entire image up by 7 pixels.

Now make **Cyan Channel** active, selecting **Offset** from **Other** under the **Filter** menu, setting it to **Horizontal:** -7 pixels, **Vertical:** 0 pixels. Then execute **Wrap Around** to move entire image 7 pixels to the left.

By using **Offset** to deliberately reposition each channel and then recombine you can achieve blurred effects and unique coloring. The weight and depth of the forest is also stronger than the original.

---

19. イエローチャンネルをアクティブにしてフィルタメニューのその他からスクロールを選択、水平方向:7ピクセル、垂直方向:7ピクセル、端のピクセルを繰り返して埋めるで実行する。

20. マゼンダチャンネルをアクティブにしてフィルタメニューのその他からスクロールを選択、水平方向:0ピクセル、垂直方向:-7ピクセル、選択範囲外からスクロールさせるで実行する。

21. シアンチャンネルをアクティブにしてフィルタメニューのその他からスクロールを選択、水平方向:-7ピクセル、垂直方向:0ピクセル、ラップアラウンド(巻き戻す)で実行する。

19. Make the **Yellow Channel** active, then select **Offset** from **Others** under the **Filter** menu to move the image 7 pixels to the right and down. Execute at **Horizontal:** 7 pixels, **Vertical:** 7 pixels, **Repeat Edge Pixels**.

20. Make the **Magenta Channel** active, choosing **Offset** from **Others** under the **Filter** menu to move the entire image 7 pixels toward the top. Set and execute at **Horizontal:** 0 pixels, **Vertical:** - 7 pixels, **Set to Background**.

21. Make the **Cyan Channel** active, selecting **Offset** from **Others** under **Filter** menu to move the entire image 7 pixels to the left. Execute at **Horizontal:** 7 pixels, **Vertical:** 0 pixels, **Wrap Around**.

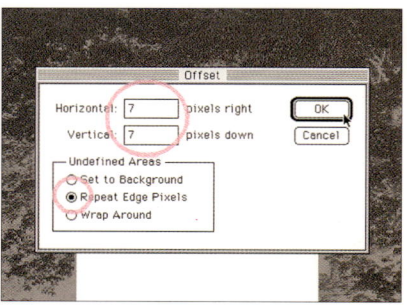

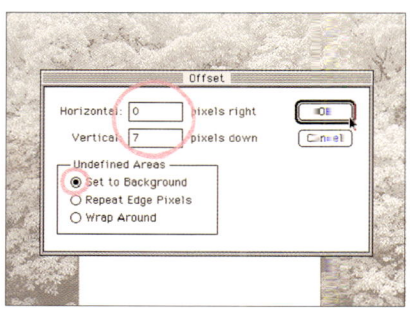

チャンネルの統合　Merging channels

チャンネルパレットのメニューからチャンネルの**統合**を選択、モード選択ダイアログボックスでモード:CMYKカラー、チャンネル4でOKする。チャンネル指定ダイアログボックスでシアンチャンネルとマゼンダチャンネルを入れ替えてOKする。これでチャンネルの入れ替えによる色変換が終了、モードメニューで*RGB*モードに変換しておく。

Select **Merge Channels** under the **Palette** menu, indicating **Mode: CMYK Color**, **Channels 4**. Click OK. In the Channel indication dialogue box click OK for switching **Cyan** and **Magenta Channels**. By doing this you can switch to **RGB Mode** after color alterations and finishing work are complete.

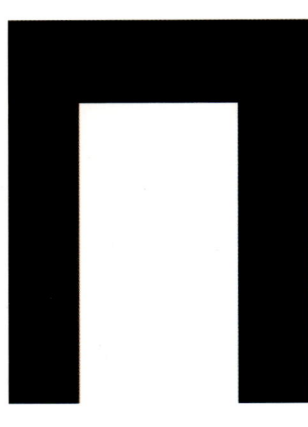

最終合成用と背景整理用を兼ねたマスクを作る。情報パレットの**ポインター**の位置を見ながらx:112、y:135ピクセルの**ポイント**を起点にして**長方形選択ツール**でW:256×H:505ピクセル選択、選択範囲の記録後RGB表示に戻る。**選択範囲**の選択を実行して**編集**メニューから**消去**を選んで背景を整理、**保存**する。

Make the final mask for both adjustments to background and final merging of composite elements. Watching the **Position of Pointer** under the **Informatoin Palette**, position the **Rectangular Marquee Tool** at point **x:**112, **y:**135 and draw an area of W:256xH:505 pixels. After executing **Save Selection**, return to **RGB Mode**. Do **Load Selection**, then select **Clear** form the **Edit** menu to adjust and **Save** the background.

チャンネルの統合を実行する際、RGBでもCMYKでもαチャンネルを持っているときは**マルチチャンネルモード**で実行しないとαチャンネルが統合されない。取り残されたαチャンネルは**イメージ**の**演算**から**複写**を使って複写することができる。**マルチチャンネルモード**で統合するとカラー表示しないので、CMYKなりRGBなりにモード変換して保存する。またチャンネルの利用法として**チャンネルパレット**で各チャンネルをクリック選択表示してコントラストを上下したり、濃度を上げ下げしてカラーバランスを整えることは従来のアナログ的実感があって人によってはかえってわかりやすいかもしれない。

When executing **Merge Channels** in either RGB or CMYK modes and using an alpha channel you must be in **Multichannel Mode** or the alpha channel will not merge.

You can use the remaining alpha channels to **Duplicate** (under **Calculate**, on the **Image** menu). When merging on **Multichannel Mode** color cannot be shown, so images must be converted and saved in RGB or CMYK modes.

Another use of channels is to click Channels under the **Channels Palette** to adjust contrast and density up or down, or change color balance. This method is similar to the analog approach and might be easier to use for some people.

---

22. 分割したファイルをエフェクトをかけながら統合するために**チャンネルパレット**のメニューから**チャンネルの統合**コマンドを選択する。

22. To merge channels which have been separated in order to achieve effects use **Merge Channels** command from the **Channels Palette**.

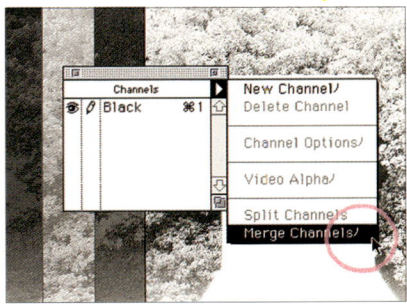

23. **チャンネルの統合**コマンドを選択すると最初にモードを指定するためのダイアログがでる。CMYKを選択するとチャンネルは自動的に4になりαチャンネルは統合されない。

23. When selecting **Merge Channels** a dialogue box will arise for **Mode** settings. When CMYK is selected 4 channels automatically open and alpha channels cannot be merged.

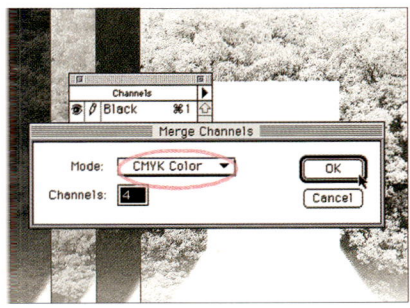

24. モードを指定してOKすると次にCMYK各チャンネルにどのファイルを割り当てるか設定するためのダイアログがでる。シアンチャンネルにマゼンダファイルをマゼンダチャンネルにシアンファイルを割り当てる。

24. After setting and OK-ing **Mode** a dialogue box will appear asking which files to apportion the different CMYK channels. Specify **Magenta** file to **Cyan channel** and **Cyan** file to **Magenta**.

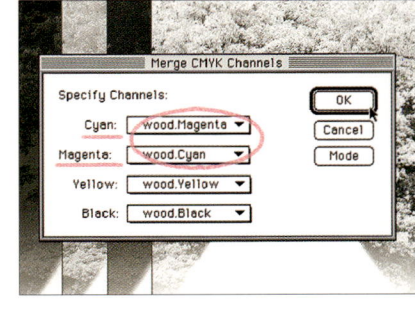

パネルの影をつける　Adding panel shadows

情報パレットのポインターの位置を見ながらx：121、y：127ピクセルのポイントを起点にして、境界線のぼかし幅を5ピクセルに設定した長方形選択ツールでx：378、y：508ピクセルまで選択する。境界線のぼかし幅：0に設定したなげなわツールでオプションキーとコマンドキーを押しながら白バック部分の選択範囲を選択除外する。残された天地逆のL字状選択部分に黒色を塗りつぶし100%して影をつける。

Following the **Position of Pointer** on the **Information** menu fix the **Rectangular Marquee Tool** at starting point **x:**121, **y:**127 pixels and set **Feather Radius** at 5 pixels. Select an area to point **x:**378, **y:** 508 pixels. With **Lasso Tool** set to **Feather Radius:** 0, hold down **Option Key** and **Command Key** to delete the selected white area. The remaining, L-shaped white area is **Filled** 100% in black.

空と合成済みのオブジェクトを全画面の選択してコピー後、完成した背景をアクティブにして#4チャンネルを選択範囲の選択で表示して、オブジェクトを選択範囲内へペーストするとできあがり。
右下はもう一度チャンネルの分割してから赤チャンネルと緑チャンネルを入れ替えてチャンネルの統合後、演算コマンドの差の絶対値を使ってひとひねりしたカラーバリエーション。

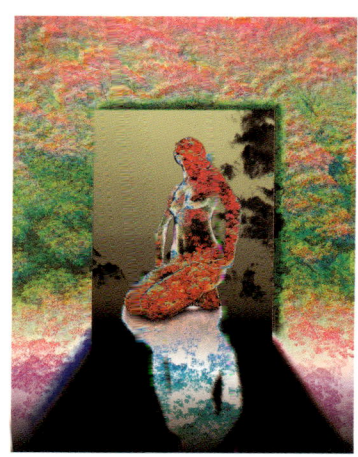

After **Selecting** and **Copying** the sky and finished composite image, make the background active and **Load Selection** with **Channel #4**. After **Paste Into** with the subject you are finished. After doing a **Split** and then **Merge** on the **Red Channel** and **Green Channel** in the lower right, use the **Difference calculation** to add a twist to the color.

---

25. 不思議さを強調するためにパネルの影を右コーナーにつける。まず長方形選択ツールをダブルクリックして長方形選択ツールオプションで境界線のぼかし幅を5ピクセルに設定する。

25. To emphasize the strangeness attach the shadow to the right corner. First double-click the **Rectangular Marquee Tool** and set **Feather Radius** under **Rectangular Marquee Tool** options to 5 pixels.

26. 情報パレットのポインターの位置を見ながらx：121、y：127ピクセルのポイントを起点にって長方形選択ツールを使ってx：378、y：508ピクセルまで選択、影のボケ足部分を選択する。

26. Watching the **Position of Pointer** (under the **Information Palette**) start at x:121, y:127 pixels with the **Rectangular Marquee Tool** and select to **x:**378, **y:**508 pixels. Then select the distorted shadow at the feet.

27. 境界線のぼかし幅：0、アンチエイリアシング設定したなげなわツールを使ってコマンド+シフトキーを押しながら白スペースを選択除外、森側に影の選択範囲を残す。黒色塗りつぶし100%をするか明度を下げて影を作る。

27. Set to **Feather Radius:** 0, **Anti-aliased:** ON, and use the **Lasso Tool**, holding down the **Command+Shift Key** to select and delete the white, leaving only the shadow on the forest side selected. **Fill** 100% in black or lower brightness to create a shadow.

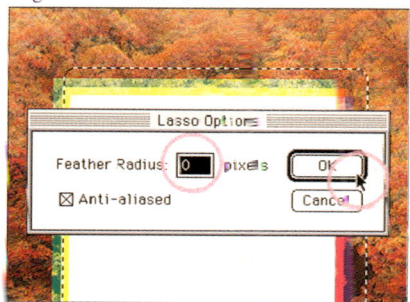

第8章 解像度を上げる

Chapter 8 Heightening Resolution

Work A：W727×H496Pixels 72 ppi,1.03MB,RGB

Work B：W2094×H1430Pixels 350ppi,8.57MB,RGB

低解像度データをガイドラインに高解像度データを作り直す

W:727×H:496ピクセル、1.03MBで作成したカンプをもとに本番印刷用の高解像度データを作り直す。カンプの作り手と同一人が作業するのであれば問題ないが、別人の場合はカンプ作成時のデータをできるだけ詳細に申し送りする。

刷り上がり寸法は横幅152ミリ／175線なので350ppi、2094×1430ピクセル、8.57MBが必要な解像度とサイズだ。

まず低解像度データを上記のサイズに**イメージメニュー**の**画像解像度**コマンドを使って拡大する。

ラインツールオプションの幅を０にしてスケールがわりに**情報パレット**の表示を見ながら合成に必要な画像の横幅を計測する。

次にパスツールを使って合成のポイントとなる絵柄をトレースする。パスツールが苦手な人は**なげなわツール**を使ってトレース後、**パスパレット**のメニューから**パスの作成**を実行しても同じことができる。

パスパレットの**パス選択ツール**を使ってすべてのパスを選択後コピーして、同サイズにスキャニングしなおしたメインの画像にペーストする。

このパスをガイドラインに使うと位置決めに迷うことなく、どんな複雑なレイアウトでも造作なく行うことができる。

単純なレイアウトはマスクチャンネルを表示のみにすることによってマスクを見ながら張り込むことも可能だ。

A W:727xH:496 pixel, 1.03MB rough image file will be reworked into a high-resolution print-film data file. There is no problem if the person making the high-resolution file is the same one who made the rough, but if they are different, it helps to learn as much as possible about the data used in the original.

The finsihed dimensions and resolution will be 152 mm/175 lines, which requires 350ppi, 2094x1430 pixels, and 8.57MB.

First of all, resize the rough to the above dimensions with the **Image Size** command on the **Image** menu.

Set the **Line Tool** options to width: 0, then watch the **Information Palette** to determine the necessary dimensions for the composite image.

Next, use the **Pen Tool** to trace the pattern of the composite. For those who are poor with the **Pen Tool**, use the **Lasso Tool**, then execute **Make Path** under the **Paths Palette** menu for the same effect.

Use the **Selection Pointer** of **Paths Palette** to Select all paths, then **Copy** and **Paste** into the Main file, which has already been scanned to the same size.If you use this path as a guideline you need not worry about positioning. You can handle even the most complex images without need of great prowess.

With simple layouts you can overlay merely by displaying the mask channel. Use either method, depending on the needs of the situation.

---

1. **イメージメニュー**の**画像解像度**コマンドでファイルサイズを**固定**のチェックを外して幅：15.2cm、解像度：350ppiで実行する。**画像解像度**コマンドは実際に実行しない場合も解像度とサイズの関係を知るために便利に使える。

1. Omit the **File Size** check under the **Image Size** (of **Image** menu), executing at **Width**: 15.2cm, **Resolution**: 350ppi. When you don't actually use the **Image Size** command this is convenient for learning the relation between the size and resolution of the image.

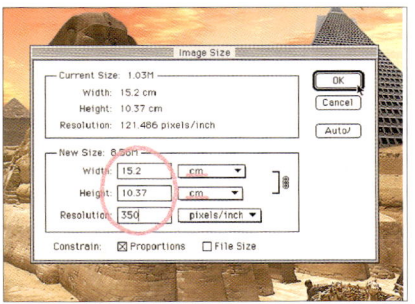

2. 選択ツールを使って範囲を選択して**パスパレット**のメニューから**パスの作成**を実行する。選択範囲がパスに代わる。

2. Using the Selection Tool to select the area, execute **Make Paths** under the **Palette** menu to create a path in the selected area.

3. ラインツールをダブルクリックしてラインツールオプションで幅を０にすると引いた線が現れないので、**情報パレット**と併用して角度も表示できるスケールがわりに重宝する。

3. By double-clicking the **Line Tool** options and setting **width** to 0 a line will appear; use this together with the **Information Palette** to show the angle, too.

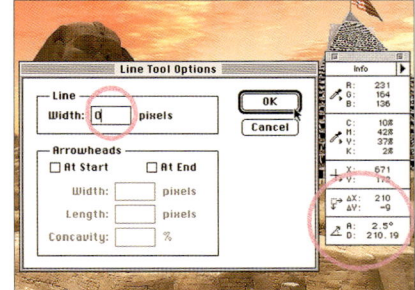

Using low-resolution data as a guideline for high-resolution data creation

選択範囲メニューから選択範囲の選択してメインカットのバックに夕焼け空を選択範囲内へペーストする。位置調整をしてからもう一度選択範囲の選択して夕焼のビル群を選択範囲内へペーストする。パスのガイドラインを参考に位置を決める。再度選択範囲の選択、パスのガイドラインを参考にピラミッド型のビルを選択範囲内へペーストする。選択範囲メニューからフロート解除コマンドを実行、ピラミッド型ビルをメインカットに確定後、選択範囲メニューから選択範囲の反転。選択範囲内に星条旗を選択範囲内へペーストする。あとはガイドライン通り、作業する人々を手前にペーストして貼り込みは終了である。

From the **Select** menu do **Load Selection**, then use **Paste Into** to add the sunset sky to the background of the main cut. After adjusting the position once again **Load Selection** and **Paste Into** with the Skyscrapers. Using Path guidelines, adjust the positioning. Again, **Load Selection** and **Paste Into** with the pyramid-shaped building. Once more refer to Path guide lines to determine exact position ing. Now use the **Defloat** command from the **Select** menu to confirm the position of the pyramid-shaped building, then do **Inverse** from the **Image** menu. **Paste Into** the selected area with the Stars and Stripes flag. Afterwards, **Paste** the people to the places indicated by the guidelines.

夕焼けの空、横幅を2094ピクセルでスキャニング後、高さを54%に縮小して偏平化する。

After scanning the sunset sky at 2094 pixels, set height at 54% and shrink horizontally.

夕焼けのビル群、横幅を419ピクセルでスキャニング後、自動選択となげなわツールを使って空を除いたマスクを作り保存する。

After scanning the skyscrapers at 419 pixels, use the **Magic Wand** and **Lasso Tool** to delete the sky and create a mask. **Save**.

ピラミッド型のビル、横幅を1047ピクセルでスキャニング後、自動選択となげなわツールを使って空を除いたマスクを作り保存する。星条旗も同様に(横幅213ピクセル)。

After scanning the pyramid-shaped building at 1047 pixels, use the **Magic Wand** and **Lasso Tool** to delete the sky and create a mask. **Save**. Do the same with the Stars adn Stripes flag.

メインカット、横幅を2094ピクセルでスキャニング、自動選択となげなわツールで空と右側のピラミッドを含めたマスクを作り保存。

After scanning the main cut at 2094 pixels, use the **Magic Wand** and **Lasso Tool** to mask and **Save** the sky and righthand side.

作業する人々、横幅を691ピクセルでスキャニング後、なげなわツールを使って必要な領域のマスクを作り保存する。

After scanning the workers at 691 pixels, use the **Lasso Tool** to mask and **Save** the necessary area.

4．今回の作業はほとんど**選択範囲内へペースト**になった。実際の合成作業でも単純な**ペースト**よりも範囲を決めて**選択範囲内へペースト**することが多い。

4. Most of this work has used **Paste Into**. In real composite work even simple pasting is best done with a set, selected area using **Paste Into** rather than **Paste**. Learning to use **Paste Into** and **Composite Controls** is the fastest path to mastering composite techniques.

5．選択範囲メニューから選択範囲の選択するとあらかじめ作っておいたマスクチャンネルを選択範囲として画面に呼び出すことができる。選択ツールで作った選択範囲も**選択範囲の記録**を実行しないとマスクとして保存されない。

5. After using **Load Selection** from the **Select** menu you can bring up the Mask Channels to your screen. If you don't do **Save Selection** with the areas you created with the selection tool the masks will not be saved.

6．選択範囲メニューからフロートの解除コマンドを実行する。フロート両域が確定して選択領域を反転することが可能になる。フロート／フロートの解除コマンドはVer 2.5から新しく備わったコマンドだ。

6. Execute the **Defloat** command on the **Select** menu. After confirming both floated regions you can reverse the selected areas. The **Float/Defloat** command is a new addition to Ver. 2.5.

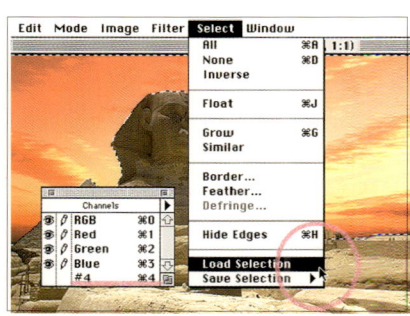

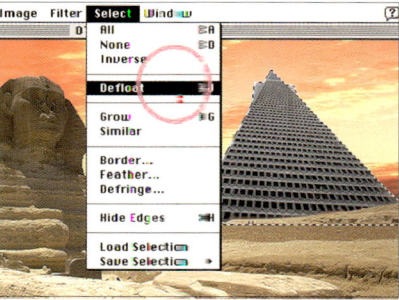

低解像度データを補間して高解像度データに変える

Supplementing low-resolution data to create high-resolution data

フォト CD を利用する。

コダックのフォトCDは35ミリのフィルムからデジタルデータを作るために最もコストパフォーマンスに優れた手段である。1カットにつき5サイズの圧縮した画像をもち、用途に応じて自由に使い分けることができる。アウトプットは少ない画素数でもきれいに出力できるコダックのデジタルプリンターの使用を前提にしているので、CCDスキャニング特有のシャドウのノイズやピントの甘さは残るものの充分に実用的だ。フォトショップでカラーコレクションをきちんと調整して、適度のアンシャープマスクをかければ、小サイズの印刷用途なら使えないことはない。

ここではフォトCDで取り込んだW：768×H：512ピクセル（Base：基準のファイルサイズで一番扱いやすい）の画像をそのままの解像度で印刷したものと、約3倍に解像度を上げて印刷したものを表示してある。同じ画像を最大サイズ（W：3072×H：2048ピクセル）のファイルを使って印刷したものが口絵頁に掲載されているので比較されたい。印刷にはWork Aは**フィルタメニューのシャープ**からアンシャープマスクの設定を**適用量**：100％、**半径**：1.0、**しきい値**：6で実行。Work Bは**イメージメニュー**の**画像解像度コマンド**でファイルサイズを固定のチェックを外し**幅**：15.2cm、**解像度**：350ppiで実行、解像度をアップしてから、**フィルタメニューのシャープ**からアンシャープマスクの設定を**適用量**：150％、**半径**：2.0、**しきい値**：6で実行。

Using a photo CD

The Kodak photo CD is the most cost-efficient method of creating digital photo data from 35mm film.

A single cut offers five compressed images which can be used freely for various applications. The output presumes a low-resolution Kodak digital printer, so while the special noise and pint shadowing of a CCD scanner are a bit weak, the technology is sufficiently practical to use. If you carefully adjust the color collection of Photoshop and add an appropriate degree of **USM**, there is no reason you cannot use even small sizes for printing.

The 768x512 pixel photo CD images shown here (the middle being the easiest size to handle) include one printed at the same resolution and one printed at three times the resolution. The same image printed at the largest possible file size (3072x2048 pixels) is shown on the front page. Please compare.

For printing Work A, the **Unsharp Mask** (under **Sharpen**, on the **Filter** menu) is set and executed at **Amount**: 100%, **Radius**, 1.0, **Threshold**: 6. Work B omits the **File Size** check (under the **Image Size** command of the **Image** menu) executing at **Width**: 15.2cm, **Resolution**: 350dpi. After increasing resolution, the **Unsharp Mask** (under **Sharpen**, **Filter** menu) is set to Amount: 150%, **Radius**:2.0, **Threshold**:6, and executed.

補間法とは　About interpolation

解像度を上下する場合、画像の補間法が問題だ。フォトショップは**ファイルメニュー**の**環境設定**の**環境**で3種類の補間法を選択することができる。デフォルトはバイキュービック法で最も画質のよい補間法だが処理時間も一番かかる。処理時間は最も速いが中間トーンを生成しないのでジャギーの目立つのがニアレストネイバー法だ。バイリニア法はスピード、画質ともその中間と考えればよい。画質を優先するならバイキュービック法を常用することだ。ただし中間トーンを生成して補間するのでアンチエイリアスのかかった眠い感じになる。イラスト等ではニアレストネイバー法がよい結果を得られるケースが多い。

When raising or lowering image resolution the fill method comes into question. You can choose any of three interpolation from **General**, under **Preferences**. The default method is **Bicubic**, and this produces the finest image, but also takes the most time. **Nearest Neighbor** is the fastest, but it leaves middle tones untouched, and tends to produce jaggies. **Bilinear** can be thought of as somewhere in between the other two. In general, one wants to sacrifice the time and use **Bicubic** for its finer image quality. However, when the image has an anti-alias, sleepy middle tone effect that makes middle tone filling unnecessary, such as in illustrations, **Nearest Neighbor** can be a very suitable choice.

---

7. **イメージメニュー**の**画像解像度コマンド**を実行、**ファイルサイズ**の**固定**のチェックを外して**幅**：15.2cm、**解像度**：350ppiで実行、解像度をアップする。事前に**環境設定**で**画像補間**を**バイキュービック法**に指定しておく。

8. **フィルタメニュー**の**シャープ**から**アンシャープマスク**を選択、**適用量**：150%、**半径**：2.0、**しきい値**：6で実行する。フォトCDデータから印刷する場合、**アンシャープマスクコマンド**は欠かせない作業である。

9. **ファイルメニュー**の**環境設定**の**環境**で**画像補間**を**バイキュービック法**に指定する。ほとんどのケースではバイキュービック法でよいが、場合によってニアレストネイバー法のほうが結果がよい場合がある。

7. Use the **Image Size** Command (under the **Image** menu), omitting the **File Size** check and executing at **Width**:15.2cm, **Resolution** 350ppi. Interpolation has already been set to **Bicubic**, under **Preferences**.

8. From **Sharpen** on the **Filter** menu select **Unsharp Mask**, executing at **Amount**: 150%, **Radius**: 2.0, **Threshold**: 6. You can't print from a photo CD file without the **USM** command.

9. In **Gerneal**, under **Preferences** (**File** menu) set **Interpolation** to **Bicubic**. In most cases **Bicubic** is preferable, but **Nearest Neighbor** can also achieve good effects in certain situations.

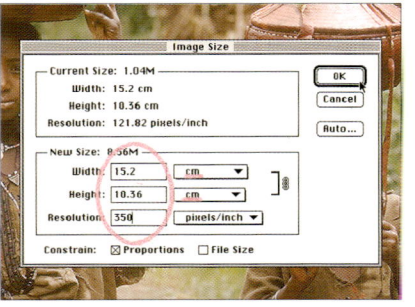

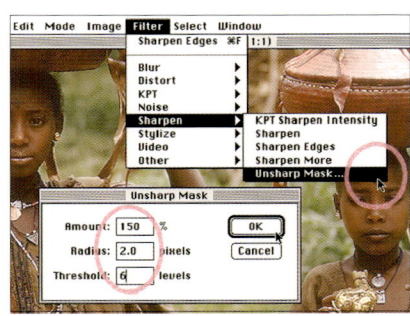

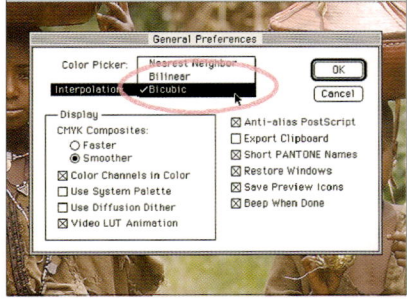

Work A：W729×H497Pixels,121ppi,1.04MB,RGB

Work B：W2094×H1428Pixels,350ppi,8.56MB,RGB

第9章 ソフトの連係プレー

Chapter 9 Teaming-up Multiple Applications

ソフトの連係プレー

Teaming-up Multiple Applications

イラストレーターとの絶妙な組み合わせ

フォトショップVer.2.5になって大きく改良された機能の1つがペンツールの使い勝手である。まるで機能を限定した「イラストレーター」が組み込まれているようだ。従来「イラストレーター」と組むことで始めて可能であった高度な作業が、フォトショップだけでほとんど完結できる。

とはいいながら「イラストレーター」と組み合わせて使うことで、まだまだ使い勝手も技術の可能性も大きく高まるのでぜひ両ソフトを有機的に使い込んで技術の向上をはかってほしい。

「イラストレーター」のオートトレース代わりに使う

選択範囲をパスに変換することができるので、スキャニングした画像をフォトショップ上でレタッチして選択範囲を**パスの作成**、ファイルメニューの**出力用プラグ**から*Illustrator*のパスコマンドを実行すると「イラストレーター」のファイルとして利用できる。極端に複雑なファイルは時間がかかりすぎて現実的ではないが、フォトショップ上で分割して書き出して「イラストレーター」上で集合させればよい。

複雑で微妙な線をフォトショップのレタッチ機能と併用することで的確にトレースすることができるので利用価値が高い。

「イラストレーター」のオートトレース機能はベテランほど利用していないようだが、フォトショップの**パスの作成**機能は使いものになることを受けあう。

「イラストレーター」のファイルをラスタライズする

「イラストレーター」のポストスクリプト画像をラスタライズしてビットマップ画像に変換するのはフォトショップの優れた機能のひとつだ。もともとフォトショップはペイントソフトではないので描画機能には秀でていない。「イラストレーター」で描いた絵を望みの解像度のビットマップ画像としてフォトショップに取り込めるのはペイント機能の不足を補ってあまりある便利さである。

変形のグラデーションマスクなどもこの機能のおかげで気軽に作ることができる。

3Dソフトを使って背景を作る

さてこの章の実習では「イラストレーター」で創った空と3Dソフトで創った背景を組み合わせてバックを創り、フォトショップで写真と組み合わせて不思議な空間を創造する。

商品写真の背景処理に色々と応用できるのではなかろうか。

版画風な似顔絵を作る..........エンボス処理

もう1つの実習はフォトショップのフィルタを使って線画にした画像を「イラストレーター」のポストスクリプト画像に変換して、版画風なタッチにするとともにサイズにとらわれず使用できる自由さを与える。写真から線画や絵を作る作業もかなり応用性が広い。

バリエーションとして再度フォトショップに戻して、エンボス加工したものを大理石パターンと組み合わせて作品とする。

The superb "Illustrator" connection

One of the major improvements to Ver. 2.5 is to the usefulness of the Pen Tool. It is now quite as if a limited "Illustrator" were contained within the program. In fact, most of the high precision work made possible by "Illustrator" can now be carried out within Photoshop.

However, this is not to deny the great usefullness and power of "Illustrator" when used in combination with Photoshop. Everyone should endeavor to improve their skills and effectiveness in the combined use of both softwares.

Substituting with Illustrator's auto-trace

You can change any selected area into a Path, and after scanning and retouching an image on Photoshop you can choose **Make Path**, then execute **Paths to Illustrator** (under **Export**, on **File** menu) with the selected item. The image can then be opened as a file on Illustrator. Extremely complex files take too much time to convert, and are thus not practical to use. Instead, break them apart on Photoshop, then bring them together once again on Illustrator.

Complex, fine lines can be retouched on Photoshop, then exported to Illustrator for accurate tracing - an extremely useful method. The greater one's skill with "Illustrator" the less one is likely to use Auto-Tracing, but Auto-Tracing is very well-suited to the **Make Path** function of Photoshop.

Rasterizing Illustrator files

One of the superb capabilities of Photoshop is its ability to rasterize and make bitmap images of postscript files created on Illustrator. Photoshop is not originally a paint program, so its illustrating capacities are not too advanced. But the ability to make bitmap images of illustrations created at desired resolution on Illustrator more than makes up for this lack of painting ability, and is highly convenient.

As a result of this function, such effects as altered gradation masks are easily produced.

Creating background with 3-D Soft

The subject of study in this chapter is a background that combines a sky done on Illustrator with a background done on 3-D software. Reproduced with a photo in Photoshop, it will become a mysterious space-zone.

This background production method can be used for product photos and various other applications.

A woodcut portrait....and embossing

Another subject of study in this chapter is the use of Photoshop's filters to convert a sketched image into a postscript Illustrator file image which has a touch of the woodblock and can be used at any size. There are various applications for changing photos into sketches or paintings.

The image will then be returned to photoshop, where it will be embossed and laid over a granite surface for the finished effect.

「イラストレーター」で背景と図面を描く

Drawing surfaces and backgrounds on Illustrator

森のシルエットを「イラストレーター」でトレース後コピーして上下に間隔をあけて配置、上のパスをペイントメニュー のペイント設定で塗りつぶしを濃いブルーに、下のパスをマゼンタに指定。ブレンドツールでステップ数を253にして実行。最後に一番手前のパスを選択し塗りつぶしを黒色にして保存する。

After tracing the scanned silhouette of the forest on Illustrator, *Copy* it. Then separate and set the upper perspective to dark blue under *Fill* (with *Style*, under the *Paint* menu), and the lower perspective to Magenta. Set the *Number of steps*, under the *Blend Tool*, to 253, and execute. Finally, *Fill* the foremost perspective with *Black*, and *Save*.

口紅の写真をスキャニングしてフォトショップに読み込む。ペンツールを使って右側半分をトレースする。パスの記録 をしてファイルメニューの出力用プラグから Illustratorのパスコマンドで「イラストレーター」のファイルとして書き出す。

A photo of the lipstick is scanned and read into Photoshop. Use the *Pen Tool* to trace the righthand size. Do *Save Path*, then choose *Paths to Illustrat* or under *Export* on the *File* menu, writing the file for Illustrator.

「イラストレーター」で上記のファイルを開いてパスを選択。ペイントメニュー のペイント設定で塗りつぶし、線の設定を黒に指定。プレビュー画像をMacintoshモノクロにして保存する。

Open the file on Illustrator and select Perspectives. Under Style on the *Paint* menu set *Fill*, *Stroke* to *Black*, and Save again as a new file. Set *Preview* to black and *White Macintosh* and *Save*.

「イラストレーター」はブレンドツールをうまく使うことで、柔らかい感じの絵も描くことができる。元図の背景は第10章で詳しい作り方を解説しているので参考にして欲しい。

線のはっきりした図面などは独壇場だが、3Dソフトに正確な形や複雑な平面図を持ち込むためにも便利に使える。

「Stratavision 3d」で「イラストレーター」のファイルを平面図として *Import* するためには、ファイルの保存時に必ずMacintoshモノクロプレビュー画像つきのEPSフォーマットで保存しなければならない。

写真からシルエットをトレースして平面図として利用すると、正確でリアルなモデリングを実に簡単に行うことができる。

By effectively using the *Blend Tool* on Illustrator you can create an image with a soft effect. Of course, surfaces with sharp lines area also a forte, but it is convenient for importing complex surface compositions and sharp images produced with 3-D software.
To import an Illustrator file as a flat image to Stratavision 3D the file must be saved in EPS Format with attached *Black&WhiteMacintosh Preview*. It is truly easy to do accurate and realistic modeling with a flat image tracing taken from a photo silhouette.

1.「イラストレーター」で森のシルエットをトレース、上のパスをペイントメニューのペイント設定で塗りつぶしを濃いブルーに、下のパスをマゼンタに指定。ブレンドツールでステップ数を253にして実行する。

1. Trace the silhouette of the forest in Illustrator. With *Fill* (under *Style*, on the *Paint* menu) indicate dark blue for the upper perspective and magenta for the lower part. Set the *Number of Steps* under the *Blend Tool* to 253, and execute.

2. 口紅の写真のパスをフィルタメニューの出力用プラグから Illustratorのパスコマンドで「イラストレーター」のファイルとして書き出す。

2. From *Export* under the *File* menu choose the Lipstick path and execute *Paths to Illustrator*, writing the file for Illustrator.

3.「イラストレーター」で口紅のパスファイルを開いて全画面の選択。ペイントメニューのペイント設定で塗りつぶし、線の設定とも黒に指定して新規保存。そのときプレビュー画像をMacintoshモノクロにして保存する。

3. *Open* the Lipstick path file under Illustrator and *Select All*. Set *Fill/Stroke* (under *Style*, on the *Paint* menu) to Black, and *Save* again. At this time save *Preview* as *Black & White Macintosh*.

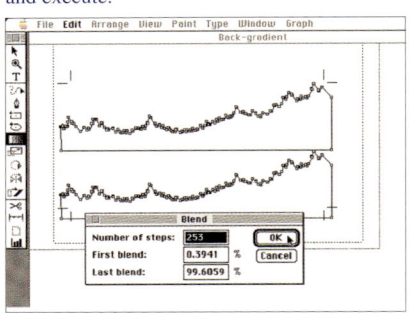

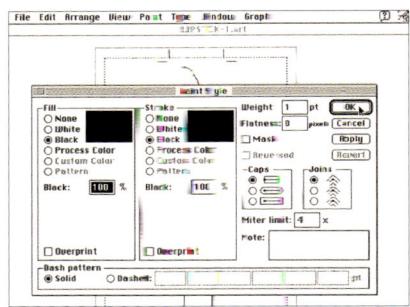

3Dソフトで背景を創る

Creating with 3-D software

「イラストレーター」で作った口紅の図面を「Stratavision3d」でImportしてLatheコマンドでモデリングする。今回はSolid Metal Textureだが、用意された様々なテクスチャーを与えることでかなり変化にとんだ絵作りが可能だ。

After ***importing*** the Lipstick diagram created on Illustrator to Stratavision 3d, the ***Lathe*** command is used for modeling. In this case, ***Solid Metal Textures*** was used, but an assortment of textures and large variety of images are possible.

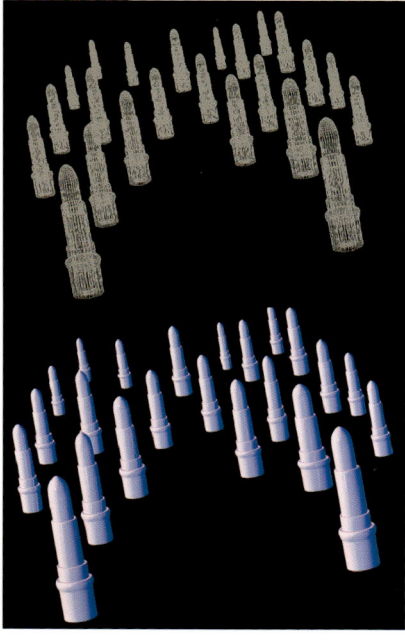

こつソフトでは最初から予定したアングルでレイアウトするのは不可能に近い。パースをつけない正面図と平面図、側面図でTransform Objectsの情報を利用しながら正確に配置していく。Camera Toolを使って予定したアングルを捜し配置を確認する。

It is almost impossible to create a layout along a predetermined angle with 3d software. Objects are placed accurately upon ***Frontal***, ***Horizontal*** and ***Sidelong*** surfaces using information shown under ***Transform Objects***. No perspctve is included at this time.
Using the ***Camera Tool***, the predetermined angle is checked and objects are adjusted.

Modelingが完成すれば作業としてはほとんど終わったようなものだ。ハイレゾリューションでレンダリングすればするほど待ち時間が長くなる。

Once the ***Modeling*** is finished the work is basically over. The higher the rendering resolution, the longer it will take to produce the image.

2Dのソフトと3Dのソフトは使い勝手がかなり違うために「イラストレーター」やフォトショップを相当に使い込んでいるベテランでも敬遠している人が多い。

制作に時間がかかるのは否定できないがレンダリングの時間はともかく、モデリングは慣れればそれなりに速くなる。食わず嫌いをせずにせいぜい利用してほしい。そこにはフォトショップ単独では絶対にできない世界が広がっている。

疑似3Dソフトの「Adobe Dimensions」などで3Dの感覚に慣れると本格的3Dの世界に入りやすいのではないだろうか。3Dで映像を作るうえでもフォトショップはかかせないソフトである。

The methods of 2D and 3D software are fairly different, so that many of those who are fairly skilled with Photoshop and Illustrator feel far from confident with the other medium.
It certainly cannot be denied that 3D production is time consuming, but rendering aside, the better one gets at modeling the quicker the work proceeds. Whether one likes it or not, it is well worth learning to do. With it comes a multitude of things that cannot be done with Photoshop alone.By learning to use other 3D programs, such as Adobe Dimensions, one can more easily get a feel for advanced 3D techniques. But to utilize 3D images there is no question but that Photoshop is required software.

4.「Stratavision3d」でFile メニューからNew、次にShapes メニューからNew Shapeを実行、新規保存する。File メニューから口紅の図面をImportする。ファイルは、白黒のプレビュー画面付のEPSファイルにしておく。

4. On "Stratavision 3d" choose New from the ***File*** menu, then execute ***New Shape*** under the ***Shapes*** menu, ***Saving as*** a new file. Under the ***File*** menu, import the lipstick image. If you can't import, check to see that it is an EPS file attached to a ***Black and White Preview***.

5. Modeling メニューからLatheコマンドを実行する。回転軸がずれている場合は回転のセンターに配置する。左上の図ができあがったワイヤーモデルである。ここで好みのテクスチャーも決めておく。

5. Execute the ***Lathe*** command under the ***Modeling*** menu. If the spin axis is off center, set it to center. The wire model shown left/above is the result. At this time choose the texture.

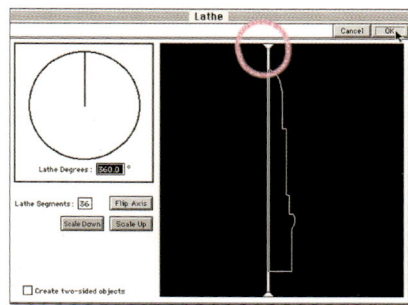

6. Worldに戻りInsert Shapeコマンドでできあがった口紅のShapeを配置、ドラッグ／コピーを繰り返して集合体にする。望みの場所に配置するにはFront,Top,Sideを行き来して調整。最後にCamera Toolでフレーミングする。

6. Return to ***World*** and ***Insert Shape*** of the finished lipstick, repeating ***Drag/Copy*** to create the assembly of lipsticks. In order to achieve the desired spread, adjust by going to ***Front***, ***Top*** and ***Side***. Then set the frame with ***Camera Tool***.

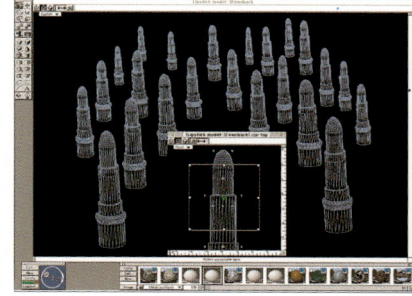

「フォトショップ」で背景を組み合わせる

Assembling a background on Photoshop

最後の仕上げはフォトショップの縄張りだ。3Dソフトですべて場面を作り上げるのもよいが、制作時間を考えると部品作りに徹したほうが現実的だ。実際、部品点数の多い**World**をレンダリングする場合は部分部分に分けてレンダリングしたほうが時間とメモリーの節約になる。

Editメニューの**Selection**で**Hide Selected**すると非表示になりレンダリングもされない。すべて同比率でレンダリングしてフォトショップで合成する。作例もフォトショップ上で口紅の数を増やしている。3Dソフトに戻ってモデリングとレンダリングをやり直すのは時間の無駄だ。

Finishing up is the forte of Photoshop. It is fine to create the entire scene on 3D software, but when one considers production time it is more realistic to approach the work from its individual parts. Actually, when rendering a world with many individual parts it is more economical in terms of memory and time to produce each part individually. If you choose **Hide Selection** under **Selection** on the **Edit** menu the selection will be concealed, and rendering cannot take place. Render all parts at the same percentage, then combine with Photoshop. Here the number of lipsticks has been greatly increased on Photoshop.

「イラストレーター」で作ったバックをフォトショップに読み込み**背景色**を黒にしておいて、イメージメニューの**画像サイズ**コマンドで縦長のファイルを作る。下部に3Dソフトで作った口紅集合体がペーストされるのでスペースを開けてレイアウトする。

Read the background created on Illustrator into Photoshop, setting **Background Color** to black. Use **Canvas Size** under the **Image** menu to open a tall file. The lipstick image created on 3D software will be pasted here, so open some extra space for layout work.

口紅集合体をペーストして3Dソフトでにつけきれなかった微妙な陰影やライティングの差、バックへいくほどダークに落とす作業をする。口紅の数が物足りないので後ろ側にパース感を合わせて何本かコピー&ペーストする。仕上げにフィルタメニューから逆光コマンドを実行する。

Fine shadowing and lighting around the lipsticks, work which could not be done on the 3D program, is now carried out in Photoshop. Darken the shadowing as you go deeper into the image. If the number of lipsticks is insufficient, **Copy** and **Paste**, keeping consistent with the perspective. Finish with the **Lens Flare** command on the **Filter** menu.

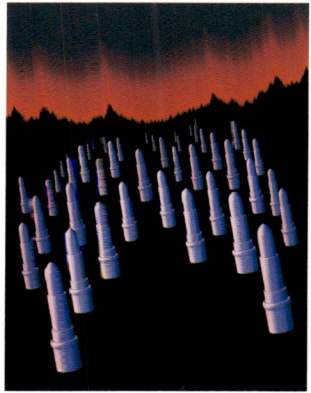

---

7. ライティングの巧拙が仕上がりを決める。少しでもリアリティを上げるためにはライティングをおろそかにしてはいけない。ここでは左サイドから1灯、左右後方からマゼンタ色の強い逆光をあてている。

7. The handling of lighting will determine the quality of the finished image. To achieve the highest effect of reality the lighting must be absolutely perfect. Here there is lighting cast from the left side, and strong magenta backlighting from the right rear.

8. **Tool Palette**の**Rendering Tool**をシフトキーを押しながらドラッグするとドラッグした範囲をレンダリングするためのオプションダイアログが現れる。**Image size**を指定して**Rendering**する。

8. Using the **Rendering Tool** (under **Tool Palette**) and pushing the **Shift Key** you can drag, selecting an area which can then be rendered in response to an option dialogue box. Set **Image size** for **Rendering**.

9. フォトショップのフィルタメニューの表現手法から逆光を実行する。設定は明るさ:100%、レンズの種類:50〜300mmズーム。

9. From **Stylize** (on Photoshop's **Filter** menu) execute **Lens Flare**. Settings are: **Brightness: 100%**, **Lens Type: 50-300mm Zoom**.

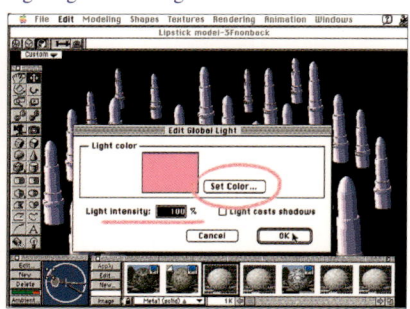

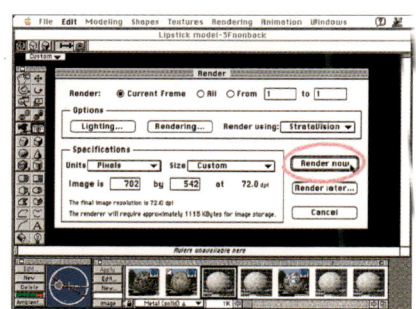

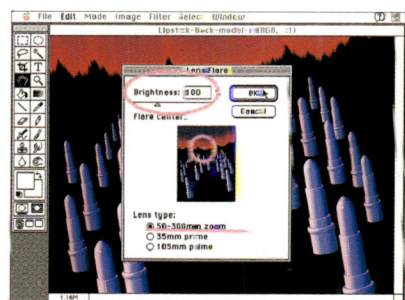

写真と合成する

Composing with the photo

角度調整をした口紅の写真。右のバリエーションの画像に使ったものと同じものだ。

The lipstick photo at the adjusted angle. The same object was used in the variation on the right.

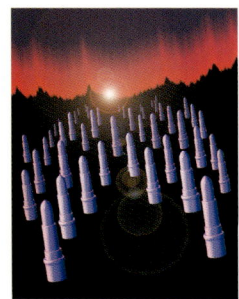

逆光フィルタで光を入れた背景の絵。写真とも絵ともつかない独特の世界を表現している。CGでありながらCGくさくない映像を作れるのがマッキントッシュのソフトの強味といえるのではないだろうか。

The background showing light introduced with the **Lens Flare** filter. This is a unique image, neither a photo nor a painting. The ability to create a CG that doesn't appear like a CG is the specialty of Macintosh software.

印象度はかなり違うが、同じ素材と同じ手法を利用したバリエーションカットである。逆光フィルタの代わりにジグザグフィルタを使っている以外はほとんど同じ手順だ。
3Dの*Textuer*を*Solid Metal*からブルーの*Pearl*に変えて*Rendering*した。

The impression is fairly different, but this variation uses the same materials and methods. With the exception of the use of the *Lends Flare* filter instead of the *Zigzag* filter the order of production is the same.
The 3D *texture* was changed from *Solid Metal* to Blue *Pearl* for *Rendering*.

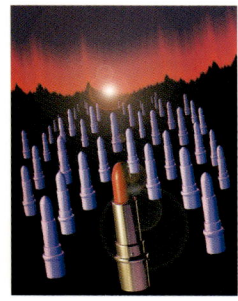
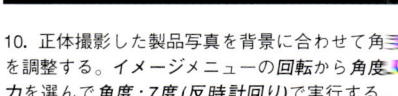

口紅の製品写真を合成する。光のフレアーを透かして合成するために合成のコントロールで描画モードを比較(明)でペーストしている。もちろん合成後に逆光フィルタをかければ合成のコントロールを使う必要はない。

Composing the lipstick product image. To spread the transparent flare of the light *Lighten Mode* (under *Composite Controls*) is used to *Paste*. Of course, if you choose to lay the *Lens Flare* filter after finishing there is no need to use *Composite Controls*.

---

10. 正体撮影した製品写真を背景に合わせて角度を調整する。イメージメニューの回転から角度入力を選んで角度:7度(反時計回り)で実行する。

10. The front angle photo of the product is adjusted to the angle of the background. A *Arbitrary* is chosen (under *Rotate*, on the *Image* menu) and set to *Angle: 7°CCW*, then executed.

11. 回転をしておいてからサイズの調整をする。本来スキャニング時に正確なサイズを出しておくべきだが、縮小方向でのリサイズは画像にそれほど大きな乱れを生ぜずにすむ。

11. After *rotation* the object's its size is adjusted. Until now emphasis has been placed on scanning an image at the correct size, but where the object is only to be shrunk, the image quality does not suffer too much.

12. オプションキーを押しながらペーストすると合成のコントロールでペースト時の細かい条件設定ができる。選択範囲内の画像の黒の三角形:10、不透明度:100%、描画モード:比較(明)で実行する。

12. When pasting to the background you can hold down the *Option Key* and *Paste*, or use *Composite Controls* to Paste and fine tune settings. *Black Triangle* (under *Floating*) is set to 10, *Opacity*: 100%, *Mode: Lighten*.

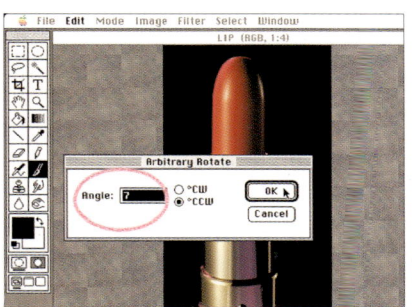
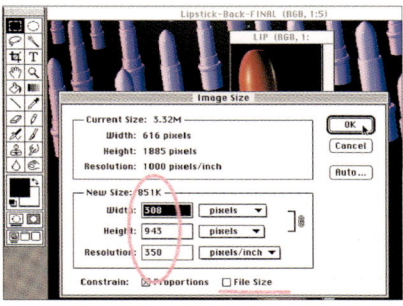
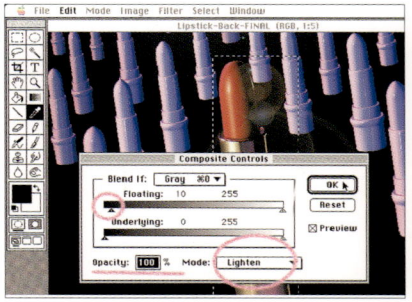

写真を元にして版画風の似顔絵を作る

Creating a woodcut-like portrait from a photo

スキャニングしたスナップ写真やビデオカメラで取り込んだ写真をもとにして似顔絵を作るのはそれほど難しい作業ではない。各種のフィルタ処理をするだけで十分絵画的な効果を与えることができる。フォトショップのフィルタが物足りなければ、サードパーティ製のフィルタも数多くある。「モネ」や「ペインター」といった絵画化するためのソフトも存在する。ここでは応用性の広い白黒の線画として表現するテクニックを紹介する。ビットマップ画像のままでは利用範囲が限定されるのでポストスクリプト画像に作り替える。さらに応用としてエンボス処理後、好みのテクスチャーと組み合わせてみる。

With Photoshop it is not particularly difficult to use a flatbed scanner to scan a snapshot, or input directly from a videocam, to create a portrait-like image. By using the various filters you can achieve effects which make a very artistic image. And if Photoshop's filters do not satisfy you, there are also many third-party filters, including "Monet" and "Painter," which offer other painterly effects.Here we will introduce black and white techniques which can be used in a broad variety of applications. Because bitmapped images are of limited applicability the image is changed to postscript. After the image is emboseed some further effects will be demonstrated.

ビデオカメラとキャプチャリングボードを使って直接取り込んだスナップフォト。モニター画面を見ながらフレーミングやシャッターチャンスを確認できるので便利だ。

A snap photo read directly to the computer via video camera and capturing board. You can conveniently adjust framing and shutter chance while watching the image on the monitor.

フィルタメニューの表現手法から輪郭検出を実行して、イメージメニューの色調補正からレベル補正コマンドで選択画面を見ながら、バックを白く線を黒くコントラストを上げる

Execute **Find Edges** under **Stylize** on the **Image** menu, then, while watching the screen, use **Levels** under **Adjust** on the **Image** menu to increase contrast, whitening background and darkening lines.

モードメニューからグレースケールを選び、ブラシツールを使って不要部分の消去と必要部分の描き込みを細心かつだいたんに行う。帽子のシャドウ部分はなげなわツールで選択して白黒反転させている。

Choose **Grayscale** from the **Mode** menu, then use the **Paint Brush Tool** to erase unnecessary parts and draw in fine and bold lines. Use the **Lasso Tool** to select the back of the hat and shadow by reversing black and white.

---

13. フィルタメニューの表現手法から**輪郭検出**を実行する。結果が思わしくないときは**取り消し**して元データのコントラストや明度を変えて思った状態になるまで再実行する。明度差が20%以上あれば、明確なラインになる。

13. Execute **Find Edges** under **Stylize** on the **Filter** menu. If the image doesn't turn out as you wish, choose **Undo**, reverting to the original contrast and brightness data. Redo until you are satisfied with the result. If contrast is raised above 20% definite lines will appear.

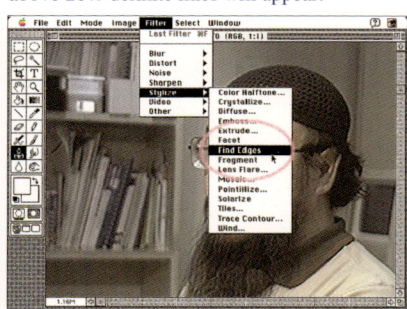

14. イメージメニューの色調補正から**レベル補正**コマンドを選択、画像を見ながらバックを白く線を黒くコントラストを上げて後の作業をやりやすいようにする。

14. Select the **Levels** command (under **Adjust**, on the **Image** menu), watching the image as you whiten background and darken lines to make later work easier.

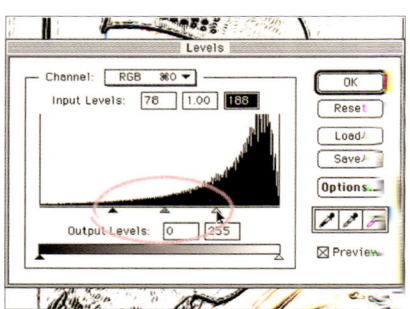

15. モードメニューから**グレースケール**を選択実行する。同じ白黒モードでも**モノクロ2階調**は使えるコマンドが限定されるので、修整作業にさしつかえる。

15. Select and execute **Grayscale** (under **Mode** menu). In the same black/white mode **Bitmap** commands are more limited, which becomes a hindrance during later revision work.

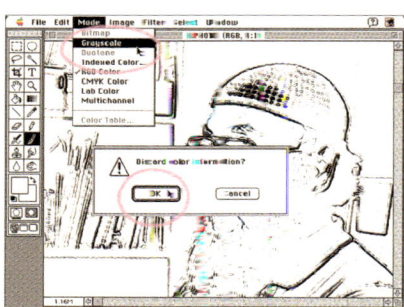

「ストリームライン」でトレースする　*Tracing with "Streamline"*

フォトショップ上で修整して完成した線画。どこまでオリジナルの線やテクスチャーを生かすかでリアルにも漫画的にも表現することができる。このままではタッチが生々しいのと、使い道が作成した解像度に左右されるので、PICTフォーマットで保存して「Adobe Streamline」を使ってポストスクリプトファイルに変換する。「イラストレーター」でテンプレートとして開いて、オートトレースコマンドを使うこともできるが、これだけ複雑な絵では細部の作業にうんざりすることだろう。

A sketch created on Photoshop. You decide which original lines to use, and what textures to adapt, in order to achieve the realistic or comic-like effects you seek. Here the effect is realistic, but the uses of the image are determined by the resolution at which the image is produced. **Save** it in PICT format, using Adobe Streamline to convert it to a postscript file. Open it in Illustrator as a template. You could use the Autotrace Command, but in this complex picture doing all the fine lines seems a bit pointless.

「Adobe Streamline」でベジェ曲線化したパス。この絵は無理だったが、もっと簡単な線画であればフォトショップでパスの作成して*Illustrator*のパスコマンドで「イラストレーター」に持ってくることもできる。

A bezier path in Adobe Streamline. With this picture it's impossible, but with simpler images you could use **Paths to Illustrator** under **Make Path**, in Photoshop, to import the file to Illustrator.

「イラストレーター」のファイルとして保存、完成した版画風の線画。ビットマップの画像をオートトレースしてポストスクリプト化するとタッチが版画風になって独特の味が出る。

Save the finished "woodblock print" as an Illustrator file. Saving the bitmapped image as an auto-traced, postscript picture gives the image its woodblock print texture.

16.「Adobe Streamline」の*Conversion Options*画面。今回はデフォルト設定で実行しているが、目的によってかなり細かい設定ができる。Ver. 2.0以上ではグレイスケール画像にも対応している。

16. The Adobe Streamline **Conversion Options** Menu. In this case the image was created in default mode, but depending on the aim fairly fine settings are possible. Ver. 2.0 and newer supports Grayscale images.

17.「Adobe Streamline」でPICT画像を開いて保存先と名前を指定する（PICTファイルならRGB、Gray、Bitmapを問わない）。*Convert Image*ボタンをクリックするとオートトレースしたファイルが作られる。

17. In Adobe Streamline open the PICT image, indicate a name and Save. Click the **Convert Image** button (Mode setting RGB, Gray, Bitmap is OK) to create an autotraced file.

18.「Adobe Streamline」で変換中の画面。最初に元の画像が表示されてどんどんパスに描き変えていく。

18. The Adobe Streamline screen while under conversion. The original image appears first, and is gradually written to the path.

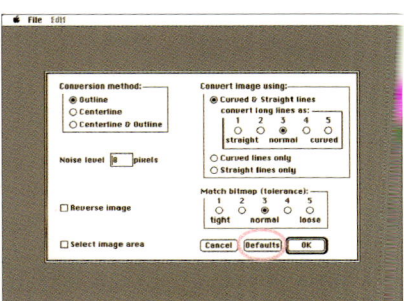

大理石にエンボス加工する

Embossing a granite slab

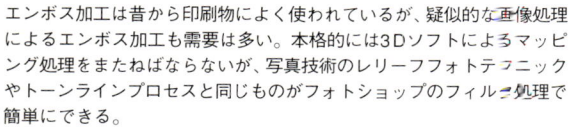

エンボス加工は昔から印刷物によく使われているが、疑似的な画像処理によるエンボス加工も需要は多い。本格的には3Dソフトによるマッピング処理をまたねばならないが、写真技術のレリーフフォトテクニックやトーンラインプロセスと同じものがフォトショップのフィルタ処理で簡単にできる。

フィルタメニューの表現手法からエンボスコマンドを実行する。角度はライティングの角度を決める、高さはエンボスの高さ、立体感を設定する。適用量はエッジの強調度を決定する。1～500%で設定できる。

Embossing has long been popular in the printing world, but its uses are also many in the image production field. The mapping abilities of true 3D software are beyond Photoshop's capacities but with its filters one can easily simulate such photo techniques as relief photography and tone line processes. Use the *Emboss* command under *Stylize* on the *Filter* menu. *Angle* decides the direction of the lighting, *Height* the height of the embossing, and both together the 3-dimensionality of the image. *Amount* determines the sharpness of the edges, and can be set from 1 - 500%.

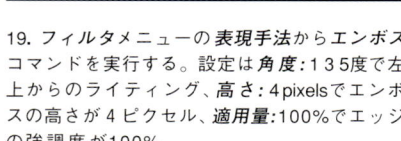

エンボス画像をじゃましない適当な素材を用意する。パターンが細かくてコントラストの強い素材はむかない。

Use material which lends itself to embossing. Material of a very fine pattern and high contrast is not well suited.

エッジが強調されすぎて固いと思われる場合はフィルタメニューのぼかしからぼかしコマンドをエッジがぼけてエンボスのやわらかい丸みが表現されるまで1回ないし数回実行する。

If the edge definition seems too harsh use Blur from the *Filter* menu, using the *Blur* command repeatedly until the expression takes on a rounded, soft appearance.

完成したレリーフ画像

できあがったエンボス画像とバック用の素材を縦横同一サイズにして両ファイルとも開いてバック用素材がアクティブな状態で、イメージメニューの演算から加算コマンドを選択。オフセット:-128で実行する。エンボス画像の50%グレイ部分を境にしてシャドウ部分とハイライト部分が合成されてレリーフができあがる。

Open both the image file and the background file in the same dimensions, making the background materials the active file. Use the *Add* command, under *Calculate* on the *Image* menu. Initiate at *Offset:* 128. The border of the embossed image is the 50% gray line. Shadowed and highlighted portions are combined, and the relief is completed.

---

19. フィルタメニューの表現手法からエンボスコマンドを実行する。設定は角度:135度で左上からのライティング、高さ:4pixelsでエンボスの高さが4ピクセル、適用量:100%でエッジの強調度が100%。

19. From *Stylize* on the *Filter* menu choose the *Emboss* command. Set to *Angle*:135°, lighting from the upper left; *Height*:4 pixels, for an embossing height of 4 pixels; and *Amount*:100%, for *Edge definition* of 100%.

20. 同サイズのエンボス画像と大理石データを開いておいて、イメージメニューの演算から加算コマンドを選択する。

20. *Open* the same size *Emboss* image and background material data files, then initiate the *Add* command under *Calculate*, on the *Image* menu.

21. 画像1にバックの画像を、画像2にエンボス画像を選択、結果に新規を選択してスケール:1、オフセット:-128で実行する。

21. Select *Source 1* for the background image, *Source 2* for emboss image. Select *New* under Destinations and initiate at *Scale*: 1, *Offset*: -128.

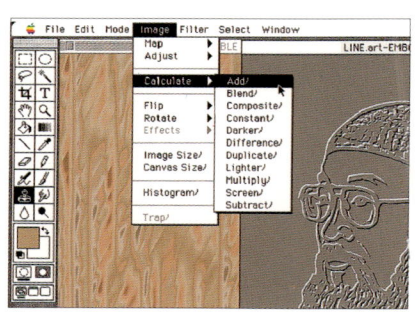

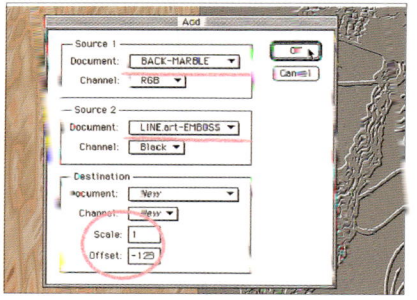

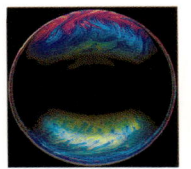   

第10章　50点合成に挑戦

Chapter 10 The 50-part Composite Challenge

50点合成に挑戦

The 50-part composite challenge

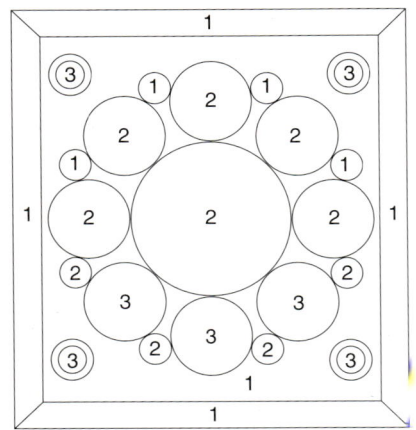

複雑な合成も単純なテクニックの積み重ね

　左の図の数字は素材の数で、組み合わせる点数はのべ50点。使い回している素材が何点かあるので、実際に用意する素材数は少ないものの、対称的なレイアウトといい、最終合成作業の困難さを予測させるアイデアである。

　慣れないと、どこから手をつけてよいのかわからないだろうが、1つ1つの技術は単純なものなので、尻込みせずに挑戦してほしい。額縁は第4章のグラデーションテクニックに比べれば簡単なものだし、背景の作成も第9章で既に経験している。シャボン玉とオブジェクトの透かし合成も第7章で実習した演算の応用である。

Complex Composites are the Result of Simple Techniques Repeated Over and Over

The numbers on the lefthand diagram represent materials; a few materials are used in a total of 50 parts. The design is symmetrical. The idea is to anticipate the final difficulty of the work. Without experience, you won't know where to begin. However, methods learned earlier, such as gradation (chap. 4), and background (chap. 9) will come in handy. Creation of a transparent center "eye" is something else you have seen.

パスの効果的な利用法

　フォトショップVer.2.5以降パスが非常に高機能になった。まるでミニ「イラストレーター」が組み込まれているようだ。**閉じたパス**だけではなく**開いたパス（ストロークパス）**も機能するようになったこと、**選択範囲**に変換しなくてもパスの内部を演算機能付きで指定色に塗りつぶせること（**塗りつぶしオプション**と同じ機能）、**パスの線**にそって指定色をすべてのペインティングツールで塗れること、さらに**ぼかし・シャープツール、覆い焼き・焼き込みツール**まで機能する（**編集メニュー**の**境界線を描く**よりもはるかに便利であり高機能）。また複合パスも機能するので中抜きのパスを作ることもできるし、EPSクリッピングパス機能を利用すると、データを他のソフトに切り抜き用のマスクつきで配置することもできる。パスから**選択範囲**に変換する際も**選択範囲の作成オプション**で**境界のぼかし幅（半径）**や**アンチエイリアシング**の設定が可能だ。さらに画期的なことは**パスパレット**が独立したことによって、作業内容とは無関係にパスを表示しておけることだ（もちろん非表示にもできる）。それがどうしたといわれそうだが、テンプレート機能のない「イラストレーター」、ガイドラインコマンドのない「イラストレーター」を想像してほしい。それらの機能に匹敵する武器をフォトショップが持ったということなのだ。Ver.2.01のユーザーはVer.2.5に移ってもしばらくその利用法に気がつかないかもしれないが、この本の読者はぜひ有効に利用してほしい。

　この章はほとんどその機能の解説のために書かれたといっても過言ではない。なぜならこの作例の原形に3年前に、フォトショップバージョン1.0とマッキントッシュIICXを使って、苦労に苦労を重ねて1ヵ月もかけて作成し、マッキントッシュとフォトショップの組み合わせによるデジタルフォトの可能性を悟った。著者にとって思い出深い作品なのだが、今回この原稿を書くために、フォトショップVer.2.5とマッキントッシュQuadra900の組み合わせで、写スキャンから始めて1日足らずでリメイクできてしまったのは、ハードの進歩というよりは、フォトショップVer.2.5のこのガイドライン機能によるところが大だと思っているからだ。

Using perspectives effectively

In Photoshoip Ver. 2.5 and up *Paths* are very powerful, almost like small Illustrators. Not only *Closed Paths* but *Open Paths (Stroke Paths)* have become functional, so that selected areas do not have to be changed in order to run calculation, fill colors (as with the *Fill* command), *Paint*, *Shadow*, *Burn* etc. All this can be done much more conveniently than on the *Edit* menu.

Moreover, composite *Paths* can also be run, so that cut-out paths can be made. With the EPS clipping function, one can also cut the data for pasting as a mask in ohter software. When changing a *Path* to a Selected area the selected area option can be used to set width of shadowing outline and anti-aliasing. More importantly, with *Path Palettes* you can now display a Path unrelated to your work (or leave it undisplayed) If you wonder why, think about Illustrator, which has no Templates or Make Guide commands. Functions equal to these are found in Photoshop. Newcomers to Ver. 2.5 might not notice at first, but readers of this book should realize their usefulness.

Anyway, this chapter was written to make these functions clear. The image created here was first done three years ago, with Photoshop Ver. 1.0 and a Mac IICX. It took a great deal of labor and over a month to complete, and belongs to my cherished memories.

The same image parts were recently scanned and recreated with Photoshop Ver. 2.5 on a Quadra 900, and took less than a day to finish. The reason? More than the hardware, it was the guideline capabilities of Ver. 2.5.

複雑な画像レイアウト作業を能率よくする工夫

　ガイドラインとして**パス**を利用する方法は様々な応用が可能だ。ガイドラインとマスクを兼ねさせることもできる。

　文字を**パス**化して配置しておいて、レイアウトを見ながら合成作業を先にすませ、効果的な色合いで文字を定着したり、エフェクトをかけたりすることもできる。

　フォトショップ上で自由にラフレイアウトを描いて検討後パス化してガイドラインとして使うのが最も直接的な使い方である。

　スキャナーでラフを読み込んで**パス**化するのも便利な使い方だ。通常の広告制作作業では最も多いケースであろう。合成作業において文字スペースや、プロポーション、見開きページののど部分など、制約がかなりあるものだが、それらを確実にクリアーできる。

　またこれから増えるであろうと思われるのが、第8章で紹介した解像度の低いローレゾ・デジタルデータから解像度の高いハイレゾ・デジタルデータに作り替える際にガイドラインとして利用することである。これもかなり正確なレイアウトができるので使用したエフェクト情報にまちがいがなければ、そのまま高解像度にしただけと思われるレベルで作り直すことができる。

　第4の方法が「イラストレーター」の高度な作図機能を利用して、精度の高い設計図を、フォトショップに持ち込むテクニックだ。「イラストレーター」を日常的にお使いのユーザーは「イラストレーターバージョン3.2」以降、1枚もののレイアウトだったら、ページレイアウトソフト無用といわれるほどの、高度なレイアウト機能が装備されたことをご存知であろう、そのレイアウト機能をフォトショップに取り込まない手はない。もちろんポストスクリプトデータはラスタライズされてしまうので、ポストスクリプトのまま出力することはできないし、文字の取り込みについては制約が多いが、レイアウト用のガイドラインとしての利用なら問題はない。

長いボケ足や複雑なグラデーションは「イラストレーター」を利用する

　フォトショップ単独では難しい作業の1つに、複雑な形のグラデーションがある。長いボケ足を利用するにも**境界をぼかす**コマンド1回では250ピクセルまでという制約がある（何回かかけることで延ばすことはできる）。そんな悩みを解決するのが「イラストレーター」とのコンビネーションプレーだ**ブレンドツール**を使えばフォトショップの**グラデーションツール**とは一味違うグラデーションを作ることができる。ボケ足マスクの作成も自由自在だ。

　フォトショップだけでも何とかできそうな機能を、他のソフトに求めるのは回りくどいような気もするが、最良の結果を最短の時間で得ることができるので能率があがる。

　フォトショップに欠けている部分を「イラストレーター」で補完することは、フォトショップ自身の使い勝手を飛躍的に高めるので、ほとんどフォトショップしか使わないと言うユーザーもぜひ「イラストレーター」を併用、使い込んでほしい。この二つのソフトをマスターすれば2Dグラフィックスの世界は完璧だ。

Ways to make complex image handling more efficient

As guidelines, **Paths** can be used in various ways. They can be combined as guidelines and masks, for example.

One can also make **Paths** with text, finish layout, then fix text over color and add effects.

The most direct method is with free layouts in Photoshop, where **Paths** can be used as guidelines to consider the possibilities.

Another easy use is to rough scan an image and create a **Path** with it. This is the most common use in advertising. In layout work, text space, proportions and necks in full page spreads are tough, but can be precisely cleared with **Paths**.

Another avenue which was discussed in Chap. 8 is the remaking of low resolution digital data into higher resolution data, where paths are required as guidelines. This kind of work will surely increase in the future. The method is precise, and if there is no mistake in the effect data, a high resolution image can be attained at any time.

A fourth application of **Paths** is in the import to Photoshop of highly-defined diagrams created on Illustrator. As users of Illustrator Ver. 3.2 and up well know, its layout functions are so advanced as to make 'page' layout seem obsolete. Happily, these same high level layout creations can be imported to Photoshop. Naturally, postscript data will be rasterized, so you can't output in postscript, and there are various limitations to importing text. But there is no problem using **Paths** as layout guidelines.

Using "Illustrator" to create long leg shadows and complex gradations

One of the tough jobs on Photoshop is complex gradations. For long leg shadows there is a limit of 250 pixels on the **Feather** Command. (You can use it repeatedly, though.) A better approach is to use Illustrator in combination. With the **Blend Tool** you can get a different effect from that of the **Gradient Tool**. And you can make any size mask for the leg shadows.

It may seem unnecessary to do on another program what can be achieved on Photoshop, but in time and quality, it's worth the effort. By supplementing functions which are lacking in Photoshop with others found in Illustrator you can vastly improve the effectiveness of Photoshop itself.

User's who are utterly devoted to Photoshop alone really ought to look into Illustrator, and learn to use the two together.

By mastering the two you have virtually perfected the field of 2D graphics.

「イラストレーター」で設計図を作る

できあがったラフを平面スキャナーで読み込んでPICTフォーマットで保存後「イラストレーター」で開く。

The finished rough scanned as a PICT file and **Opened** in Illustrator.

長方形ツールを使って枠線を描き、ペンツールで対角線を引いてセンターを出す。

The frame is drawn with the **Rectangle Tool**, the bisected with the **Pen Tool** to determine the center.

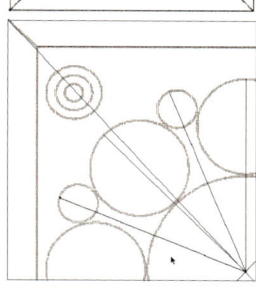

センターポイントから隣接する中間サイズの円の外側まで、ペンツールで線を引く。線を選択状態のまま回転ダイアログツールを使って角度：**22.5°**にしてコピーボタンをクリックする。コマンド+Dキーで変形の繰り返しコマンドを14回連続して実行するとレイアウト用の16等分線ができあがる。

With the **Pen Tool** draw lines from the center through each of the circles. With the lines selected, use **Rotate Dialog Tool**, setting **Angle** at 22.5°. Click **Copy** button. Using **Command+D Key** (the **Transform Again** Command) 14 times, create spokes throughout the diagram.

頭の中に完全な構想ができあがっているのなら「イラストレーター」で直接レイアウト用の設計図を描き始めることができる。通常作例のような構成物は、紙の上で様々なラフ案を検討することから始まる。

アイデアが固まったら平面スキャナーのモノクロモードで取り込み、「イラストレーター」でトレースして図面化する。

完璧な設計図を紙の上で描き上げてしまえば直接フォトショップに読み込んで**パス化**することも可能だ。

この作例では「イラストレーター」の配置機能を有効に利用して製図しているので、下絵用の設計図は参考程度に利用している。

If you have the entire diagram pictured in you imagination you can begin to draw the layout in Illustrator. Often, the actual layout will be the result of many rough ideas first drawn on paper. Once completed, scan the diagram in monochrome mode on a flat scanner, then trace in Illustrator. If the diagram is perfect, you can input directly to Photoshop, and use **Paths**.

The example here was created with Illustrator's commands. Shown are several of the stages of work.

１．ラフを平面スキャナーで読み込んでPICTフォーマットで保存後「イラストレーター」でテンプレートとして開く。

1. Read the rough on the flat scanner, saving in PICT format. **Open** as a Template in Illustrator.

２．ツールパレットの回転ツールをクリックすると、その右側に回転ダイアログツールが選択できるようになる。円の16等分／**22.5°** を入力してコピーボタンをクリックすると**22.5°**回転したところに複製ができる。

2. Click the **Tool Palette**'s **Rotate Tool**, opening the **Rotate-Dialog Tool** box. Input 16 parts/22.5° and Click **Copy** button to repeat the 22.5° rotation.

３．ショートカットコマンド+Dキーで変形の繰り返しコマンドを14回連続して実行する。アレンジメニューから変形の繰り返しを14回選択するのと同じことが、すばやく実行できる。

3. Use the short-cut **Command+D Key** and **Transform Again** Command 14 times. This is the same as selecting the **Transform Again** Command from the **Arrange** menu 14 times, but faster.

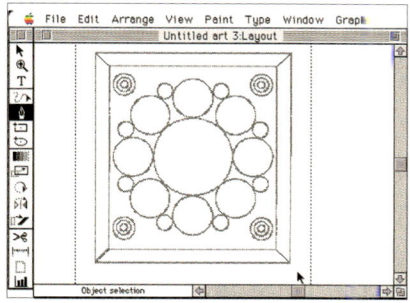

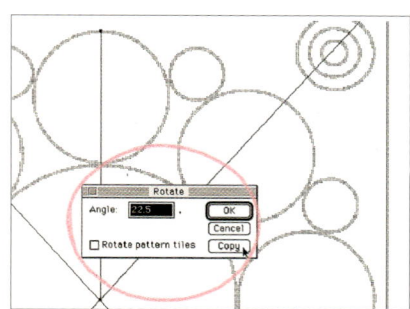

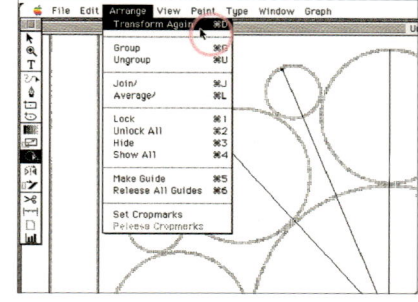

Creating blueprints on "Illustrator"

センターポイントを出すために引いた対角線を消去する。センターの円を描くためにツールパレットから楕円（中心から描画）ツールを選択して、センターポイントをクリック。幅、高さとも2.5インチと入力して**OK**ボタンをクリックする。中間サイズの円の中心点を楕円（中心から描画）ツールでクリック、幅、高さとも1.28インチと入力して中円を描く。円を選択状態のまま回転ダイアログツールでセンターポイントをクリック、45°と入力してコピーボタンをクリック、コマンド+**D**キーを6回実行、8個の中円が大円の周囲に配置される。

Lines used to determine the centerpoint are now useless; Delete them. Use the **Centered-Oval Tool** to draw the central circle; Click at the center. Input **Width** and **Height** at 2.5 inches. Click **OK**. Click at the center of a middle-sized circle, this time setting **Width** and **Height** to 1.28 inches. Click OK. With the circle still selected, click **Rotate-Dialog Tool** at the center, input an angle of 45°, click **Copy**, and execute **Command+D Key** six times.

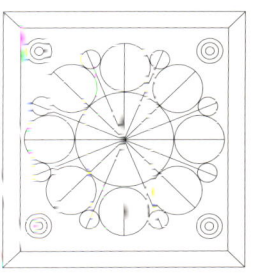

同様に小円の中心点を楕円（中心から描画）ツールでクリック、幅、高さとも0.5インチと入力。円を選択状態のまま回転ダイアログツールでセンターポイントをクリック、45°と入力してコピーボタンをクリック、コマンド+キーを6回実行すると3個の小円が配置される。四隅の円の中心点を楕円（中心から描画）ツールでクリック、幅、高さとも0.666インチと0.444インチ、0.222インチの三重円を描き他の三隅にドラッグ／コピーする。16等分のレイアウトラインを選択し消去する。線の太さを決めるためにすべてを選択してペイントメニューのペイント設定で塗りつぶし：なし、線の設定：黒、線幅：0.1ptに設定する。長方形ツールを使って外側を囲む外形線を描き、アレンジメニューからトンボを選択、保存する

Do the same operation with a smaller circle, clicking with the **Centered-Oval Tool**, setting **Width** and **Height** to 0.5 inches and entering. Leaving the circles selected, use **Rotate-Dialogue Tool**, clicking at center point. Input 45° and **Copy**. Do **Command+D Key** six times to set out eight circles. Now click with the **Centered-Oval Tool** on one of the outer four circles, setting **Width** and **Height** to .666 inch, .444 inch, and .222 inch, drawing a three-ringed circle. Now **Drag/Copy** to each of the four corners. Now **Select** and **Delete** the 16 layout lines. To determine line thickness select all, the under **Style** (**Paint** menu) set **Fill: None, Stroke: Black, Weight:** 0.1pt. Use the **Rectangle Tool** to draw the outer lines, then use **Arrange** menu to Set **Cropmarks**, and **Save**.

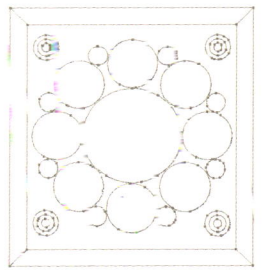

作成した「イラストレーター」のデータをフォトショップで開く。EPSファイルのラスタライズの設定は、幅、高さはそのまま、解像度を500dpiアンチエイリアシング：オフ、縦横比を固定：オンで実行する。ラスタライズされたデータのホワイトスペースを自動選択ツールで選択、選択範囲メニューから選択範囲の反転を実行して黒い線のみを選択、パスパレットのパスの作成を実行、パスの記録後、別名で保存する。

Open the data produced on Illustrator in Photoshop. Leave **EPS Rasterizer Width** and **Height** settings at default, **Resolution** at 500dpi, **Anti-aliased:** Off, **Constrain Proportions:** On. Execute. Select the white space in the rasterized data with the **Magic Wand**, then Inverse on **Select** menu, selecting only black lines. Now create a **Path** on **Make Paths**. After **Saving Path**, **Save As**.

４．ツールパレットから楕円（中心から描画）ツールを選択して、センターポイントをクリック。幅、高さとも2.5インチと入力して**OK**ボタンをクリックすると中心円ができる。

4. From the **Tool Palette** select the **Centered-Oval Tool** , clicking on the center point. Set **Width**, **Height** at 2.5 inches, enter and click **OK**. A centered circle is thus made.

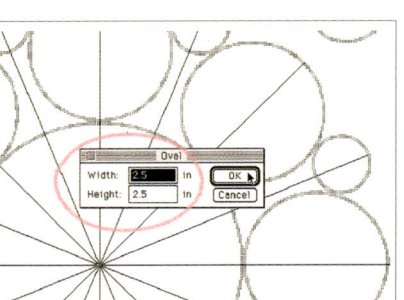

５．中間サイズの円の中心点を楕円（中心から描画）ツールでクリック、幅、高さとも1.28インチと入力して**OK**ボタンをクリックすると隣接する中円ができる。

5. Clcik at the center of the middle-sized circle with the **Centered-Oval Tool**, setting Width, Height at 1.28 inches. Click the **OK** button. The connecting middle circle is created.

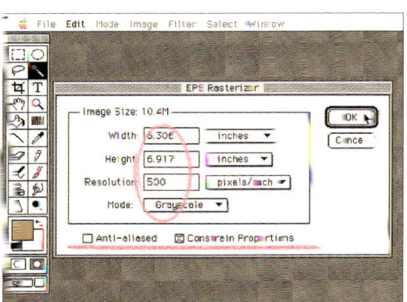

６．「イラストレーター」のデータをフォトショップで開く。EPSファイルのラスタライズの設定は、幅、高さはそのまま、解像度を500dpi、アンチエイリアシング：オフ、縦横比固定：オンで実行。

6. **Open** the Illustrator data in Photoshop. Set the **EPS Rasterizer** at **Width, Height** default, **Resolution** 500 pixels, **Anti-aliased :** Off, **Constrain Propotions** On. Execute.

サイズに合せてスキャニングする

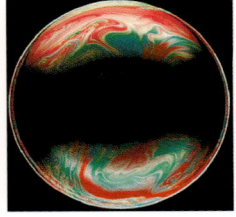

B１：小円用250ピクセルと
三重円用333ピクセルでス
キャニングする。

B1: Small circle of 250 pixels and triple circle of 333
pixels.

B２：中円用640ピクセルで
スキャニングする。

B2: Central circle scanned
at 640 pixels.

B３：中円用640ピクセルで
スキャニングする。

B3: Central circle scanned
at 640 pixels.

HEAD 1＆2：センター用に顔の左右632ピクセル周囲の円用に
顔の左右325ピクセルでスキャニングする。

Head 1&2 : For a center face in a circle of 632 left/rigth
pixels a face of 325 left/right pixels is scanned.

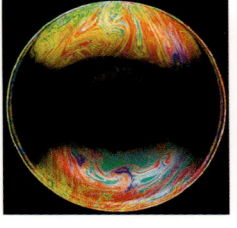

B１H：小円用と三重円用を
色相：-95で色変換する。

B1H: Small and triple circles
converted to *Hue:* -95.

B２H：イメージメニューの
色相・彩度コマンドで色相：-
70で色変換する。

B2H:*HueSaturation*(*Image*
menu) adjusted to *Hue:* -70.

B３H：色相：95で色変換す
る。

B3H: *Hue* converted to
Hue: -95.

7. フォトショップで開いた設計図上で幅：0に設定したラインツールと**情報**パレットを利用してそれぞれの円のサイズを計ってメモする。合成する顔の取り込みサイズも検討する。

8. 卓上型ドラムスキャナーDTS-1015AIを使ってポジフィルムのスキャニングをする。フィルムをドラムに巻き付けて原点設定、キャリブレーション後、プリスキャンして*Color Setup*を設定する。

9.*Trimming Setup*と*Magnification*を使って取り込む画像のサイズを設定する。単位は画素数（ピクセル）が絶対値なので間違いが少なくて便利だ。インチやセンチは解像度とセットで初めて意味を持つ単位になる。

7. The diagram opened in Photoshop with **Line Width: 0**. **Line Tool** and **Info Palette** are used to check and note various circle sizes. Size of faces is also considered.

8. The desktop drum scanner DTS-1015AI was used to scan posi-film. After attaching the film to the drum, basic settings and calibration were completed. After print scanning **Color Setup** was specified.

9. Indicate image size in **Trimming Setup** and **Magnification**. Units are in pixels, an absolute unit which leaves little room for mistakes. After setting resolution, inches and centimeters take on real meaning.

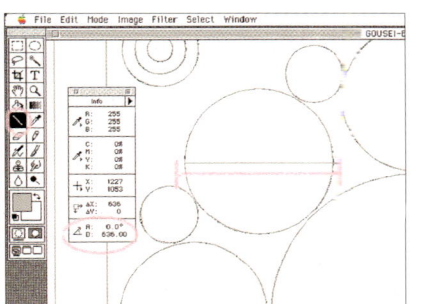

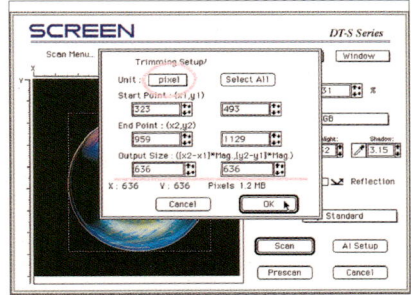

Matching size and scanning

B4：センター用1250ピクセルと中円用640ピクセルでスキャニングする。

B4: Central and middle circles scanned at 1250 and 640 pixels.

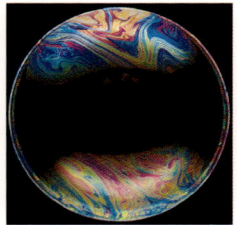

B5：小円用250ピクセルと三重円用333ピクセルでスキャニングする。

B5: Small and triple circles scanned at 250 and 333 pixels.

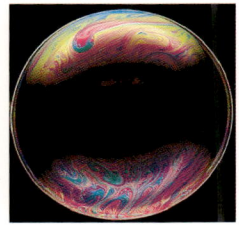

B6：小円用250ピクセルと三重円用333ピクセルでスキャニングする。

B6: Small and triple circles scanned at 250 and 333 pixels.

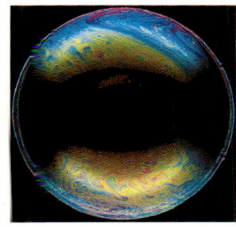

B7：中円用640ピクセルと小円用250ピクセルでスキャニングする。

B7: Middle and small circles scanned at 640 and 250 pixels.

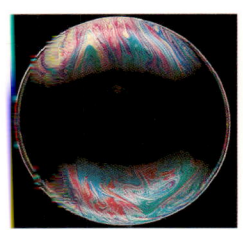

B3：小円用250ピクセルと三重円用333ピクセルでスキャニングする。

B3: Small and middle circles scanned at 250 and 333 pixels.

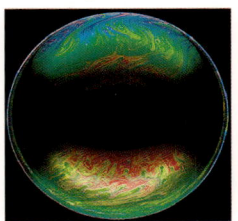

B4H：中円用を色相：-95で色変換する。

B4H: Middle circle with **Hue:** -95.

B5H：小円用を色相：-130で色変換する。

B5H: Small circle with Hue converted to **Hue:** -130

B6H：小円用を色相：-180で色変換する。

B6H: Small circle converted to **Hue:** -180

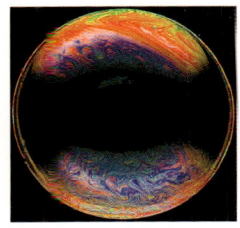

B7H：中円用を色相：-180で色変換する。

B7E: Small circle converted to **Hue:** -180

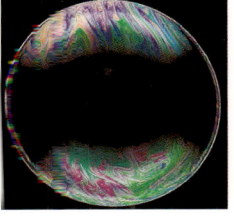

B8H：小円用を色相：40で色変換する。

B8H: Small circle with **Hue** set to -40.

---

10. **AI Setup** を実行、自動的に最適な取り込み設定をしてくれる。ハイエストライトのない作例のような画像は意図的なローキーフォトなのか、露出不足の補正をするのか選択することができる。

10. Execute **All Setup** to automtically get the best input setting. Examples with highest lighting might be those deliberately taken rough, and underexposed for later supplementation.

11. トリミングを決めて本スキャンを実行する。作例は約1.4MBのRGBファイルだが、キャリブレーションから保存までの作業時間は数値の設定が出来ていれば1分42秒ほど、36MBのファイルで5分40秒ほどである。

11. Decide the trimming, then scan. The working example is a 1.4 MB RGB file, which from calibration to actual saving requires, assuming setting of values, 1 min. 42 sec. A 36MB file takes 5 min. 40 sec.

12. ドラムスキャナーで読み込んだ8種類のシャボン玉のポジ画像を、イメージメニューの色相・彩度コマンドで色変換してバリエーションを作る。

12. The nine big eye images scanned from posifilm. Variations were created with **Hue/Saturation** Command, on the **Image** menu.

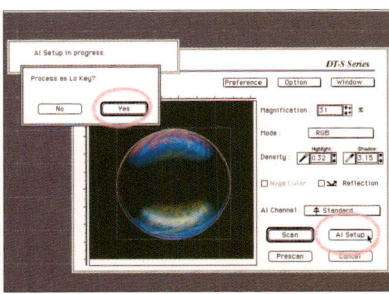

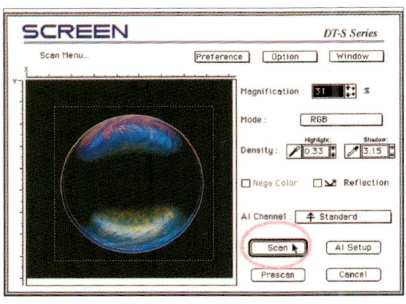

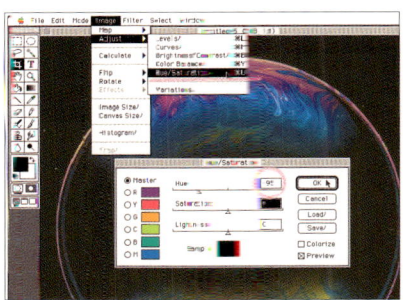

「イラストレーター」でバックを描く

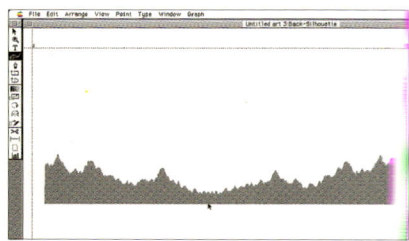

バック用の稜線を直接手で描くか写真からトレースしたものを平面スキャナーで読み込んでPICTフォーマットで保存後「イラストレーター」で*開く*。

A hand-drawn or photo-scanned silhouette image scanned on a flatbed scanner, saved as a PICT file, and **opened** on "Illustrator".

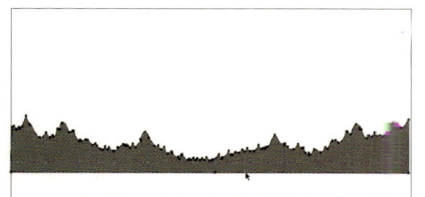

オートトレースツールを使ってトレースする。

Tracing with the **Auto Trace Tool**.

選択ツールでオプションキーを押しながら全体を選択して、さらにシフトキーも押してまっすぐ上に5.8cmドラッグ／コピーする。
編集メニューで背面へ送るコマンドを実行して上部のパスを背後に配置してからペイントメニューのペイント設定コマンドで塗りつぶしの設定を上部のパスをダークブルー、下部のパスをマゼンタに色指定する。シフトキーを押しながら上下のパスの相対するポイントをクリックしてブレンドツールを選択する。

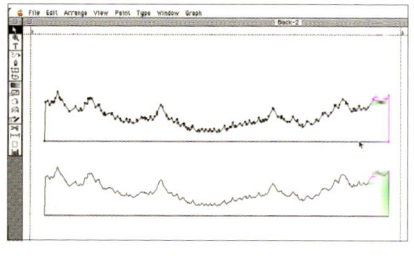

Using the **Selection Tool** and pressing the **Option Key** selects everything; further adding the **Shift Key** one can drag the selection upwards by 5.8cm. Then use **Send To Back** command (on **Edit** menu) to move the upper path to the back. With **Style** command (under the **Paint** menu) set **Fill**, making the upper path dark blue, and the lower path magenta. Now hold down the **Shift Key**, clicking on the opposite points in the upper and lower paths; then select **Blend Tool**.

作例に使ったテンプレートは森の稜線をトレースしたものだ。山岳の稜線などに比べるとずっと複雑なシルエットなので、ブレンドした結果がオーロラのような複雑なグラデーションになって効果を高めている。

フォトショップのGradient Toolだけでは、とても真似のできないところだ。

「イラストレーター」をフォトショップのプラグインツール代わりにフルに活用すると不可能が可能になっていく楽しさを味わうことができる。

特に透かしマスク用を含めて様々な形のグラデーションを、フォトショップに持ち込むことができるのはフォトショップの機能が大幅に拡大したようなものだ。

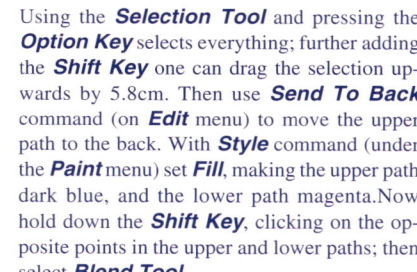

The background example is a tracing taken from a forest picture. Compared to a mountain range, the forest silhouette is quite complex.
After blending, the image appears almost like an aroura an effect impossible with Photoshop's **Gradient Tool**.
"Illustrator" can be used in place of plug-in tools to enhance Photoshop's performance in many ways.
Especially in many-shaped gradations and transparent masks the ability to import to Photoshop is one of the program's great advantages.

---

13. 「イラストレーター」のファイルメニューから新規コマンドでバック作成用のテンプレートを開く。直接「イラストレーター」で描く場合はなしボタンをクリックする。

13. From Illustrator's **File** menu use **New** to **Open** a template for the background. Click the **None** button to draw directly in "Illustrator".

14. オートトレースツールでテンプレートの端をクリック。パスを作成する。編集メニューの環境設定でオートトレースしていく点の間隔を0〜2ピクセルの範囲で変えることでトレースの精度を変えることができる。

14. With the **Auto Trace Tool** click the edge of the template. In the **Preference** (under **Edit** menu) change the precision of the tracing by adjust **Auto Trace Overgap** from 0-2 pixels.

15. 選択ツールでオプションキーを押しながら全体を選択して、さらにシフトキーも押して垂直に上に5.8cmドラッグ／コピーする。編集メニューで背面へペーストコマンドを実行して上部のパスを下部のパスの背後に配置する。

15. Holding down the **Option Key** and Select Tool select everything, then press **Shift Key** and **Drag/Copy** upwards 5.8cm. Use **Send To Back** command (under **Edit** menu) to move the path to the background.

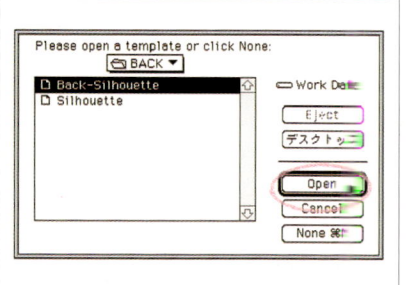

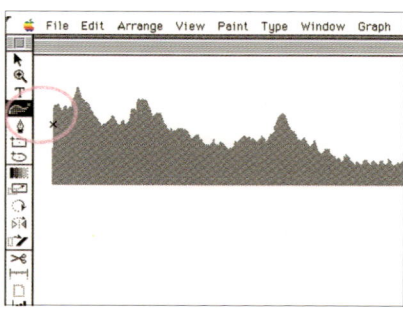

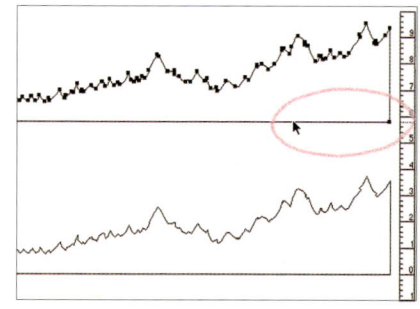

Drawing background on "Illustrator"

このページで一番難しいのは最上部のパスを選択して、稜線を基点に天地反転させるところだ。操作が飲み込みにくいところもそうだが、それ以上にパスの下左端と下右端のポイントを選択するのが技術的に難しい。

このパスは一番背後にあるので作業しやすい最大サイズに**ズームイン**したら、パスを選択して、まず編集メニューの**前面へ出す**を実行してパスを一番手前に出す。そうすればなんなく目的のポイントを選択することができるはずだ。

リフレクトツールは一回目のクリックで基点を決め、二度目のクリックで反転する方向を決めるので、作例のケースはダブルクリックでよい。二度目のクリックの場所がずれると、思わぬ反転をしてあわてることになる。

On this page the most difficult point is selecting the upper path and selecting its base point to reflect against the sky.
The manipulation is hard to get a feel for, and selecting the lower right and left points is tricky. This path is the furthest back.
First, enlarge it with **Zoom-in**, then select the path and **Bring to Front**, making selection of points easier. Click the **Reflect Tool** once to set the starting point, again to decide direction of reflection. A mistaken second click will lead to a failure.

ブレンドツールで上下の選択されたポイントを順番にクリックしダイアログボックスの**ステップ数**に253と入力する。

With the **Blend Tool** click on the selected points above and below, opening the dialog box and indicating 253 steps.

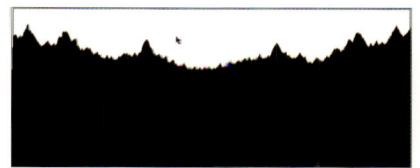

下側一番手前のパスだけを選択してペイントメニューのペイント設定コマンドで**塗りつぶし**を黒に色指定する。200〜400%にズームイン、シフトキーを押しながら最上部のパスの最下部左端と右端のポイントを選択しておいて、リフレクトツールで左端最上部のポイントのあたりを二度クリックして反転させる。グラデーションの上部にダークブルーのスペースができる。

Choose only the bottom path and set **Fill** to **Black** under **Style** on the **Paint** menu. **Zoom-in** 200-400% to make work easier. Holding down the **Shift Key**, select the lower left and right points of the highest path, then click the **Reflect Tool** twice on the upper left point, creating the dark blue gradation in the upper part.

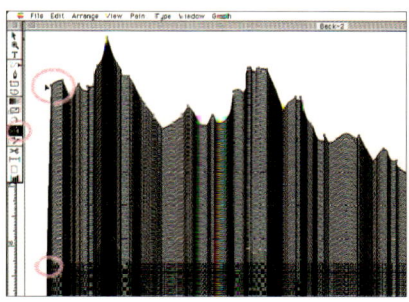

完成した背景は保存した後でフォトショップに読み込む。**EPS**ファイルのラスタライズの設定は、幅：2700ピクセル、アンチエイリアシング：オン、縦横比を固定：オンで実行（他の設定はいじる必要がない）。

Save the background and read into Photoshop. Set **EPS Rasterizer** at **Width:** 2700 pixels, **Anti-aliased:** On, **Constrain Proportions:** On. (Leave other settings alone.)

16. ペイント設定で塗りつぶしの設定を上部のパスを**プロセスカラー：シアン100%、マゼンタ100%、イエロー20%、黒20%のダークブルー、下部のパスをマゼンタ100%、イエロー20%の赤紫に色指定する。

16. For the upper path set **Fill** (**Paint** menu, **Style** command) to **Process Color:** Cyan 100%, Magenta 100%, Yellow 20%, Black 20%, for a dark blue. Make lower path Magenta 100%, Yellow 20%, for a magenta coloring.

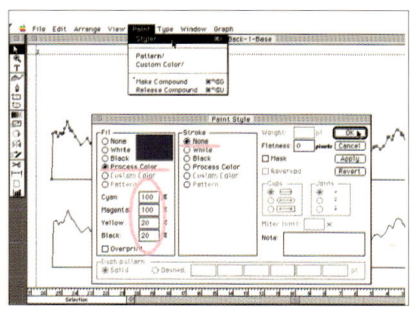

17. シフトキーを押しながら上下のパスの相対するポイントをクリック、ブレンドツールを使って各ポイントをクリックする。ステップ数を253と入力して実行する。

17. Holding down the **Shift Key**, click opposite points on the upper and lower paths, then use **Blend Tool** and click points. Set **Number of steps** to 253.

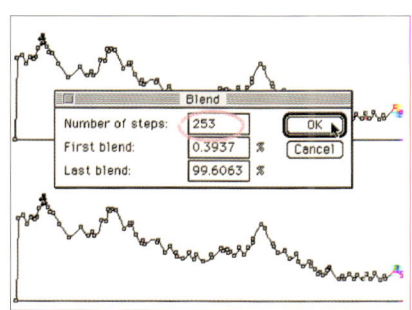

18. シフトキーを押しながら最上部のパスの最下部左端と右端のポイントを選択しておいて、リフレクトツールで左端最上部のポイントのあたりを二度クリックして下側のパスだけを天地反転させる。

18. Holding down the **Shift Key** select the bottom left and right points on the uppermost path, then click twice on the highest lefthand point with the **Reflect Tool**, making only the bottom side reflect against the sky.

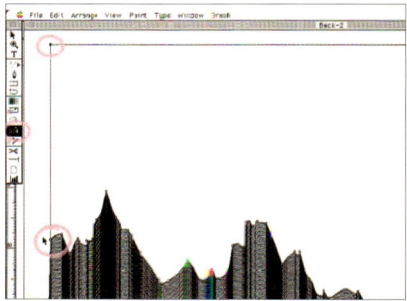

オブジェクトとシャボン玉を合成する

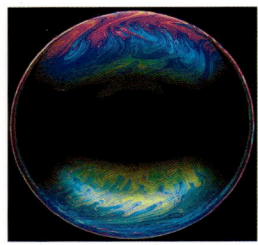

合成目のシャボン玉とオブジェクトのファイルを開いて横位置に並べる。

Open the jumbo eye and subject files and line up side by side.

背景色を黒色にして**イメージ**メニューの**画像サイズ**コマンドでシャボン玉のファイルサイズと縦横とも同寸にする。全体を選択してシャボン玉の中央に顔がくるように移動調整する。

Make the **Background color** black, then use **Canvas Size** (**Image** menu) to make the file sizes width and height the same. Select everything and bring the faces into the middle of the eye.

イメージメニューの**演算**から**スクリーン**を選択する。**画像1**と**画像2**に目的のシャボン玉とオブジェクトファイルが表示されていることを確認して、**結果**は**新規**で実行する。スクリーンという演算法はちょうど写真のネガフィルムを二枚重ねてプリントしたような効果を表現できるので、作例のような黒バックどうしの合成にはぴったりの**コマンド**だ。

From the **Image** menu choose **Calculate**, then **Screen**. Indicate the Jumbo Eye and Subject files as **Source 1** and **Source 2**. Execute **Destination** as **New**. **Screen** calculation gives you something exactly like a double negative print. It is perfect with this type of black background.

第7章で実習した演算の応用である。第7章では白バックの写真を**加算**コマンドで処理したが、この作例は黒バックの写真どうしを**スクリーン**コマンドで処理している。

白バックの写真どうしだったら、マスクを使わないかぎり利用できるのは**乗算**コマンドくらいのものだが、黒バックなので演算の選択肢が広い、**加算**コマンドでも、**差の絶対値**コマンドでも、**比較（明）**コマンドでもそれなりの合成画像ができる。そのなかで**スクリーン**コマンドを選択した理由は、仕上がり結果が一番自然だったからだ。

An application of the calculation studied in Chap.7. In Chap.7 a photo and white background were combined with the **Add** calculation; here a photo with a black background was done with the **Screen** calculation.If both photos have white backgrounds, without using a mask only **Multiply** can be used, but with black backgrounds there are more choices. **Add**, **Difference**, and **Lighter** all offer different effects. Here, **Screen** provided the most natural finish.

19. 合成する二つのファイルを開いてファイルサイズを確認する。縦横比も含めたピクセル数が完全に一致していないと演算することができないので片方のファイルサイズを調整する。

19. **Open** the files to be combined and check their sizes. Height and width, and all pixel values, must match. Adjust file size if necessary.

20. **イメージ**メニューの**演算**から**スクリーン**コマンドを選択する。合成したいファイルが二つとも開いていることを確認する。開いていないファイルは合成することができない。

20. From **Calculate** on **Image** menu choose **Screen**. Check that the files you want to calculate are both **Open**. You can't combine a closed file.

21. 開いているファイルが二つしかない場合、アクティブなファイル名が**画像1**に現れる。ファイル名が現れないのはサイズが異なる場合だ。

21. When only two files are opened, the active file becomes **source 1**. If no file appears it means file sizes don't match.

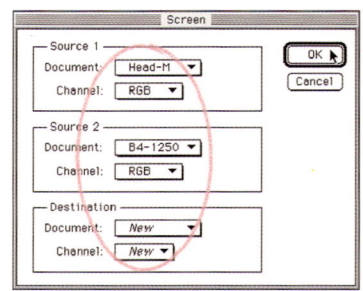

Combining subjects and jumbo eye

　演算の結果、**スクリーン**コマンドがベストであることがわかったので、演算より能率のよい合成方法で残りの7点の作業を行う。

　最初にオブジェクトファイルを開いてすべてを選択しコピーする。

　ファイルを閉じてシャボン玉のファイルを開く。**オプションキー**を押しながら**ペースト**するとオープンする、**合成のコントロールオプション**で描画モードを**スクリーン**にして**OK**ボタンをクリックする。**選択ツール**でオブジェクトの位置調整をして保存する。次々にシャボン玉ファイルを開いて同様の作業を繰り返す。**イメージメニューの演算**を使うよりはるかに能率がよいのはおわかりいただけると思う。

Seeing that **Screen** offers the best result, this efficient method is used for the remaining seven eye-globes. First the Subject file is opened and everything is copied. Then that file is closed and a Jumbo Eye file is opened. Holding down the **Option Key** and **Paste** opens the **Composite Controls** option. Click **OK** for **Screen** under **Mode**. With the **Selection Tool**, adjust the position of the Subjects and **Save**. Open the Jumbo Eyes over and over, doing the same operation. This is much more efficient than using **Calculate** under the **Image** menu, as you would guess.

オブジェクトファイルを開いて選択範囲メニューから全画面の選択を実行、編集メニューからコピー後ファイルを閉じる。

Open the subject file, excute **Select All** under **Select** menu. **Close** the file after **Copying**.

シャボン玉ファイルを開く、オプションキーを押しながらペーストする。合成のコントロールオプションで描画モードをスクリーンにして実行する。演算でスクリーンコマンドを実行したのと同じ効果を得ることができる。

Open the Jumbo Eye file, hold down the **Option Key**, and **Paste**. Set **Mode** (under **Composite Controls** option) to **Screen**. This gives the same result as **Screen** command under **Calculations**.

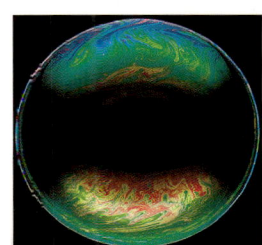

どちらの作業方法を取るかは作業者の好みとハードの処理能力による。この方法のほうが、メモリーを消費せず作業効率もよいので著者は好んで使っている。

Which method is chosen depends on the creator and his hardware. This method, which uses less memory and is work-efficient, is popular with the author.

---

22. 左記の方法との比較のため、ファイルを同時に開いたが、実作業ではオブジェクトファイルを開いてコピー後、閉じてからシャボン玉ファイルを開いている。ファイルサイズがまったく違うところを見てほしい。

22. For comparison, here both files are opened at the same time. When actually working, the Subject file is copied and closed, then the Jumbo Eye file is opened. It is obvious that the file sizes are completely different.

23. オプションキーを押しながらペーストする。編集メニューからペーストコマンドを選択してもコマンド＋Vキー（＋オプションキー）でも、どちらでもよいが作業能率を考えると、ショートカットを常用することを薦める。

23. Hold down the **Option Key** and Paste. From **Edit** menu choose either **Paste** command or use **Command+V Key** (+ **Option Key**), depending upon your preference. Learn shortcuts.

24. 合成のコントロールオプションで描画モードをスクリーンに設定する。プレビューをチェックしておくと演算効果をそのまま確認できるのでいろいろな演算方法を試すことが簡単にできる。

24. In **Composite Controls** option set **Mode** to **Screen**. If you check **Preview**, you can easily test various calculations.

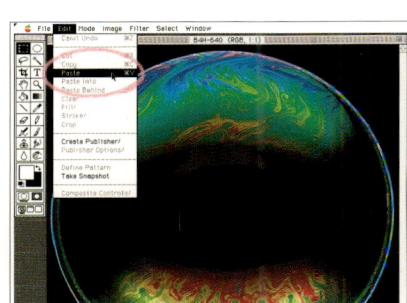

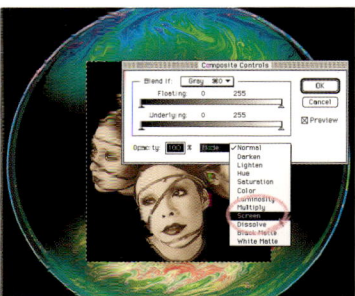

オブジェクトとシャボン玉と背景を透かし合成する

背景のファイルを**開いて**合成するシャボン玉のファイルサイズに縮小する。下側の黒い稜線部分を**自動選択ツール**で選択、そのまま平行に上にドラッグしてグラデーション部分を狭くする。**長方形選択ツール**で真ん中より左側を選択して**イメージメニューの変形**から**自由な形に**を選択して左側上部のポイントをドラッグして変形する。同様に右側も変形する。

Open the Background file and shrink it to the size of the Jumbo Eye. Select the bottom of the silhouette with the **Magic Wand** and Drag upwards, narrowing the gradation area. With the **Rectangular Marquee Tool** choose a point left of dead center, then use **Distort** under **Effects** (**Image** menu), dragging from a point in the upper left. Do the same on the right side.

顔の部分のマスクを作ってペーストする。顔の部分を除いてなるべく小さめのマスクのほうが自然な感じに合成できる。

Make masks for the faces and **Paste**. Cut out the face, keeping the mask as small as possible for a natural effect.

イメージメニューの**演算**から**スクリーンコマンド**を実行する。他の2点も同様に合成する。

Execute **Screen** command under **Calculate** (**Image** menu). Do the same for the other two faces.

下側の中円3点に背景の稜線を変形縮小して合成、透明感と球の感じを表現する。オブジェクトとすでに合成されているために演算だけでは思った効果は得られない。**スクリーン**コマンドを使うのだが背景側のファイルにボケ足のマスクを作る必要がある。

まずオブジェクトと合成済みシャボン玉の内部の抜けを**自動選択ツール**で選択して**境界をぼかす**コマンドを2ピクセルで実行、**選択範囲**メニューから**選択範囲の反転**コマンドを実行して**コピー**する。変形縮小した背景のファイルに**ペースト**して黒色を塗りつぶし100%で実行するとマスクができる。あとは二つのファイルを**スクリーン**コマンドで合成するだけだ。

The lower, middle-sized spheres are filled with the background, and the spheres are made transparent, and given a rounded expression. Since they are already combined with the faces you can't achieve the desired effect with just a calculation. Assuming you will use **Screen** command, create a shadow mask for the background file. First, take the finished composite of the subject and eye and select the inner, cut-out portion with the **Magic Wand**. Execute **Feather Selection** at 2 pixels, then do the **Inverse** command under **Select** menu, and **Copy**. **Paste** it into the altered and shrunken background file and use a black **Fill** at 100% to create the mask. Then combine the two files using **Screen** calculation.

---

25. イメージメニューの**画像解像度**で背景を合成するシャボン玉と同じサイズに縮小する。**縦横比を固定とファイルサイズを固定**のチェックははずしておく。

25. With **Image Size** under the **Image** menu reduce the background to the same size as the jumbo eye. Leave out **Proportions** and **File Size** check.

26. **自動選択ツール**で稜線の下側を選択して平行に上に移動、グラデーション部分の面積を狭くする。

26. Select the lower part of the silhouette with the **Magic Wand** and drag upwards, narrowing the gradation.

27. **長方形選択ツール**で真ん中より左側を選択、**イメージメニューの変形**から**自由な形に**コマンドを実行、左端上部のポイントをドラッグして変形する。球状の感じを出すためである。右側も同様に実行する。

27. With the **Rectangular Marquee Tool** select just to left of center, then execute **Distort** under **Effects** (on the **Image** menu). Drag the upper left point to alter shape and bring out roundness. Do the same on the right side.

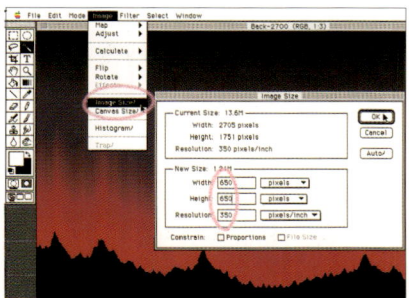

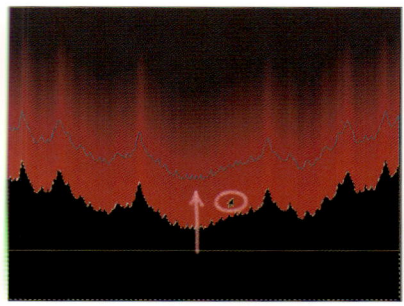

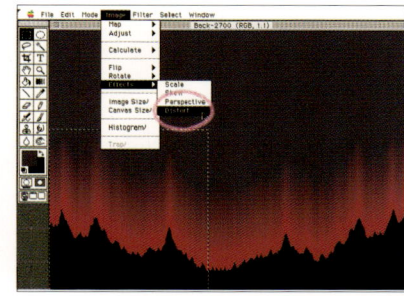

Combining subjects and background in a pellucid sphere

同様に下側の小円4点に背景の稜線を変形縮小して合成、シャボン玉の透明感と球状であることを表現する。

これらは単純に**スクリーン**コマンドを使うだけで合成できる。

シャボン玉の外側の黒スペースを**自動選択ツール**で選択して、**選択範囲**メニューの**選択範囲の反転**コマンドを実行、シャボン玉のみを選択状態にして、変形縮小した背景を**オプションキー**を押しながら**選択範囲内**へペーストする。

合成のコントロールオプションで描画モードを**スクリーン**にして実行すれば透かし合成が完成する。

In the same way, fit the altered and shrunken background to the smaller spheres, bringing out the roundness and transparency of the eye. You can create these with the **Screen** Command alone. Select the black space around the eye with the **Magic Wand Tool**, then use **Inverse** command under the **Select** menu to select only the jumbo eye, **Pasting Into** the altered and shrunken background with the **Option Key**. Use **Screen** under **Mode** in the **Composite Controls** option to complete the transparent composite.

背景を小円のサイズに縮小して、下側の黒い稜線部分を**自動選択ツール**で選択、そのまま平行に上にドラッグしてグラデーション部分を狭くする。シャボン玉の外側黒スペースを**自動選択ツール**で選択して**選択範囲**メニューから**選択範囲の反転**を実行、オプションキーを押しながら**選択範囲内**へペースト、合成のコントロールオプションで描画モードをスクリーンにして実行する。左サイドも同様に作業する。

Reduce the background to small eye size, select the lower portion of silhouette with the **Magic Wand** and drag upwards, narrowing the area of gradation. Select the dark area outside the eye with the **Magic Wand** and do **Inverse**, holding down the **Option Key** to **Paste Into**. Then do **Screen** under **Mode** (**Composite Controls** option). Do the same operation on the left side.

一番下の小円の作業。背景の変形を左ページの要領で実行し、全体に上に移動。シャボン玉の外側を**自動選択ツール**で選択して、上記とまったく同じ作業を左サイドと右サイドのシャボン玉にたいして繰り返し行なう。

Do the background change on the left page, moving everything upwards. Select the outside of the eye with the **Magic Wand** and **Inverse** (under **Select** menu). Then use **Option Key** to **Paste Into**, and execute **Screen** under **Mode** (**Composite Controls** option). Do the same on the right side.

28. 　**自動選択ツール**でシャボン玉内の背景に抜けるべきスペースを選択する。**選択範囲**メニューの**境界をぼかす**で半径を2ピクセルで実行。**選択範囲**メニューの**選択範囲の反転**を実行して**コピー**、背景に**ペースト**する。

28. With the **Magic Wand Tool** select the space to be cut out of the center of the eye. Set **Feather Radius** (under **Select** menu) at 2 pixels, and execute. Then do **Inverse**, and **Copy** and **Paste**.

29. 　背景との混じり具合を計算してシャボン玉の一部を**境界のぼかし幅**を2ピクセルにした**なげなわツール**でコマンドキーを押しながら選択除外、編集メニューから黒色の塗りつぶし100%を実行する。

29. Calculate the mix, then with the **Feather Radius** set at 2 pixels use the **Lasso Tool** and **Command Key** to select and remove a part of the eye. From **Edit** menu **Fill** with black 100%.

30. 　イメージメニューの演算からスクリーンコマンドを実行する。合成すべき二つのファイルが同一サイズであり、両方とも開いていることを確認する。

30. Choose **Screen** under **Calculate** on the **Image** menu. Check to see that both files are the same size, and that both are **open**. Then execute.

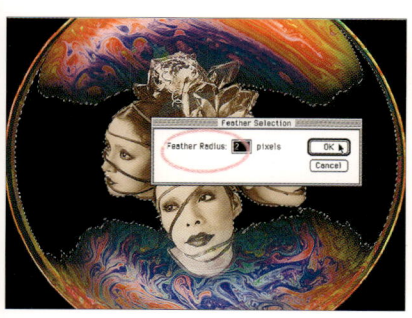

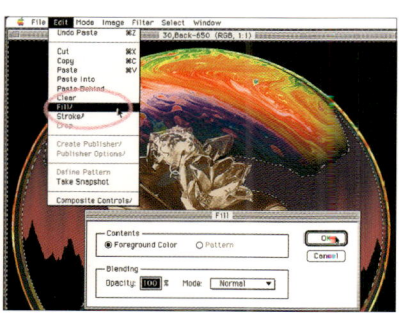

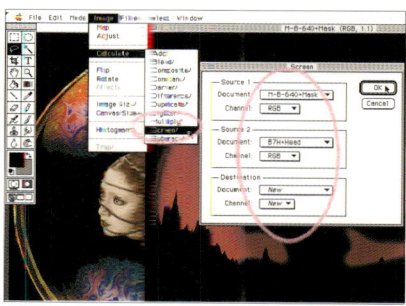

シャボン玉を３つ重ねる　*Overlaying three jumbo eyes*

666ピクセルのシャボン玉を開く。イメージメニューの回転から角度入力を選択し、20度(反時計回り)で実行後、すべてを選択してコピーする。

Open the 666 pixel Jumbo Eye. Choose **Arbitrary** under **Rotate** (**Image** menu), executing at **20° CCW**. Then select and **Copy** .

ペーストしてイメージメニューの変形から拡大・縮小を選択、プロポーションを保つためにシフトキーを押しながら右下角のポイントをドラッグ、62%に縮小してセンターに配置する。

After *pasting*, select **Scale** under **Effects** (**Image** menu). To maintain proportion, hold down **Shift Key** while clicking on lower right point and dragging for a reduction to 62%.

さらにペーストしてイメージメニューの変形から拡大・縮小を選択、プロポーションを保つためにシフトキーを押しながら右下角のポイントをドラッグ、31.3%に縮小してセンターに配置する。

After *pasting*, select **Scale** from **Effects** on the **Image** menu, again holding down **Shift Key** while clicking and dragging from the lower right point for a reduction to 31.3%.

右上角に配置する都合上、イメージメニューの鏡像から水平方向を実行して角度をあわせる。

From the upper right corner select **Flip Horizontal** under **Flip** on the Image menu, and execute.

単純なシャボン玉だが同心円上に配置すると立体感と動きが出て予想以上に面白いオブジェになった。四隅に最後の味つけに配置することにする。それぞれ角度を変えてセンターを目指すように配置する。

円の縮小率は機械的に３分の２、３分の１にしてみたが、動きが止まって面白くないので見た目で微妙に手加減している。半端な数字はその結果である。

三重円を作ってから最後に**水平方向 に反転**しているのも最終合成してみた結果から出てきた結論である。

いずれにせよこのとおりやらなければ作例の仕上がりと同じものはできないが、技術を実習するためだけなら細かい数字や手順にこだわる必要はない。必要な部分だけを参考にのびのびと試してほしい。

This simple eye becomes more spherical and motive with the added circles.

Final touches are added to the four corners. Angles are adjusted to achieve a centered effect.

The circle was reduced to 2/3 and 1/3, with a little difference added to improve the effect. After completing the triple circle **Flip Horizontal** is executed to finish the composition.

In any case, to get the same effect you must go through these steps. But its not necessary to take such care if you are merely learning the skills. Use what you need and continue to explore.

31．シャボン玉を20°左に回転する。イメージメニューの回転から**角度入力**を選択して、20度(反時計回り)で**OK**ボタンをクリックする。

31. **Rotate** the eye 20° to the left. Use **Arbitrary** under **Rotate** (**Image** menu), clicking **OK** on **20° CCW**.

32．すべてを選択してコピー＆ペースト、イメージメニューの変形から拡大・縮小を選択してシフトキーを押しながら右下角のポイントをドラッグ、62%に縮小してセンターに配置。さらにペーストして同様に31.3%に縮小配置する。

32. Select all and **Copy&Paste**, then select **Scale** under **Effects** on the **Image** menu. Hold down the **Shift Key** and drag the lower right point, reducing to 62% and centering. After pasting, do the same operation, reducing to 31.3%.

33．イメージメニューの鏡像から**水平方向**を実行する。

33. Execute **Flip Horizontal** under **Flip** on the **Image** menu.

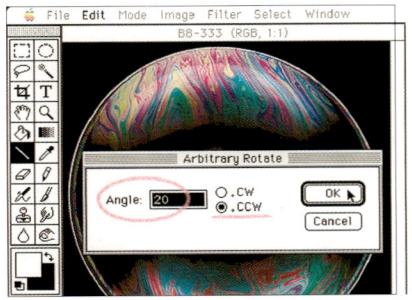

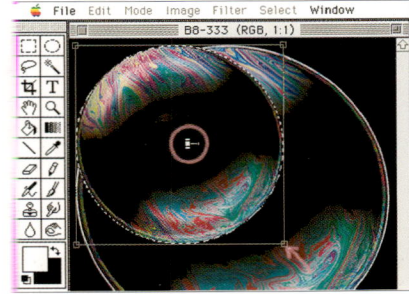

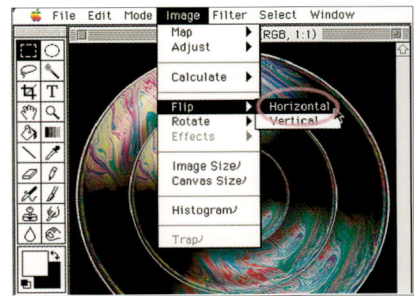

額縁用の素材を作る　*Making frame materials*

長方形選択ツールで幅14ピクセル選択して赤色を塗りつぶす。
Select a 14 pixel area with the **Rectangular Marquee** and **Fill** red.

右隣に幅17ピクセル選択して黄土色のグラデーションを作る。
Select and make a 17 pixel yellow gradation on the right side.

ドラッグ／コピーして右側に配置、水平方向に反転する。
Drag/Copy this to the right side; do **Flip Horizontal**.

以下同様に幅12ピクセル選択して茶色を塗りつぶす。
Do the same operation below, **Filling** a 12 pixel area with red.

幅19ピクセル選択して緑色のグラデーションを作る。
Select a width of 19 pixels and create the frame gradation.

ドラッグ／コピーして右側に配置、水平方向に反転する
Drag/Copy to the right side; do **Flip Horizontal**.

幅12ピクセル選択して濃いワインレッドを塗りつぶす。
Select a 12 pixel area and **Fill** with dark wine red.

幅20ピクセル選択して赤色のグラデーションを作る。
Select a 20 pixel width and create a red gradation

ドラッグ／コピーして右側に配置、水平方向に反転する
Drag/Copy it to the right side; do **Flip Horizontal**.

幅10ピクセル選択して焦げ茶色を塗りつぶす。
Select a 10 pixel width and Fill with burnished brown.

幅16ピクセル選択して黄土色のグラデーションを作る。
Select a 16 pixel width and create and earth yellow gradation.

ドラッグ／コピーして右側に配置、水平方向に反転する
Drag/Copy to the right side; do **Flip Horizontal**.

幅17ピクセル選択してベージュ色を塗りつぶす。
Select a 17 pixel width and **Fill** with beige.

第4章で実習したグラデーションテクニックのの復習である。グラデーションをかけるときの基点と終点を調整することで円柱状にも少ししゃくれた額縁の縁取りのようにも見せることができる。

作例ではシャドウ側を多めに取ることで額縁らしく見せかけている。

使う色も全体に彩度を落としてなかの絵のじゃまをしないように心がける。

単純なグラデーションなので各部分の横幅は原寸で厳密に作る必要があるが高さは作業しやすい適当なサイズでよい。完成後に必要なサイズまで**画像サイズ**で拡大してから**ドラッグ／コピー**すれば良いのだ。また**画像解像度**で縦方向だけ拡大しても画像はほとんど劣化しない。

This is a repeat of gradation techniques learned in Chap 4. By adjusting your starting and ending points you can even achieve a rounded effect in your frame.
In the example extra weight is given to the shadow side of the frame, making it more realistic.
Subdued coloring is used in the frame so as not to detract from the picture.
The gradation appears simple. Feel free to work at any height, but take great care in the width of the gradations. After completion, use **Canvas Size** to **Drag/Copy**, expanding to the desired size. Or use **Image Size** to increase the length, which will hardly reduce image quality at all.

---

34. グラデーションを作るために必要なカラーを**カラーパレット**にあらかじめ作成しておくと、手際よく作業が進行する。

35. グラデーションツールオプションはデフォルトのままだ。色の変化は**通常**、種類は**ライン状**、**中間位置**は50%である。

36. ドラッグ／コピーして水平方向に反転するとパイプ状のグラデーションができる。

34. Save yourself time by creating the necessary colors for the gradations on the **Color Palette** beforehand.

35. The **Gradient Tool** Option is left at the default setting. **Style** is **Normal**, **Type** is **Linear**, **Midpoint Skew** is 50%.

36. After **Drag/Copy** use **Flip Horizontal** to create a pipe-like gradation effect.

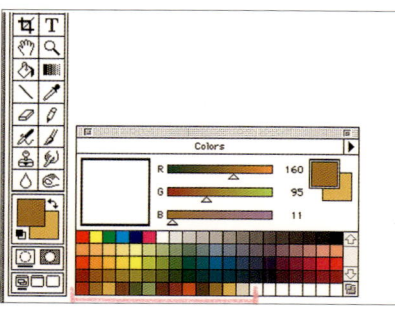

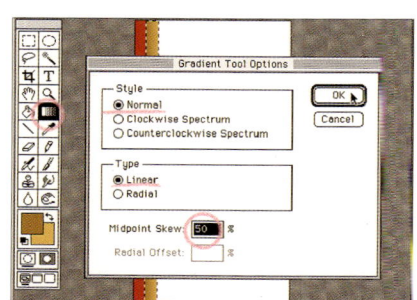

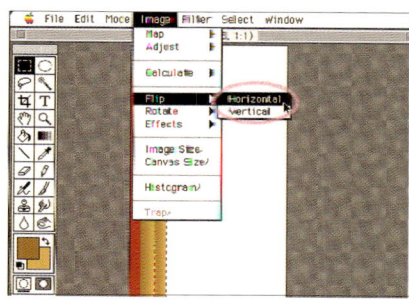

すべての素材を設計図にしたがって合成する

設計図を開く。すべてを選択して黒色の塗りつぶし100%を実行する。パスパレットでパス1をクリックして表示しておく。

Open the Blueprint file. Select all and **Fill** at 100% black. Click **Path 1** on **Paths Palette**, leaving it displayed.

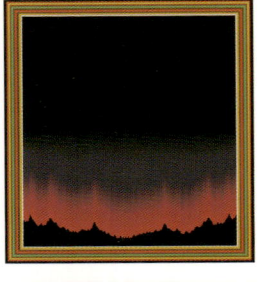

パスのガイドにしたがって額縁を左、右、上、下の順にペーストする。

Following the guide of the **Path**, **Paste** in this order: left, right, top, bottom.

センターのシャボン玉を開いてシャボン玉の外側黒スペースを自動選択ツールで選択、選択範囲メニューの選択範囲の反転を実行、シャボン玉だけを選択してコピー、パスのガイドに従ってペーストする。

Open the center jumbo eye and select the outer dark space with the **Magic Wand Tool**. Use **Inverse** under the **Select Menu** to reverse selected area, then select the jumbo eye and **Copy**, **Pasting** according to the **Path** guide.

素材の下ごしらえは、すべて整っているのでレイアウト作業は極めて簡単だ。唯一神経を使うのは、額縁のトメ加工（縦棒と横棒を45°で突き合わせる部分）くらいなものだ。

30分もあればレイアウト作業は終了するはずだ。そして**パス**をガイドラインに使えることの便利さをつくづく噛みしめることと思う。

最終レイアウト段階でも26点の対称配置をフリーハンドで作業することを考えると、天才的なレイアウト感覚の持主でもない限り、フォトショップよりアナログのレイアウトのほうがまだましだと思うであろう。

フォトショップと「イラストレーター」の組み合わせが2Dグラフィックス最強とうたわれているのも理解できるはずだ。

Doing the layout is extremely simple because all the materials are prepared. The only area of concern is the connecting of the frame (the 45° splices). Layout should only take about 30 minutes. The convenience of the **Path** guidelines is now obvious. In the final layout of the 26 symmetrical parts anyone but a genius layout artist would have to find Photoshop an advantage over freehand. You can see why many people consider a combination of Photoshop and "Illustrator" to be the strongest hand in 2D graphics.

---

37. 背景を下部にコピー＆ペーストする。位置決めのポイントは背景の稜線と三重円のシャドウのラインが程よく揃う感じがよい。

38. 左端に額縁素材をコピー＆ペーストする。右端にペーストした額縁素材を**イメージメニュー**から鏡像の**水平方向**コマンドを実行して内向きに反転する。

39. なげなわツールを使ってオプションキーを押しながら額縁の上辺を選択する。ポイントは左右端の45°で接辺を選択する部分だ。

37. **Copy** and **Paste** to the lower background Positioning is determined by the silhouette and the shadow outline of the triple ball.

38. **Copy** and **Paste** the frame material on the left side. Frame materials **pasted** on the right are selected and reversed with **Flip Horizontal** command.

39. Use the **Lasso Tool** and **Option Key** to select the upper part of the frame. The select points are the 45° angles on the right and left sides of the frame.

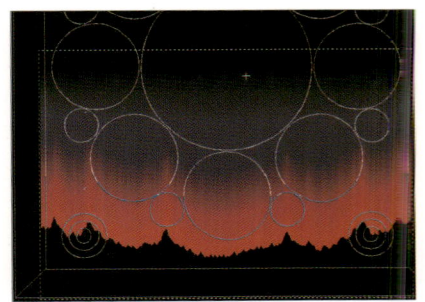
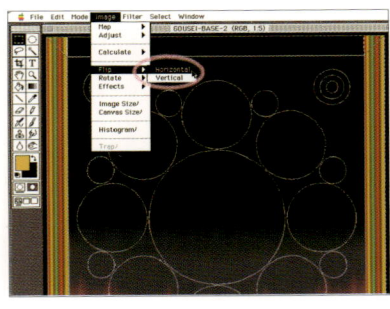
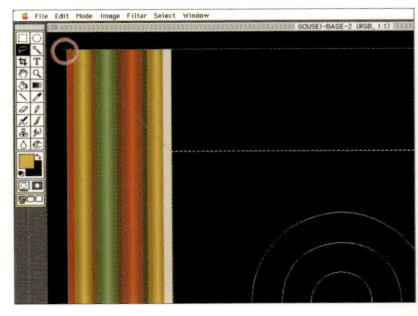

Combining all elements according to the blueprint

サイドのシャボン玉を開いてシャボン玉の外側黒スペースを自動選択ツールで選択、選択範囲メニューの選択範囲の反転を実行、シャボン玉だけを選択してコピー、パスのガイドに従ってペーストする。同じ要領で8個のシャボン玉をすべてレイアウトする。

Open the side jumbo eye and select the outer dark space with the **Magic Wand Tool**. Then use Inverse under the **Select Menu** to remove only the eye. **Paste** it according to the **Path** guideline. Do the same with all eight eyeballs.

一番小さいシャボン玉を開いてシャボン玉の外側黒スペースを自動選択ツールで選択、選択範囲メニューの選択範囲の反転を実行、シャボン玉だけを選択してコピー、パスのガイドに従ってペーストする。同じ要領で8個のシャボン玉をすべてレイアウトする。

Open the smallest jumbo eye and select the outer dark space with the **Magic Wand Tool**. Use Inverse (**Select Menu**) to remove only the eye, **Copying** and **Pasting** to the **Path** guideline. Do the same with all eight small eyeballs.

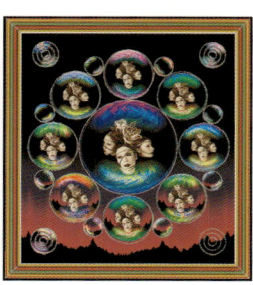

四隅のシャボン玉を開いてシャボン玉の外側黒スペースを自動選択ツールで選択、選択範囲メニューの選択範囲の反転を実行、シャボン玉だけを選択してコピー、パスのガイドに従ってペーストする。同じ要領で4個のシャボン玉をすべてレイアウトする。

Open the four corner eyeballs and select the outer dark space. Use the **Inverse** command to remove only the eyeballs. **Copy** and **Paste**, using the **Path** as a guideline. Do the same with all four jumbo balls.

完成した50点合成レイアウト
The complete 50-part layout

アイディアは浮かんだが、いざ実行という段階であまりに面倒そうなので、そのままになってしまった企画はよくある。

この作例をコンピュータ合成を行う会社に依頼したら、いくらの合成料を請求されるか想像してみてほしい。

写真家が自ら合成処理まで行うことで始めて実現した画像だといえる。

Good ideas are easy, but when it comes to executing them, a good many are left as unfinished plans.

But if this job were requested by a company, what would the charge for such a composite be? This could be the first composite completed by a photographer all on his own.

---

40. 額縁素材を選択範囲内へペーストする。イメージメニューの回転から90度時計回りを実行。選択範囲に移動配置する。

40. **Paste Into** with the frame materials. Do **90° CW** with **Rotate** on the **Image Menu**.

41. 額縁角の接合部を正確にあわせる。なげなわツールで正確に45°で選択していれば、上下の調整をするだけでぴったりあうはずである。

41. Accurately bring together the pieces of the frame. If you use the **Lasso** to precisely select 45°, adjustment is merely a matter of moving the pieces up or down.

42. シャボン玉ファイルを開いてシャボン玉の外側黒スペースを自動選択ツールで選択する。選択範囲メニューの選択範囲の反転を実行、シャボン玉だけを選択、パスのガイドラインに従ってペーストする。

42. **Open** the jumbo eye file and select the dark space around the eye with the **Magic Wand**. Use **Inverse** on the **Select Menu** to reverse and select only the eye. Then **Paste** it according to the **Path** guideline.

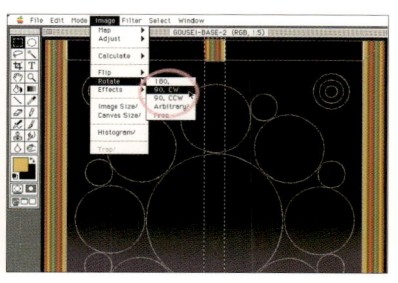

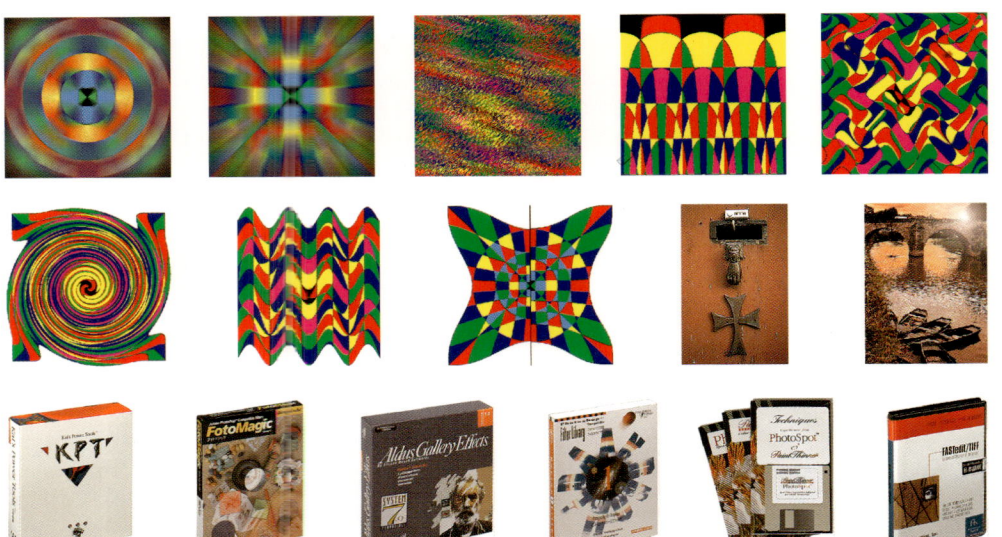

これだけ揃ったフォトショップのプラグインツール

第11章　フィルタ＆プラグイン

Chapter 11　Filters&Plug-in Tools

入出力プラグインモジュール

Plug-in Modules for Import and Export

フォトショップの**ファイル**メニューの**入力用プラグ,出力用プラグ**から利用できる入出力用のプラグインモジュールの数は非常に多い。

プログラムに最初からついてくる入出力モジュールが、Amiga IFF、BMP、FilmStrip、CompuServe GIF、マックペイント、PCX、PICTリソース、PIXAR、PixelPaint、Targa、Kodak CMS Photo CD、TWAIN、EPS JPEG、Ham出力、Illustratorのパス、ImageWriterカラー、アンチエイリシアングPICT、の多岐にわたる。

日本語版にはサードパーティソフトとしてEPSONスキャナプラグイン2.01Jがついてくる。日本でマック用の平面スキャナとして最も普及しているEPSON GT4000/6000/8000シリーズに対応したスキャナドライバだ。

現在ほとんどの主要スキャナ、プリンタ等入出力機器はドライバとしてフォトショップのプラグインモジュールを添付している。添付していない場合もヒューレットパッカードのScanJet IIcなどTWAIN対応の機器はTWAINインターフェースを通して使うことができる。

プラグイン：Kodak CMS Photo CD

フォトショップVer.2.51になって新たに添付されたプラグインモジュールの最大級は、Kodak CMS Photo CDであろう。Kodakカラーマネージメントシステムをベースにして、Photo CDのデータ変換に必要な部分だけを取り出したような高度なソフトである。

QuickTimeを利用したPhoto AccessのPICT変換に比べてはるかに高精度の変換を可能にしている。

Photo CDはテレビ画像のデータ形式に似たPhoto YCCという独自の圧縮フォーマットで5種類の画像サイズが1つのファイルに保存されている。Kodak CMS Photo CDプラグインはKodak Precision CMS技術によりPhoto YCCデータを最適化してRGBもしくはLabデータに変換する。CMYKへ直接変換するオプションもKodak社より購入可能だ。

このソフトはプラグインモジュールだけではなくシステムフォルダにインストールするCMSCPフォルダ、KPCMSフォルダと機能拡張フォルダにインストールされるKODAK PRECISION CP、CP1、CP2、システム機能拡張ファイルがあるのでインストール時に注意が必要だ。

ファイルメニューの**指定形式で開く**からKodak CMS Photo CDを選択してPhoto CD ディスク内のPhotosフォルダではなくPHOTO_CDフォルダ内のIMAGES フォルダから必要な画像を開く。変換したい**解像度**を指定して、変換元オプションに元画像に使用したフィルムタイプを指定する。タイプが分からない通常のカラーポジはPhotoCD Ektachrome PTでよい。Kodachrome PTはKodachromeフィルム使用時に指定する。ネガの場合はPhotoCD Color Negativeを指定する。

変換先オプションはRGBよりPhotosop CIELABの方が精度が高い。**環境設定のモニタの設定**で**環境光（設定）**を**明るい**に設定して**Lab**カラーモードで**開く**と最高画質になる。Photo CD Accessで開いたものに比べてアンダー気味だが情報量がはるかに多くすっきりした画像が得られる。

There are a great number of import and export plug-in modules that can be used under Aquire/Export on the File Menu. Included since the program was first issued are Amiga IFF, BMP, Filmstrip, Compuserve GIF, MacPaint, PCX, PICT Resource, PIXAR, PixelPaint, Targa, Kodak CMSPhoto CD, TWAIN interface, EPS JPEG, HAM output, Illustrator for persectives, Imagewriter Color and Anti-aliasing PICT.

For the Japanese version there is a third party plug-in, Epson Scan Plug-in 2.01J. This is for the Epson GT4000/6000/8000 series scanners, the most popular flatbed scanners in Japan. Almost all leading scanners and printers now come equipped with a plug-in import/export tool for Photoshop. For those which don't, like Hewlett-Packard's ScanJet IIC, the TWAIN interface card can be used.

A Plug-in: Kodak CMS PhotoCD

The newest major plug-in tool for Photoshop is the Kodak CMS Photo CD. This high-level software is based on Kodak's color management system and extrapolates only the necessary elements for Photo CD data conversion.

For Photo Access PICT conversions, QuickTime enables very high quality conversions.

The Photo CD uses an original method, somewhat similar to TV image handling, to compress images into a Photo YCC format. Five sizes of image can be saved as a single file. With Kodak Precision CMS technology the Photo CD plug-in converts data to an optimal RGB or Lab data format. Kodak also sells an option for converting to CMYK mode.

But this software is not simply a plug-in. Care must be taken when installing it. There are Kodak Precision CP, CP1, CP2 and Extension folders which must be installed correctly to CMSCP, KPCMS and Extensions folders.

Select Kodak CMS Photo CD from File Menu Open As. Then, select not the Photos folder on the Photo CD Disk, but the Images folder inside the Photo CD folder, and open the images you need.

Set the size to which you wish to convert, then, under Conversion Options, set the film type based on the original film. When you don't know the type, as with a color positive, just set it to Photo CD Ektachrome.

Use the Kodachrome filter when the film is Kodachrome PT, or the Photo CD color negative setting for negative film.

The Photoshop CIELAR conversion produces a better image than the RGB mode. If you set the Ambient Light to High on Monitor Setup, under Preferences, then Open to Lab mode, you will get the best quality. The image appears a little darker, but the information is far greater and the image much clearer than when opened with the Photo CD Access.

Kodack CMS PhotoCD Plug-in　　Photo CD Access

プラグイン：プロフォトCDを利用する

About PRO Photo CD

いよいよ日本国内でも『プロフォトCD』のサービスが本格的に稼働し始めた。最大6144×4096ピクセル72MBの写真データを気軽に利用できる環境をフルに利用しない手はない。

アマチュア対象のフォトCDに比べるとコストははるかにかかるが、その分プロ向けのきめの細かいサービスに対応している。4×5、6×9、6×7、6×6、6×4.5、35ミリとスキャニングできるフィルムサイズは幅広く、フィルムタイプもカラーネガ、カラーポジ、白黒全てOKだ。

画像フォーマットはフォトCDと同じPhoto YCCフォーマットで、テレビ画像サイズのBASE（512×768ピクセル、1.2MB）を中心に1/4BASE（256×384ピクセル、295KB）、1/16BASE（128×192ピクセル、73KB）、4BASE（1024×1536ピクセル、4.7MB）、16BASE（2048×3072ピクセル、18.9MB）5種類の解像度を持つ画像データが、4MB程度の一つのイメージパックデータとして圧縮保存されている。64BASE（4096×6144ピクセル、72MB）のデータは8MB程の差分データとしてIMAGESフォルダとは別にIPEフォルダ内に収められている。

プロフォトCDのサービスは16BASEと64BASEの二通りがあるので、注文する際は16BASEにしたいのか64BASEにしたいのか、はっきり明記する必要がある。

1枚のプロフォトCDマスターに25点の画像を収録することができる。25点未満収録のディスクに追記することもフォトCD同様に可能だ。もちろんディスクの複製を作るサービスもある。

前述のKodak CMS PhotoCDプラグインやPhoto Accessでは残念ながら64BASEは開けない。Kodak社から発売されているKodak Photo CD Acquire Module Ver.2.01をフォトショップにインストールして初めて64BASEを開くことができる。

さすがに72MBもあるとファイルを解凍オープンするのに10～15分くらいかかる。しかし300ppiでほぼB3サイズをカバーする大きさなので無理はないが。

ファイルをハードディスクにコピーしてからオープンしても、CD-ROMから直接オープンしても20%弱しか時間は変わらないので、ディスクアクセスよりも解凍の計算に時間がかかっているのだろう。

35mmポジフィルムの同じデータをフォトCDとプロフォトCDで作成して画質の比較をしてみた。フォトCDの最大サイズ16BASEを450ppiで口絵ページに掲載してあるが、同一ポジをプロフォトCDで作成した16BASEの部分（450ppi）が左下図、64BASEを同一サイズに縮小した部分（450ppi）が右下図なので口絵も合せて比較されたい。16BASE、64BASEともフォトCDに比べて品位の高さがはっきりとうかがえる。4×5ポジから作成した64BASEデータはさすがに35mmポジデータよりもはるかにきれいで印刷にも充分対応できる。

At last PRO Photo CD service is about to arrive in Japan. Now photographic data up to 6144x4096 pixles and 72 MB can be conveniently and fully utilized.

Compared to the amatuer-oriented Photo CD service, the cost of PRO Photo CD is far higher, but the service is all the more complete. Scanning film sizes include 4X5, 6X9, 6X7, 6X6, 6X4.5 and 35mm in color negative, color positive and black and white.

The image format is the same Photo YCC format, centered on the TV image size of BASE (512x768 pixels, 1.2MB) in five image data resolutions: 1/4BASE (256x384 pixels, 295KB), 1/16BASE (128x192 pixels, 73KB), 4BASE (1024x1536 pixels, 4.7MB), and 16BASE (2048x3072 pixels, 18.9MB). Photos are compressed and saved in 4MB image packages. 64BASE (4096x6144 pixel, 72MB) data is compressed and saved a 8MB in a separate IPE Folder, rather than the normal Image Folder. PROPhoto service offers either 16BASE or 64BASE, and it is necessary to indicate which size when using the service.

25 items can be saved on one PROPhoto master CD. Like Photo CD, extra images may be saved to a PROPhoto CD when less than 25 images are contained on the disk. And, of course, the service will create duplicates.

As stated earlier, Kodak CMS PhotoCD plug-in and Photo Access cannot be used to open 64BASE. But if you open 64BASE images if you aquire the Kodak Phoito CD Aquire Module Ver. 2.01 and install it to Photoshop.

Not suprisingly, it takes from 10 to 15 minutes to unfreeze a compressed 72MB image file. But at 300ppi, which will cover B3 size, you can hardly complain. Even if you copy from the CD to your hard drive, unfreezing speed is increased by less than 20%, so its obvious that the time is more a matter of calculating the decompression than of accessing.

We compared data created from the same 35mm positive film processed on Photo CD and PRO Photo CD. The image on the facing page is a 16BASE, 450ppi data file from Photo CD. Below left is a 16BASE (450ppi) image created on PRO Photo CD, and right a 64BASE (450ppi) image from the same size and shrunk down. As you can see, both the PRO Photo images (16BASE, and 64BASE) are clearly superior in quality. A 64BASE image created from a 4x5 posi is even clearer than 35mm, and entirely adequate to printing needs.

フィルタ：ぼかし、シャープ、ノイズ、その他

121〜123ページは縦591Pixels、500ppiの画像にフィルタをかけている。画像サイズによって同じ設定値でもかかり具合が異なるフィルタが多いので、サイズの大きさに比例して設定値を変えるか、回数を増減して調節する。

Filters:Blur,Sharpen,Noise,Others

Pages 121-123 show vertical 591 pixel, 500ppi images through various filters. Depending on the image size each filter will offer different effects, so settings must be adjusted to size, or the number of filtrations repeated.

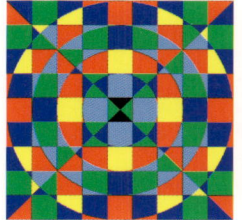

オリジナル画像
Original Data

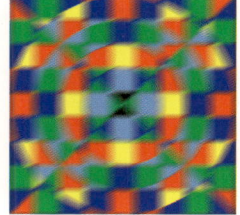

ぼかし(移動)：25° 35pixels
Motion Blur:25° 35pixels

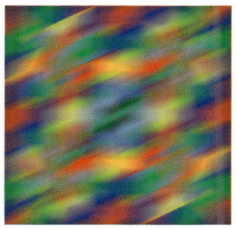

ぼかし(移動)：25° 100pixels
Motion Blur:25° 100pixels

ぼかし(放射状)：ズーム20
Radial Blur:Zoom20

ぼかし(放射状)：ズーム100
Radial Blur:Zoom100

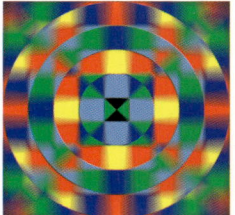

ぼかし(放射状)：回転10
Radial Blur:Spin10

ぼかし(放射状)：回転100
Radial Blur:Spin100

ノイズを加える：均等に分布100
Add Noise:Uniform100

ノイズを加える：ガウス分布100
Add Noise:Gaussian100

明るさの中間値：10Pixels
Median:10pixels

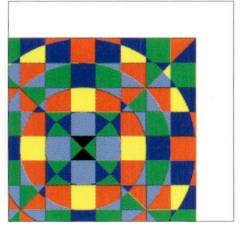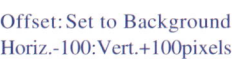

スクロール：選択範囲外からスクロールさせる、水平方向-100:垂直方向+100pixels

Offset: Set to Background
Horiz.-100:Vert.+100pixels

スクロール：端のピクセルを繰り返して埋める、水平方向-100:垂直方向+100pixels

Offset: Repeat Edge Pixels
Horiz.-100:Vert.+100pixels

スクロール：ラップアラウンド(巻き戻す)、水平方向-100:垂直方向+100ppixels

Offset: Wrap Around
Horiz.-100:Vert.+100pixels

明るさの最小値：10pixels
Minimum: 10pixels

明るさの最大値：10pixels
Maximum: 10pixels

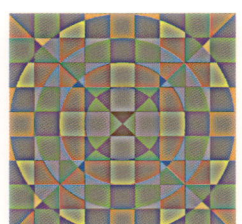

ハイパス：10pixels
High Pass:10pixels

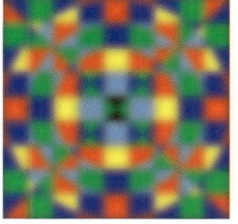

ぼかし(ガウス)：10pixels
Gaussian Blur:10pixels

オリジナル画像
Original Data

輪郭以外をぼかす
Despeckle

シャープ(輪郭のみ)
Sharpen Edges

シャープ(強)
Sharpen More

アンシャープマスク
適用量：250% 半径：1pixels しきい値：0
Unsharp Mask
250%/1pixels/0

フィルタ：変形

Filter:Distort

形を変えるフィルタ。波形以外はほとんど最大値で効果をかけている。最大値で1回かけるより何回かに分割して同量の効果をかけたほうが滑らかな変形ができるがシャープネスは悪くなる。

A distortion filter. With the exception of the ripple effect all values are set to maximum. By repeating the filtration a smooth effect is achieved, but sharpness is lost.

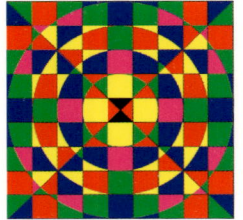

オリジナル画像

Original Data

回転：999度

Twirl:999°

球面：両方向（球）＋100

Spherize:Normal ＋100

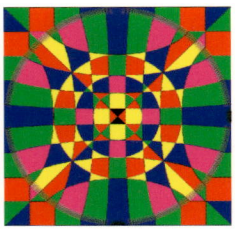

球面：両方向（球）-100

Spherize:Normal -100

シアー

Shear

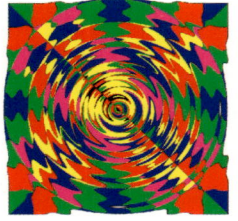

ジグザグ：左上、右下方向
大きさ50、折り返し10

Zigzag:Pond ripples

Amount50,Ridges10

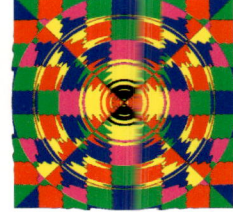

ジグザグ：中心 方向
大きさ100、折り返し20

Zigzag:Out from center

Amount100,Ridges20

ジグザグ：回転
大きさ100、折り返し20

Zigzag:Around center

Amount100,Ridges20

つまむ(放射状に移動)：右半分+100
で1回、左半分+25で5回かける

Pinch:Right half Amount
+100,Left half +25,5times

つまむ（放射状に移動）：-100

Pinch:Amount -100

置き換え用マップデータ
Displacement map data

波形：正弦波 波数1、波長 1:159
振幅1:144、比率 0:100%
端のピクセルを繰り返して埋める

Wave:Sine Number of Generators
1,Wave length 1:159,Amplitude1:144
Scale 0:100,Repeat edge pixels

波形：三角波 波数1、波長 1:294
振幅1:264、比率 0:100%
端のピクセルを繰り返して埋める

Wave:Triangle Number of Generators
1,Wave length 1:294,Amplitude1:264
Scale 0:100,Repeat edge pixels

波形：矩形波 波数1、波長 1:113
振幅 1:97、比率 0:100%
端のピクセルを繰り返して埋める

Wave:Square Number of Generators
1,Wave length 1:113,Amplitude1:97
Scale 0:100,Repeat edge pixels

波形：正弦波 波数5、波長
10:120、振幅5:35、比率
100:100%、ラップアラウンド

Wave:Sine Number of Generators
5,Wave length 10:120,Amplitude5:35,
Scale 100:100,Wrap Around

置き換え：水平比率100、垂直比
率100、繰り返し（タイリング）
端のピクセルを繰り返して埋める

Displace:Horizontal Scale100,
Verticale Scale100,Displacement
map:Tile, Repeat Edge pixels

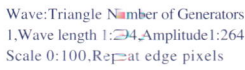

波紋：大きさ650、振幅数：小

Ripple:Amount650

Size Small

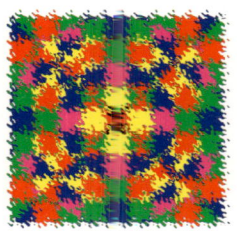

波紋：大きさ999、振幅数：中

Ripple:Amount999

Size Medium

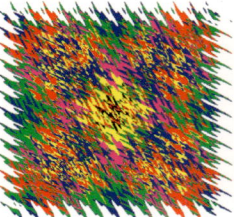

波紋：大きさ999、振幅数：大

Ripple:Amount999

Size Large

極座標：直交座標を極座標に

Polar Coordinates:Rectan-
gular to Polar

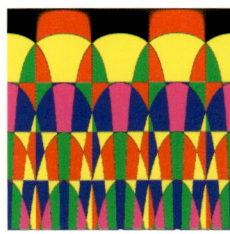

極座標：極座標を直交座標に

Polar Coordinates:Polar to
Rectangular

フィルタ：表現手法

Filter:Stylize

様々な表現を可能にしてくれるフィルタ。データが付記してあるフィルタは、設定を変えることでもっと変化に富んだ表現も可能だ。元データに透明度を加減して合成するのも効果的な使い方だ。

A filter that allows for various effects. A filter that includes recorded data allows the greatest possibilities for expression. It is also effective to raise or lower the transparency of the original when using this filter.

オリジナル画像

Original Data

面を刻む

Facet

輪郭検出

Find Edges

拡散：通常

Diffuse:Normal

逆光：150%50-300zoom

Lens Flare:150%,50-300zoom

ぶれ

Fragment

モザイク：10ピクセル平方

Mosaic:10pixels square

エンボス：135°,3pix.,100%

Emboss:135°,3pix.,100%

カラーハーフトーン：4pix.

Color Halftone:4pix.

ソラリゼーション

Solarize

水晶：4pix.

Crystallize:4pix.

点描：4pix.

Pointillize:4pix.

風：標準、右

Wind:Wind,Right

風：強く、右

Wind:Blast,Right

風：激しく揺らす、右

Wind:Stagger,Right

分割：分割数10,最大移動値10%,元画像を反転して塗る

Tiles:Number of tiles10,Maximum Offset10%,Inverse Image

押し出し：ブロック
大きさ30pix. 深さ100pix.
ランダム

Extrude:Blocks,Size30pix.
Depth100pix.,random

押し出し：ピラミッド
大きさ10pix. 深さ30pix.
レベルに合せる

Extrude:Pyramids,Size10pix.
Depth30pix.,level-based

輪郭のトレース：レベル128
指定レベルより小さな画像の周り

Trace Contour:Level128
Edge Lower

輪郭のトレース：レベル10
指定レベル以上の画像の周り

Trace Contour:Level10
Edge Upper

☆ショートカット：一度かけたフィルタの再実行や他の画像にかける場合はCommand+F、設定変更する場合はCommand+Option+Fキー。

☆A shortcut: When reusing a filter, or applying it to a different image, use Command + F. When changing the value settings, use Command + Option + F.

Kai's Power Tools　カイ パワー ツール

開発元：**Harvard Systems, Corp. (HSC Software)**　　販売元：株式会社ビーピーエス　　　Developer: Harvard Systems Corp. (HSC Software)

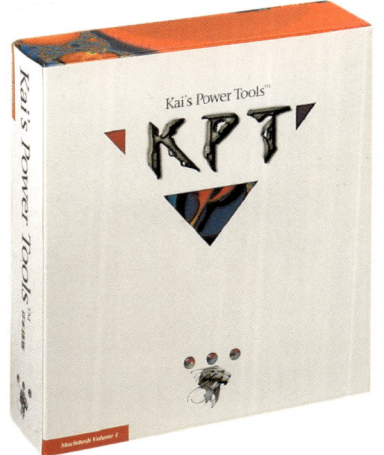

数有るフォトショップのプラグインフィルタの中でカイ パワー ツールほどパワフルなフィルタはない。単に33個のフィルタの集合体というにとどまらず、フォトショップの創造能力を飛躍的に高める可能性を秘めたツールといっても過言ではない。

カイパワーツールのメインプログラムは、グラディエントデザイナーとテクスチャー探求である。この1つずつでもユーザーは充分もとが取れると思えるほど高機能なものだ。

第4章のグラデーションテクニックで苦労して作ったマルチグラデーションは、グラディエントデザイナーを使うと1回の操作で作成できる。人物が付けている仮面もジュリアセット／探求で作ったものだ。この本が発売されるころには計算スピードがアップして新機能が加わった新しいバージョンが発売になっているはずだ。

Among all the plug-in tools offered by Photoshop there is none as powerful as Kai Power Tools. Not only does it include 33 individual filters; as a bundle, it enhances immensely the creative potential of Photoshop.

The main programs in Kai Power Tools are the Gradient Designer and Texture Explorer. Either of these alone offers enough value to satisfy any user.

With Gradient Designer, the multi-gradations which we struggled to produce in Chapter 4 can be done in a single operation. An image of a person can be created with Julia Set and Explorer. And at the time this book is published, new and faster version should be out.

オリジナル画像 Original Data 	KPT グラス レンズ／鮮明 Glass Lens Bright 	KPT サイクロン KPT Cyclone 	KPT シャープ インテンシティー KPT Shapen Intensity 	KPT ノイズ／黒 KPT Grime Layer 
KPT ノイズ／赤 KPT Spescial Red Noise 	KPT ピクセル／微風 KPT Pixel Breeze 	KPT ピクセル／風 KPT Pixel Wind 	KPT 明部スマッジ／右方向 KPT Smudge Lighten Right 	KPT 拡散／強 Diffuse More KPT 
KPT 拡散／水平方向 Scatter Horizontal KPT 	KPT 最大色調保護ノイズ KPT Hue Protected Noise Maximum 	KPT 暗部スマッジ／右方向 KPT Smudge Darken Right 	KPT 輪郭検出／反転 Find Edges & Invert KPT 	KPT 輪郭検出／木炭調 Find Edges Charcol KPT 

KPT Julia&Mandelbrot Explorer

ジュリア＆マンデルブロート

☆プリセットデータの作例の順番は左から右、一段下の左から右という配列。作例の英語名はそれぞれの作例の下に、日本語名はページのセンターに表記してある。

☆The preset examples are ordered from left to right, and again below from left to right, etc. The Japanese translation of the names is found in the middle, following this order:

ジュリアセット／探求　Julia Set Explorer

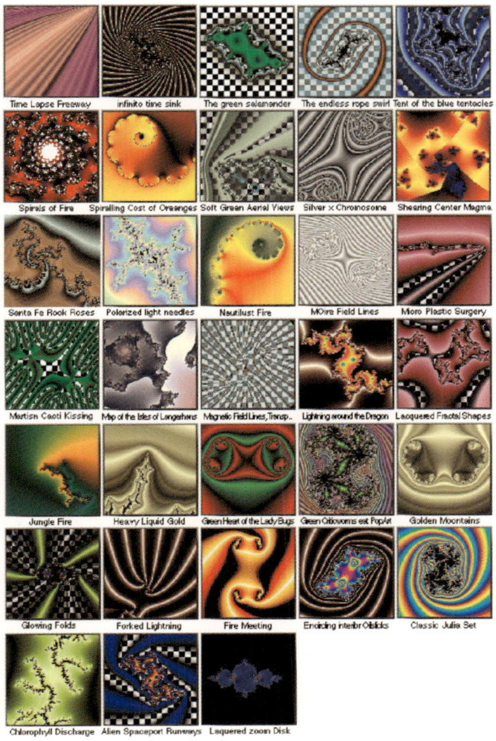

Time Lapse Freeway / infinito time sink / The green salamander / The endless rope swirl / Tent of the blue tentacles / Spirals of Fire / Spiralling Cost of Oraanges / Soft Green Aerial Views / Silver x Chromosome / Shearing Center Magma / Santa Fe Rook Roses / Polarized light needles / Nautilust Fire / MOire Field Lines / Moro Plastic Surgery / Martisn Caoti Kissing / Map of the Isles of Langerhans / Magnetic Field Lines,Transp.. / Lightning around the Dragon / Lacquered Fractal Shapes / Jungle Fire / Heavy Liquid Gold / Green Heart of the Lady Bugs / Green Citiworms est PopArt / Golden Moontains / Glowing Folds / Forked Lightning / Fire Meeting / Encircling interior Oilslicks / Classic Julia Set / Chlorophyll Discharge / Alien Spaceport Runways / Laquered zoom Disk

ジュリアセット／探求 II　Julia Type II Explorer

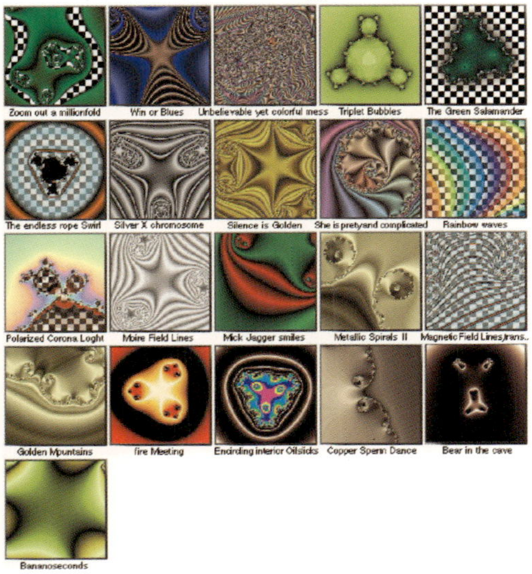

Zoom out a millionfold / Win or Blues / Unbelievable yet colorful mess / Triplet Bubbles / The Green Salamander / The endless rope Swirl / Silver X chromosome / Silence is Golden / She is pretyand complicated / Rainbow waves / Polarized Corona Loght / Moire Field Lines / Mick Jagger smiles / Metallic Spirals II / Magnetic Field Lines,trans.. / Golden Mpuntains / fire Meeting / Encircling interior Oilslicks / Copper Sperm Dance / Bear in the cave / Bananoseconds

☆ジュリアセット／探求

タイム　フリーウエイ
無限時空
緑色イモリ
無限ロープの渦
青触角のテント
炎の渦巻
オレンジのらせん状コスト
ソフトな緑色気体
シルバーX染色体
マグマの中央切断
サンタ フェの岩薔薇
偏光針
火のおうむ貝
波紋型ライン
ミクロ整形手術
火星人のさぼてんキッス
ランガーハン小島の地図
磁界ライン／透明
稲妻の竜
漆塗りフラクタル図形
ジャングルの火
重い液体金
四つ蛙
フラクタルZ星人
黄金の山々
まぶしいくぼみ
稲妻の嵐
炎の宴
囲む水面の油膜
ジュリアセット／クラシック
黄金蛍の夜
ブルー スペース　マウンテン
漆塗りズーム ディスク

☆ジュリアセット／探求 II

水槽中のエメラルド
勝利か否か
信じられない雑然色彩
泡の三つ組
緑色イモリ
無限ロープの渦
シルバーX染色体
沈黙は金なり
スカーフに包まれた宝石
虹色の波
偏光された光環
波紋型ライン
ミック ジャガーの微笑み
金属性渦巻き
磁界ライン／透明
黄金の山々
炎の宴
囲む水面の油膜
砂丘海岸
洞窟の中の熊
発光体ヒトデ

☆ジュリアセット／探求 III

生命の樹
粋なベージュの渦巻
らせん形
渦７／プラチナ
渦６／宇宙
渦５
渦４
渦３
渦２
渦１
滑らかな道
すべすべの花びら
シルバーX染色体
ウォールペーパーの種類
プラリーヌ／ズームアウト
プラリーヌ／ズームイン
終夜灯のアーク
パンガエア諸島
緑の羨望の的
炎の宴
カラフルペイント／衝突
カラフルペイント
シマウマの世界

☆マンデルブロート／探求

無限の詳説
ハリケーン上塗り
ゆっくりズーム アウト
五つの虹の橋
ニュー ギニアのジャングル
縮図の湖
雪中の雷
光と影
非常に深い
増加繰り返し、徐々に備える
２４金の亀裂
永遠の金髪の三網
銅色中のカビの群れ
無数の泡の群れ
青い拡散と銀のしだ
黒い稲妻
不調和の美
ピストルの穴

ジュリアセット／探求III　Julia Type III Explorer

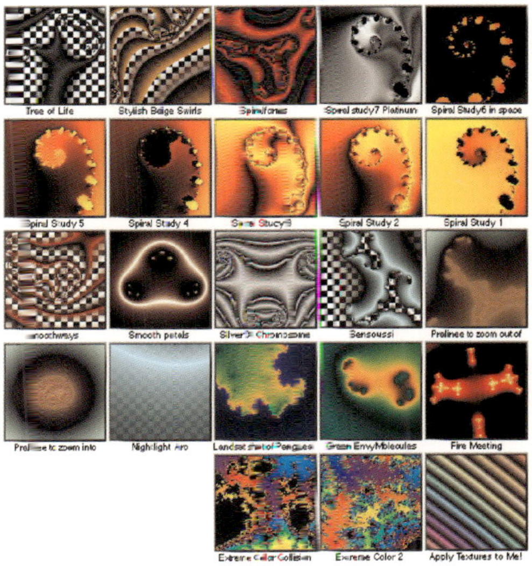

Tree of Life / Stylish Beige Swirls / Spiralforms / Speral study7 Platinum / Spiral Study6 in space / Spiral Study 5 / Spiral Study 4 / Spiral Study 3 / Spiral Study 2 / Spiral Study 1 / Smoothways / Smooth petals / Silver X Chromosome / Sensoussi / Praline to zoom out of / Praline to zoom into / Nightlight Arc / Landsat shot of Pengaea / Green EnvyMoleoules / Fire Meeting / Extreme Color Collision / Extreme Color 2 / Apply Textures to Me!

マンデルブロート／探究　Mandelbrot Set Explorer

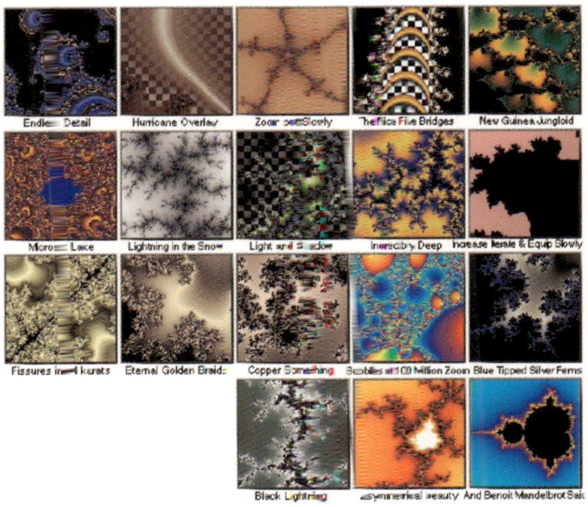

Endless Detail / Hurricane Overlay / Zoom out Slowly / The Nice Five Bridges / New Guinea Jungloid / Microcosm Lake / Lightning in the Snow / Light and Shadow / Incredibly Deep / Increase Iterate & Equip Slowly / Fissures in 24 karats / Eternal Golden Braids / Copper Something / Bubbles at 100 Million Zoom / Blue Tipped Silver Ferns / Black Lightning / Asymmetrical beauty / And Benoit Mandelbrot Saic

コンピュータが純粋に計算だけで生成する画像として有名なフラクタル画像を創りだすツールだ。0から始めるのは大変だが95種類のプリセットデータがあらかじめセットされているので、気に入った傾向の作例を選んでパラメーターを変化させることによって独自のフラクタル画像を手軽に創造することが可能だ。

作例中の市松模様は生成した画像の透明度を表現するためのバックグラウンドで画像の一部ではない。

This is a tool which creates the famous computer-calculated fractal image. It's too much to begin at 0, but here you can choose from among 95 preset calculations, changing parameters to develop an original fractal image. Among the examples is one which demonstrates transparency; it is not a piece of the image.

KPT Gradient Designer　グラディエントデザイナー

カイパワーツールの基本機能、最も使い勝手のある
フィルタだ。サブメニューとして169種類のプリセッ
トデータを持ち自作のデータも保存、再利用できる。
透明部分も含めた512階調のグラデーション、4種類
のグラデーション形態と、複雑なグラデーションをす
ばやく、しかも再現性のある形で利用できる。

プリセットデータ・タイトル

☆基本グラディエント
スペクトル調
黒影カット
春の光
野いちごのドロップ
粋な層
青い海と紅空
精密スペクトル
ソフト グレーの層
サンタ フェ
コバルト円錐体
白に青斜線
曲線マルチ カラー
アボカドの風合い
グレーに白水線
グレーの傾斜路

☆強い色調グラディエント
クーピー ペンシル
輝く虹円錐体
氷界への入口
暖かいグレー タラップ
日食の頃
オレンジの虹
イルミネーション
濃いチョコレート
藤色の夕闇
アップル社のカラーブレンド
ブルー＆パープル
薄黄色の霞
発光金属の的
新緑の候

☆金属色グラディエント
磨かれたアルミニウム／固体
鋼製シンバル
反射色付暗い吹き散り
中央黄金色
黄金の吹き散り 2
幅広 金属円筒
金属吹き散り／銅
金属吹き散り／シンバル
透明メタリック ブレンド
金属性ブラウン
金属性反射 1
金属性トゥラス
緑色月光／嫉妬
月光冶金
サックスとバイオレット
青銀色の円錐体
銀色の輝き
影付ソフト ライト グリーン
反射の紫色金属杖
反射の金属杖
亜鉛と銅について

☆テクスチャーのブレンド
明快なニュー メキシコ
レインボー スペクトル
木目模様
グリーン＆ホワイト
木と金属の調和
木の色彩
パステル II
紺チャンネル
青と黄のリング
オレンジ色・深紅・白のブレンド
赤に青の上塗りバンド
ピーチ＆ブルー
マルチ ループ 2

☆ジュリア グラディエント
深紫波
ジャングル風
完全な虹スペクトル
完全な虹スペクトル／暗い
完全な虹スペクトル／未還す
輝く真珠玉
ジュリア グラディエント
修正された曲線スペクトル
マルチ金属バンド
曲線ファイヤー スペクトル
緑色中オープン パイプ／中央半透明
桃とカボチャ
赤と緑の幅広チューブ
太陽の黒点風バンド
逆グラディエント テスト
バラ色の未来風エッジ バンド
すべすべしたメキシコ国旗
こなごなシャッター
燃える黄色チューブ

Here are some of the most useful filters of Kai Power Tools. In the sub menu are 169 varieties of preset data, and here you can also save your own ideas. Including transparencies there are 512 gradations and four types of gradation shapes, so that you can create complex gradations quickly, and reuse them again and again.

基本グラディエント　Basic Gradients

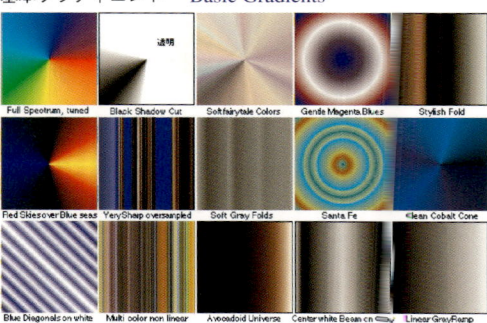

Full Spectrum, tuned / Black Shadow Cut / Soft fairytale Colors / Gentle Magenta Blues / Stylish Fold

Red Skies over Blue seas / Very Sharp oversampled / Soft Gray Folds / Santa Fe / Klean Cobalt Cone

Blue Diagonals on white / Multi color non linear / Avocadoid Universe / Center white Bean cn Gray / Linear Gray Ramp

強い色調　Strong Hues Gradients

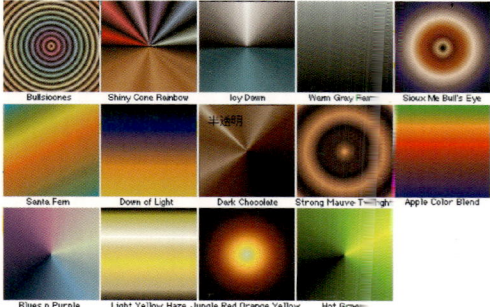

Bullscones / Shiny Cone Rainbow / Icy Dawn / Warm Gray Fear / Sioux Me Bull's Eye

Santa Fem / Dawn of Light / Dark Chocolate / Strong Mauve Twilight / Apple Color Blend

Blues n Purple / Light Yellow Haze / Jungle Red Orange Yellow / Hot Green

金属色　Metalic Gradients

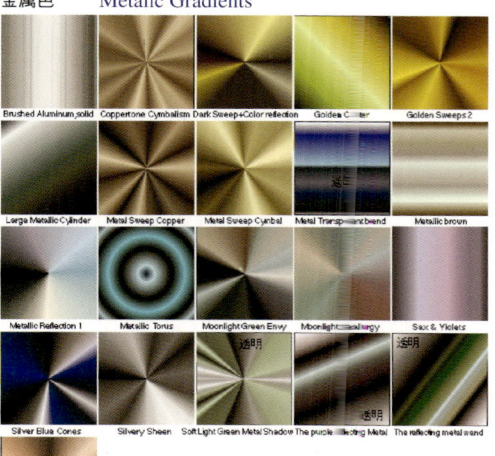

Brushed Aluminum solid / Coppertone Cymbalism / Dark Sweep+Color reflection / Golden Center / Golden Sweeps 2

Large Metallic Cylinder / Metal Sweep Copper / Metal Sweep Cymbal / Metal Transparent blend / Metallic brown

Metallic Reflection 1 / Metallic Torus / Moonlight Green Envy / Moonlight Metallurgy / Sax & Violets

Silver Blue Cones / Silvery Sheen / Soft Light Green Metal Shadow / The purple Reflecting Metal / The reflecting metal wand

Think zino popper

テクスチャーのブレンド　Texture Blend Gradients

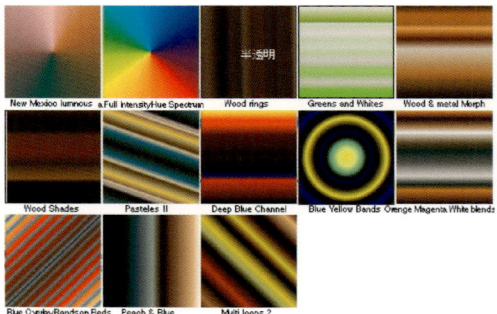

New Mexico luminous a Full Intensity Hue Spectrum / Wood rings / Greens and Whites / Wood & metal Morph

Wood Shades / Pasteles II / Deep Blue Channel / Blue Yellow Bands / Orange Magenta White blends

Blue Overlay Bandson Reds / Peach & Blue / Multi loops 2

ジュリアグラディエント　Julia Set Gradients

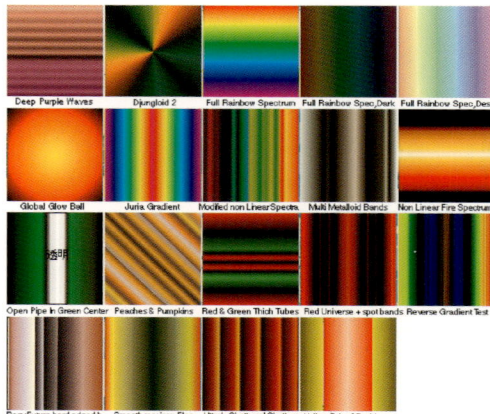

Deep Purple Waves / Djungloid 2 / Full Rainbow Spectrum / Full Rainbow Spec, Dark / Full Rainbow Spec, Dest

Global Glow Ball / Juria Gradient / Modified non Linear Spectra / Multi Metaloid Bands / Non Linear Fire Spectrum

Open Pipe In Green Center / Peaches & Pumpkins / Red & Green Thick Tubes / Red Universe + spot bands / Reverse Gradient Test

Rosy Future hard edged b / Smooth mexican Flag / Utterly Shattered Shutters / Yellow Tube & Red Insets

透明マスク指定　Transparency Masks

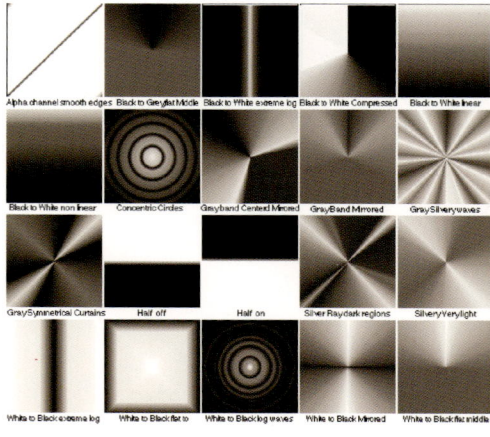

Alpha channel smooth edges / Black to Gray flat Middle / Black to White extreme log / Black to White Compressed / Black to White linear

Black to White non linear / Concentric Circles / Grayband Centered Mirrored / GrayBand Mirrored / Gray Silvery waves

Gray Symmetrical Curtains / Half off / Half on / Silver Ray dark regions / Silvery Very light

White to Black extrema log / White to Black fast to / White to Black log waves / White to Black Mirrored / White to Black flat middle

特殊効果　Special Effects Gradients

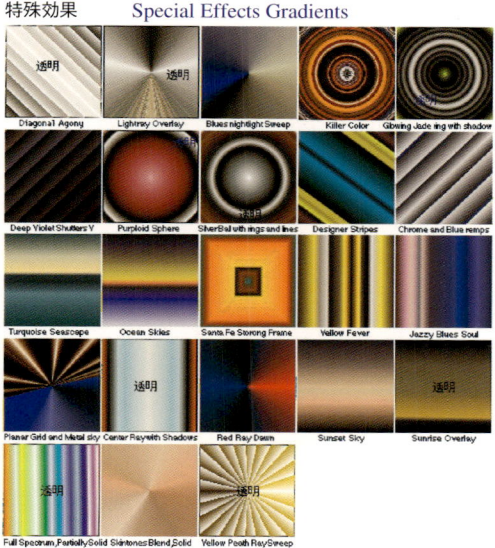

Diagonal Agony / Lightray Overlay / Blues nightlight Sweep / Killer Color / Glowing Jade ring with shadow

Deep Violet Shutters V / Purploid Sphere / SilverBall with rings and lines / Designer Stripes / Chrome and Blue ramps

Turquoise Seascape / Ocean Skies / Santa Fe Strong Frame / Yellow Fever / Jazzy Blues Soul

Planar Grid and Metal sky / Center Ray with Shadows / Red Ray Dawn / Sunset Sky / Sunrise Overlay

Full Spectrum,Partially Solid Skintones,Blend,Solid / Yellow Peach Ray Sweep

☆透明マスク指定
α チャンネル／滑らかなエッジ
黒から灰色へ／中間フラット
黒から白へ／極端な対数
黒から白へ／圧縮
黒から白へ／直線
黒から白へ／曲線
同心円
グレー バンド／中央反射
グレー バンド／反射
銀白色グレー ウェーブ
相称のグレー カーテン
ハーフ オフ
ハーフ オン
暗域の銀白色光線
より薄い銀白色
白から黒へ／極端な対数
白から黒へ／フラットから指数関数へ
白から黒へ／対数波
白から黒へ／反射
白から灰色へ／中間フラット

☆特殊効果グラディエント
閃える斜線
光輝の上塗り
夜光の吹き散り／ブルース調
殺人色
影付照り輝くひすいの輪
濃い紫シャッター
紫球体
輪と線付銀玉
デザイナー ストライプ
クロム＆ブルー タラップ
ターコイズの海景色
海空
サンタ フェ強化フレーム
黄熱病
ジャズ・ブルーズ・ソウル
プラナー グリッド＆金属空
影付中央光線
夜明けの赤光線
夕日空
夜明け色上塗り
完全スペクトル／半透明
肌色ブレンド／固形
死の黄光線の吹き散り

半透明度　Translucent Gradients

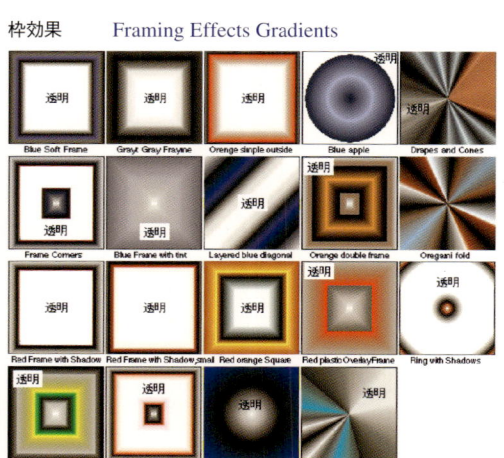

A Translucent Rainbow... / Argon Laser in Glass Tube / Brown Tint Sweep / Bulgarian Bulges / Disk Center Patterns

Double Pink Tunic Overlay / Fabric Folds,Transparent / Freshtone Haze Layer / Floating Doughnut / Floating Doughnut+Shadow

Green Metallic Sweep / Jade Sector+Waves / Laser Ray with Sadow / Moire Shadows / Neon Moonglow,slightly

Orange Sector / Pillow Shape Overlay / ReignBeauty Packy / Sepia 2 / Sepia Tint Shdow

Shadow Tubes Diagonal / Silver & Green Slice / Soft Neon Gloss & Shadow / Thin Glass Fiber/HeNe Laser / Ultra thin Red Line

☆半透明度グラディエント
虹色半透明上塗り
ガラス管中のアルゴン レーザー
茶色の吹き散り
ブルガリア風膨らみ
中央円盤パターン
トルコ風二重ピンク上塗り
布の織り／透明
肌色かすみ層
漂うドーナツ
影付漂うドーナツ
緑色金属吹き散り
波状ですい色扇形
影付レーザー光線
波紋影
月光ネオン／僅かに半透明
オレンジの扇形
枕風上塗り
レインボー／少数
セピア 2
セピア色の影
銀と緑のスライス
斜線トンネルの影
ソフトなネオンの輝き＆影
薄細グラス ファイバー／HeNe 赤光線
超薄赤ライン

枠効果　Framing Effects Gradients

Blue Soft Frame / Gray'r Gray Frayne / Orange simple outside / Blue apple / Drapes and Cones

Frame Corners / Blue Frame with tint / Layered blue diagonal / Orange double frame / Oregami fold

Red Frame with Shadow / Red Frame with Shadow,small / Red orange Square / Red plastic Overlay Frame / Ring with Shadows

Soft Edge Yellow frame / Square Red Frame Shadows / True Blue Frame round / Turquoise Cone Frame

☆枠効果グラディエント
柔らかい青枠
巨大なグレー枠
単純オレンジ外枠
青りんご
かけ布と円錐体
枠角
青フレームの色合い
ブルー層斜線
オレンジ二重枠
折り紙の折り目
影付赤枠
影付赤枠（小）
赤と橙の四角枠
赤のビニール上塗り枠
影付輪
ソフト エッジの黄色枠
影付四角赤枠
丸い青角枠
影付円錐形ターコイズ枠

Argon Laser with Halo / Auburn Streaks / avocaded Glow / Bananoid / Bloothpaste

Copernican Bands / Craynnaise / Deep Delila Blues / Ever-so-faint-oilslicky / Ex Excrent Creme

Golden Strands / Faint Shadow Moire Waves / Greasy Blipes / Green Laser with Shadow / Jade Tuboid and Ripples

Lil Lilac Loops / Low Neon Grow / Luminoous Metal Tube / Mermury Vapor Glow / Mustard Waves

Poisance / Orange Ray with Glow / PinkFloydian Glows / Prairie Fire / Red Hot Plasma Snake

Red Green Blue RainGlow / Smooth Apple Rainbow / Smooth Faded rainbow / Solid Rainbow / The Foggiesy Idea

True Blue / Umber sica depth / Zebra sings Ere Crossings

グラディエントパス　*Gradients on path*

境界をぼかしたなげなわツールのラインにそってグラデーションを付けるフィルタ。上記のプリセットデータの作例は、65ピクセルの円に6ピクセルの境界のぼかしを加えてフィルタを実行している。

Here a gradation filter has been added to create shading along a border. In the preset data above, a 6 pixel border shadow is added to a 65 pixel circle and saved as a filter.

プリセットデータの作例は100×100ピクセルで作成している。
　画像中の「透明」もしくは「半透明」という文字は、白地の部分が透明もしくは半透明で下地が透けて見えるという意味だ。
　マルチグラデーションの中に透明部分を含めることができるのは非常に便利な機能だ。

Here the preset data is set at 100 × 100 pixels.
　Japanese "透明","半透明" letters are created with transparent or half transparent "background," for a see-through affect.
Being able to include transparency in a gradation is extremely useful.

KPT Texture Explorer テクスチャー探求

カイパワーツールの2大パワー機能の一つ、テクスチャー探究は数学的な手法により様々なテクスチャーを生成する。15分類、総計224のプリセットパターンと無限のバリエーションを持っている。

One of the great strengths of Kai Power Tools is found in the Texture Explorer, which creates a variety of patterns through calculations. 15 types and 224 preset variations make for an infinte variety of possibilities.

空　Sky Textures

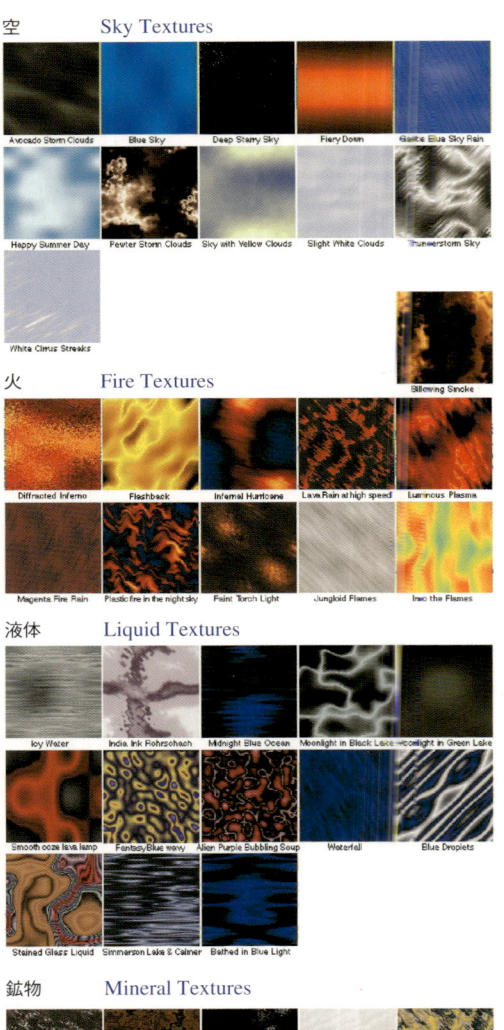

火　Fire Textures

液体　Liquid Textures

鉱物　Mineral Textures

☆空
アボガド嵐雲
青空
澄みきった星空
炎の夜明け
やさしい青空の雨
嬉しい夏の一日
しろめ嵐雲
黄色雲を持つ空
微かに白い雲
嵐の空
白い絹雲筋

☆火
渦巻く煙
火山の爆発
フラッシュバック
地獄のハリケーン
高速溶岩雨
輝くプラズマ
深紅色火の雨
夜空に踊る炎
淡い灯火の光
水の炎
炎の中へ…

☆液体
冷たい水
インド産インク
真夜中の青い海
ブラック湖の月光
グリーン湖の月光
スムーズ溶岩ランプ
ファンタジー ブルー／波型
エリアンの泡立つ紫のスープ
滝
青色の小滴
液体ステンド グラス
シマーソン レーク＆カーマー
青い光線を浴びて

☆鉱物
玄武岩＆花崗岩
茶色上ブラック オニキス
冷えたもろい溶岩
ドーバー断崖のチョーク
薄片状の硫化物
ガーネット クオーツ
緑灰色石版
小さなグリーン斑点
カイバブAZ砂岩
ライム上ターコイズ
輝くトルマリン
ウルグアイ産マラカイト
酸化トルマリン
パイライト＆ベリル
ルビー風マラカイト
錆びたヘマタイト
ラストレュメスクー

☆アニマリア
珊瑚の成長
ダルメシアン犬の染み
悲しい鴨達
炎の珊瑚礁
キリン火
藤の花の細胞
ハイエナの皮
豹染めのクロース アップ
躍動するロブスター
マンバ グリーン スネーク
火星の虎の皮
新菌種族
錦蛇／白黒
斑点のあるブダイ

☆メタリック
薄い鋼片
黄金の木材
緑色の鉄格子
液体金の水たまり
液体塊
天然チタン
ふわふわした銅
水銀雲
美感に訴える…
薄い白銀スズ
巨大門

☆ノイズ
小さなブラック斑点雲
屋根上の血
もろい溶岩ノイズ
カラー ボールをクリックして…
燃える石炭ノイズ
小さなグリーン斑点ノイズ
明快な極性ノイズ
騒がしいクリスマス
曲線分распол
黒上のオレンジ チョーク
雑駁なサンタ フェ ノイズ
微妙な砂岩のノイズ
タイ染めTシャツ
三色クレヨン
ターコイズ チョークの雨
二重 ルビーレッド

☆グリット
立方体上に浮く球体
釘刺結び目
液体サファイア
クロム格子
病原菌
ぼやけたプラチナ十字架
輝くグリーン格子
発光体ひすい蛇
強烈なパズルピース
黄金の瞳
黄金の瞳／液体
等圧玉
金属穴
オレンジ滴
紅白ファンタジー
レッド＆グリーン光沢
ターゴイズの涙
アマゾン鎮環
緑色二次元円
ソフト石墨グリット
モノポルカ
連結壁
ソフトなチェス ボード
前景と背景
一番低い球体をクリックして…

☆象形文字
クリスマスのルーン文字
チューマシュ算数
ダエニケン落書き
エジプト ブルース
火星人の速記
白熊の足跡
黄金の遺稿
スパイナル タップのデザイン
π(3.1415〜)
図B ロボット組み立て方法

アニマリア　Animalia Textures

メタリック　Metal Textures

ノイズ　Noise Textures

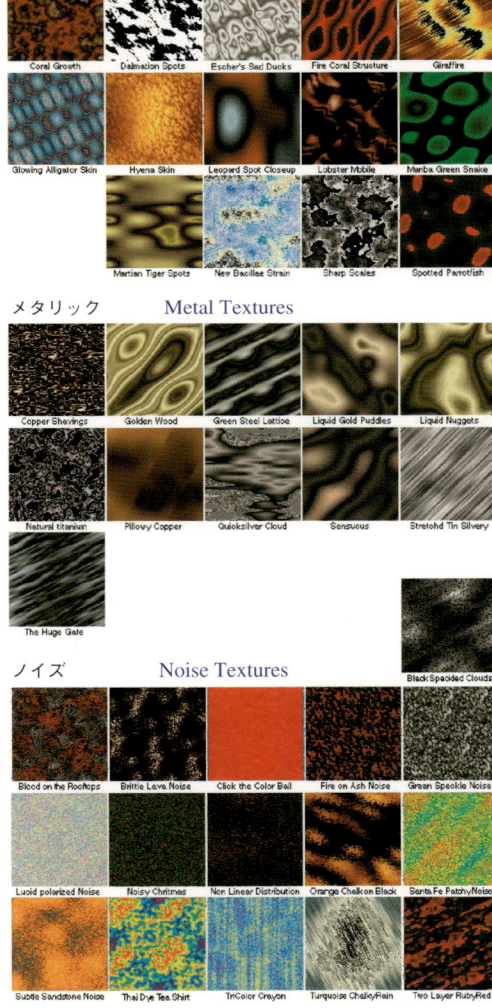

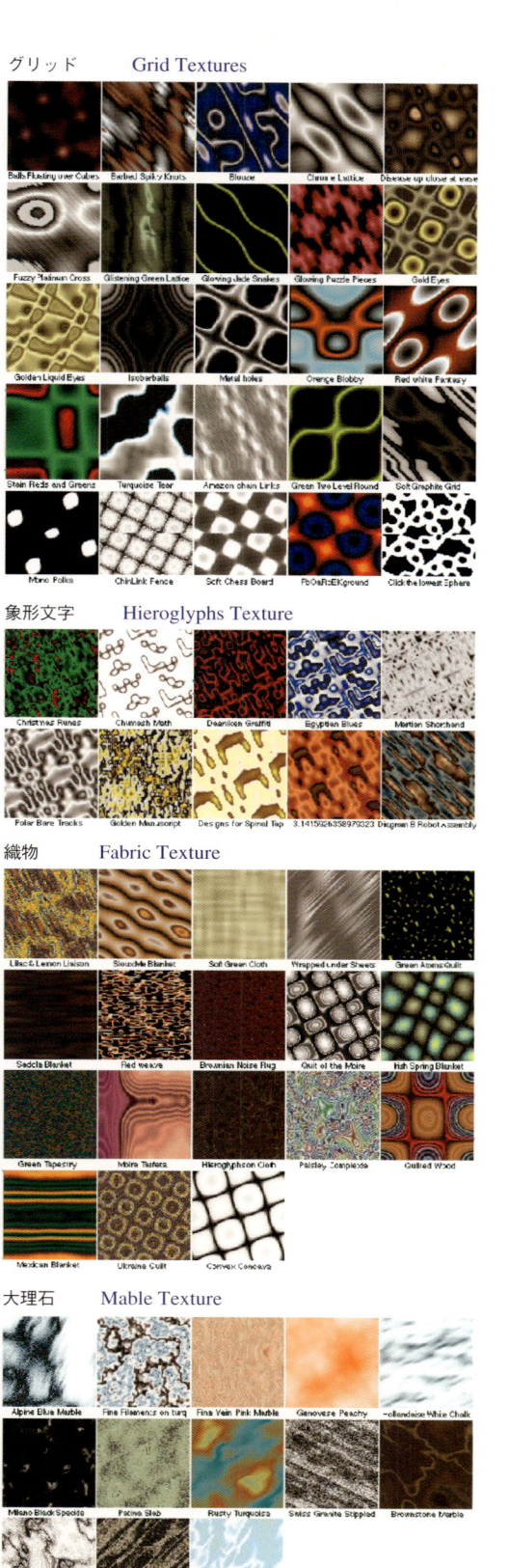

グリッド　Grid Textures

Balls Floating over Cubes ・ Barbed Spiky Knots ・ Blouse ・ Clouse Lattice ・ Disease up close at knee
Fuzzy Platinum Cross ・ Glistening Green Lattice ・ Glowing Jade Snakes ・ Glowing Puzzle Pieces ・ Gold Eyes
Golden Liquid Eyes ・ Isobarbeits ・ Metal holes ・ Orange Blobby ・ Red white Fantasy
Stain Reds and Greens ・ Turquoise Tear ・ Amazon chain Links ・ Green Two Level Round ・ Soft Graphite Grid
Mono Polka ・ ChinLink Fence ・ Soft Chess Board ・ FoOaRsEKground ・ Click the lowest Sphere

象形文字　Hieroglyphs Texture

Christmas Runes ・ Chumash Moth ・ Dandelion Graffiti ・ Egyptian Blues ・ Martian Shorthand
Polar Bare Tracks ・ Golden Manuscript ・ Designs for Spinal Tap ・ 3.1415926535897023 ・ Dingman B Robot Assembly

織物　Fabric Texture

Lilac & Lemon Liaison ・ Slouchie Blanket ・ Soft Green Cloth ・ Wrapped under Sheets ・ Green Atomic Quilt
Saddle Blanket ・ Red weave ・ Brownian Noise Rug ・ Quilt of the Moire ・ Irish Spring Blanket
Green Tapestry ・ Moire Taffeta ・ Hieroglyphican Cloth ・ Paisley Complexity ・ Quilted Wood
Mexican Blanket ・ Ukraine Quilt ・ Convex Concave

大理石　Mable Texture

Alpine Blue Marble ・ Fine Filaments on turq ・ Fine Vein Pink Marble ・ Genovese Peachy ・ Hollandaise White Chalk
Milano Black Speckle ・ Patina Slab ・ Rusty Turquoise ・ Swiss Granite Stippled ・ Brownstone Marble
White Vapollicalls Marble ・ Dark Golden Green Slab ・ White Turquoise

壁　Wall Textures

Anasazi Cliff Dwellings ・ Cave in Bryce Canyon ・ Clear Icescape with Lichen ・ Deep Shades ・ Forking Iceholes
Green LED Wall ・ Hole in the Snow ・ Lichen Mosses ・ Orange Blob Wall ・ Rock Ridge Bump Map
Rosettes ・ Shadow & Light brown ・ Shredded Orange Stuph

不気味　Eerie Textures

Aerial View of Micronesia ・ Batman in a Tunnel ・ Eyed on charcoal ・ Bloods teel brushed ・ Deanscape at midnight
Deep Cave Stalagmites ・ Dripping ・ Sigmas when Blood II ・ Glowing Magma Barnacles ・ Golden Alien Baby
Hieronymous Bosch Ghosts ・ Lightning Spike ・ Liquid MetalPesto ・ Messy Exploding Frogs ・ Ultra Violet Haze
Melting Skull ・ Igneous Raspberry ・ Skin and Blisters ・ Bio Chip in G3 2021 ・ Jovian DNA Coils

木　Wood Textures

Aged Cork ・ Ark Bark ・ Bleached river Pine ・ Bleached White Ash ・ Bloodpine Vertical
Bright Teak Tiles ・ Cheap Paneling ・ Dark Knotty Teak Wood ・ Dead Cacti Trunks ・ Huge Hollow Redwood
Knotty Cedar Planks ・ Lathed Legs ・ Silver Aged ・ Stretched Planks 2 ・ Walnut
Walnut Roots ・ White Birch Bark ・ White Mezzanite ・ White Pine Eyes

蜃気楼　Mirage Textures

African Sunset ・ Black Lightning ・ Dante's Infernal EKG
Deep Galaxy Nebulae ・ Deliberate Cuts ・ Deliberate Cuts 2 ・ Desert Dune Dawn ・ Early Morning Sand Dunes
Flying Jade Diddos ・ Gray Wet Four ・ Polarized Light Crystal ・ Santa Fe Dawn ・ The Trappec Alien

FotoMagic *Series 1*　フォトマジック シリーズ1

開発元：Ring of Fire, Inc.　　　販売元：ミノルタ事務器販売株式会社　　　　　　　　Developer: Ring of FIre, Inc.

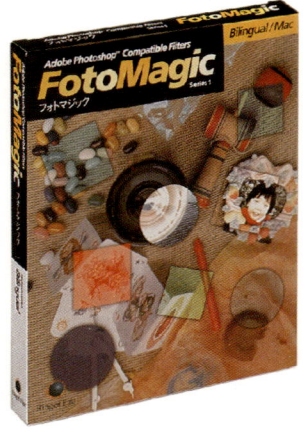

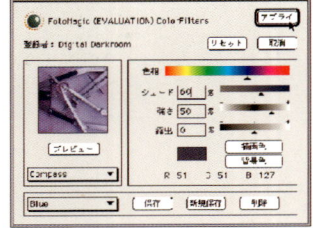

デザイナーの栗原公氏と物理学者でプログラマーのケン・トラクトン氏が共同開発した、写真撮影の際に使用する光学的フィルタをシミュレートしたフィルタだ。

光学理論に基づいているので、フォトショップのカラー補正とは一味違う効果を付けることができる。フォトショップのサードパーティ製フィルタはほとんどが変形を主体とした画像効果を狙ったものだが、全部で8種類含まれているフィルタの全てが色の変化を主体としていることが特徴だ。フォトショップでフォトクリエイティブを目指すなら是非持っていたいソフトの1つだ。

カラーフィルタはフォトショップのサードパーティソフトフォルダにも添付されているが、写真家にはおなじみのCCフィルタ（カラー補正フィルタ）の効果をシミュレートしている。もちろん色を選択することでLBフィルタ（変換フィルタ）のエフェクトをシミュレートすることも不可能ではない。プリセットでデーライト：タングステン変換フィルタや蛍光燈のグリーンかぶり補正フィルタ等が付いていれば写真家には便利だったろう。もちろん自分で作成した設定を保存、登録、再利用することは全てのフィルタにおいて可能だ。

色補正をすると露出補正を伴うことが多いのだが、同時に露出補正もかけられるようになっているきめの細かさがうれしい配慮だ。

カラーレンジャーは画像をシャドウからハイライトまで8つのレンジに分けてそれぞれのレンジに指定した色を被せることができる。

カラースケーラーは画像を選択した色でモノトーンにするフィルタである。

カラーシフターは画像を指定した色で全体に染め上げる。写真でいえばレタッチングダイ（染料）でポジフィルムを全面着色するのと同じような効果がある。

カラースイッチャーはインフラレッドフィルム（赤外線フィルム）で撮影したような効果をシミュレートしている。

カラーノイズは指定した色のカラーノイズを画像に加える。カラーエキスパンダーは画像のコントラストをシャドウ側とハイライト側別々に調整してコントロールすることができる。

カラーリバーサルはネガ：ポジの変換をきめ細かく設定することのできるフィルタだ。

FotoMagic is an optical filter simulator which was developed by designer Ko Kurihara and physicist Ken Tracton.
Because it's based on optical theory, it gives you somewhat different effects from Photoshop's color supplementation filters. Most third party filters developed for Photoshop are designed to alter shape, but all eight filters in FotoMagic are for color alterations. This software is a must for anyone who wishes to explore the creative photographic potential of Photoshop.
Photoshop has its own attached color filters in the third part filters folder, but these filters do the same work as CC filters (color filters), with which photographers are so familiar. Naturally, you can simulate the effects of LB filters (conversion filters) by choosing different colors. The preset D-light: Tungsten conversion filter and flourescent green color supplement filter are capabilities any photographer would appreciate. Of course, one can also set and save his own values, and reuse them later.Often color supplementation involves resetting exposure, but in this software the two functions are conveniently combined.

オリジナル画像　　Original Data

Color Ranger allows one to set and expose color range through eight levels, from shadow to highlight.
Color Scaler makes a selected color monotone.
Color Shifter puts an entire image into a selected hue. In photography, a retouch dye would be used to add a hue to color positive film. This gives the same effect.
Color Switcher simulates the effect of an image photographed with infrared film.
Color Noise adds noise to the image in the set color. With Color Expander, one can alter the constrast on the shadow and highlight sides independently.
Color Reversal provides exact settings for the conversion of negative and positive films.

カラーフィルタ　　　　　　　　ColorFilters

カラーエキスパンダー　　　　　ColorExpander

カラーシフター　　　　　　　　ColorShifter

カラースケーラー　　　　　　　ColorScaler

カラーノイズ　　　　　　　　　ColorNoise

カラーレンジャー　　　　　　　ColorRanger

カラースイッチャー　　　　　　ColorSwitcher

カラーリバーサル　　　　　　　ColorReversal

Aldus Gallery Effects Volume 1 アルダス ギャラリーエフェクト ボリューム 1

開発元：Silicon Beach Software, Inc.　　　　販売元：アルダス株式会社　　　　Developer: Silicon Beach Software, Inc.

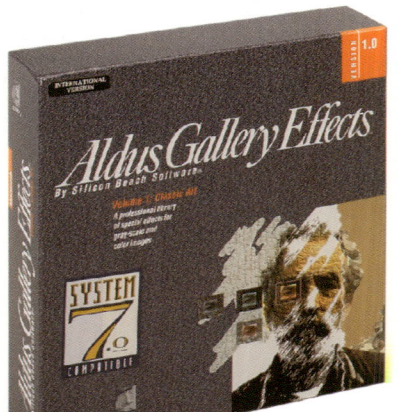

アルダスギャラリーエフェクトボリューム1は16種類の絵画調エフェクトが用意されている。フラクタルデザイン社のペインターで写真を絵画化するのに比べれば、仕上がりは単調になりがちだが、手間ははるかにかからない。パラメータをうまく設定すればかなりきれいなエフェクトをかけることができる。

　プレビューは事前に効果を確認できるので便利なのだが、75ピクセル四方のサイズなので、全体の効果を確認するのに役立つとは言い難い。もちろんテクスチャの確認は十分可能だ。

　全体に、エフェクトをかけるとオリジナルより暗めに仕上がるので、フィルタをかける前に画像を明るくしておいたほうが良いケースが多い。

　さらに多彩な絵画風エフェクトとキャンバスやレンガ、Pictファイルを利用したカスタムパターン等のテクスチャを合成するTexturizerフィルタをそなえた、アルダス ギャラリー エフェクト ボリューム 2 も発売になった。

16 painting effects can be achieved with Aldus Gallery Effects Volume 1. Compared to Fractal Design's Painter, the finished effects are simple, but it's a much easier program to use. And if one sets the parameters carefully, fairly clean effects can be achieved.

Preview is convenient for determinig the effect beforehand, but at 75 pixels, if difficult to get a clear idea of the whole picture. But it is enough to determine texture.

Adding effects will make the image darker than the original, so in most cases it's a good idea to lighten the image beforehand.

Aldus Gallery Effects Volume 2 is now out, and offers further effects such as Canvas and Brick, as well as a Texturizer Filter which uses PICT files for custom texturing.

オリジナル画像　**Original Data**

GE Chalk & Charcoal
Charcoal Area 6,Chalk Area 6,
stroke Pressure 1

GE Charcoal
Charcoal Thickness 1,Detail 5
Light/Dark Balance 50

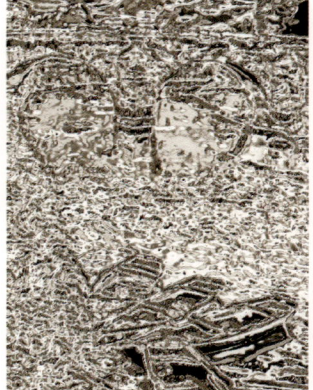

GE Chrome
Detail 10,Smoothness 1

GE Craquelure
Crak Spacing 15,Crack Depth 6,
Crack Brightness 9

GE Dark Strokes
Balance 5,Black Intensity 6,
White Intensity 2

GE Dry Brush
Brush Size 2,Brush Detail 18,
Texture 1

GE Emboss
Relief 25,Light Position:Top Left

GE Film Grain
Grain 10,Highlight Area 1,
Highlight Intensity 5

GE Fresco
Brush Size 1,Brush Detail 1
Texture 3

GE Graphic Pen
Stroke Length 15,
Stroke Direction:Right Diag.
Light/Dark Balance 50

GE Mosaic
Tile Size 12,Grout Width 3,
Lighten Grout 9

GE Poster Edges
Edge Thickness 2,Edge Intensity 1,
Posterization 2

GE Ripple
Ripplesize 9,Ripple Magnitude 9

GE Smudge Stick
Stroke Length 2,Highlight Area 0,
Highlight Intensity 10

GE Spatter
Spray Radius 10,Smoothness 5

GE Water color
Brush Detail 16,Shadow Intensity 1,
Texture 1

133

ANDROMEDA Series 1 Filters

アンドロメダ シリーズ 1 フィルタ

開発元：Andromeda Software, Inc.　販売元：有限会社フォーチュンヒル

Developer: Andromeda Software Inc.

アンドロメダシリーズ1フィルタは、写真撮影時にレンズ前につけるエフェクトフィルタの効果をシミュレートしている。

全部で10種類のフィルタが含まれているが、ちょっと毛色の違うDesignsフィルタを除いて、写真家にはおなじみのフィルタエフェクトばかりだ。非常に良くできたプレビューとあいまって、使い方でとまどうことはないと思う。

Rainbowフィルタは光学フィルタで同じ事ができたら素晴らしいが、デジタルならばこそ自由自在に画面のどこにでも虹を発生させることができる。

Diffract（放射）フィルタとStar（星）フィルタはエフェクトが荒削りでいただけない。

オリジナル画像　　Original Data

リアリティのある画像を作るためには、フォトショップの逆光フィルタと組み合わせるなどユーザー側の工夫が必要だ。

その他にHaloフィルタ、Prismフィルタ、Reflectionフィルタ、Velocityフィルタ、cMulti(サークルマルチイメージ)フィルタ、sMulti(ストレートマルチイメージ)フィルタがあり、使い勝手は良くできている。

Andromeda series filters simulate the effects of filters postioned in front of the camera lens. There are ten types of filters in the package, and with the exception of the Designs filter, all offer effects familiar to the photographer. Not only is the preview funciton excellent, but the program is generally very easy to use.

The Rainbow filter is as the name suggests; it lays a rainbow over any place in the entire image. The Diffract and Star filters, moreover, are too rough for most uses. To create a realistic image, one has to utilize Photoshops *Lens Flare* filter, and a little bit of original craft.

However, other filters, including the Halo, Prsim, Reflection, Velocity, csMulti (circlular multi image) and sMulti (straight mult image) are quite effective.

Velocity フィルタ　　Velocity Filter

122 ページで使用したパターン画像にシアーフィルタで波型に変形をかけ、アンドロメダシリーズ 1 のVelocityフィルタをかけた画像。効果がはっきりわかるように明確にかけてあるが、実際にはエッジがもっとぼけるのでぼかし（移動）の代わりに使うことができる。

Here the pattern on page 122 was altered with the Shear Filter, and the with Andromeda's Velocity Filter. The effect is clear, and because edges can be made to blur even more, this can be used instead of the Motion Blur command.

Halo フィルタ　　Halo Filter

画像のハイライトをシャドウ側に拡散させるフィルタ。暗い部分を明るい側に拡散することはできない。１定方向にも全方向にも効果をつけることができる。

This filter shifts highlighting to the shadowed area of the image. But it won't shift darkness to the lighter side. One can choose to spread the light in one direction or all directions.

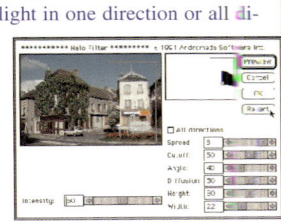

Prism フィルタ　　Prism Filter

画像をプリズムを通して見たようなイメージに作り替えるフィルタ。スペクトルが並ぶ方向と間隔は自由に変えることができる。他のフィルタも共通しているが、エフェクトをかける範囲と透過度は調整可能だ。

This filter gives the effect of an image passed through a prism. One is free to change the direction and band width of the spectrum. As with other filters, the range and transparency of the effect can be adjusted.

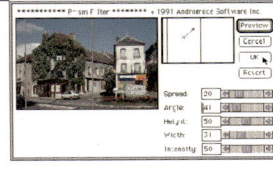

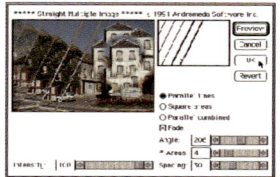

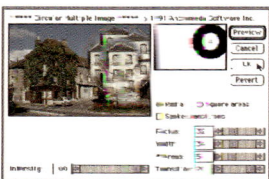

sMultiフィルタ sMulti Filter

ストレートマルチイメージフィルタの名の通り、イメージの直列パターンを生成する3種類のモードを持っている。作例はParallel linesモードで角度を左上方向にしてフェードをかけている。

As the name suggests, the straight multi image filter repeats images in a straight line. It has three modes. In the example the Parallel Lines mode is used. This upward effect also employs a fade.

cMultiフィルタ cMulti Filter

サークルマルチイメージフィルタ、イメージを万華鏡に似た円形のパターンに作り上げる。光学フィルタにはいろいろな面数のものが売られているが、さすがにデジタルで、1～20面（プラス中心部）のマルチサークルに対応している。Radius（中心イメージの半径）Width（周辺エリアの幅）#Areas（周辺エリアの数）Intensity（透過度）Transition（フェザリング）が自由に変えられるので、本物の光学マルチフィルタよりもはるかにきめの細かいエフェクトをイメージにかけることができる。

This filter produces a circular effect similar to a kaleidoscope. There are various optical filters on the market, but this one can be used to produce 1-20 surfaces, including the center. Radius, Width Areas (no. of areas), Intensity (transparency level) and Transition (Feathering) settings can be freely adjusted to achieve far more exact effects than real optical filter can offer.

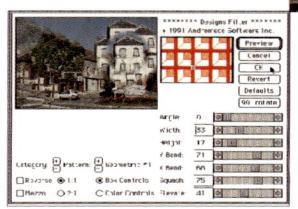

Designsフィルタ Designs FIlter

Demensionalテクスチャ、Mezzo Screenテクスチャ、Mezzo Grainテクスチャ、3種類のテクスチャを画像にかけることができる。作例はDemensionalテクスチャの110種類のパターンライブラリの1つをスライダーで変形してかけている。

Three texure types - Dimensional texture, Mezzo Screen texture and Mezzo Grain texture - can be achieved. One of 110 types of Dimensional texture was chosen and adjusted with the slider for this effect.

立体的な表面マッピングに対応したアンドロメダシリーズ2フィルタも発売されている。

Adromeda Series 2 filters for 3-D objects mapping is also on sale.

Diffractフィルタ Diffract Filter

強い光の周りに光のスペクトルを作るフィルタ。いかにも人工的な効果なので用途を限定して使ったほうが良い。ここでは逆光フィルタを併用してリアリティを出している。

This filter creates a spectre around an area of light. It's highly artificial, and should be reserved for special situations. This work use with **Lens FLare** filter.

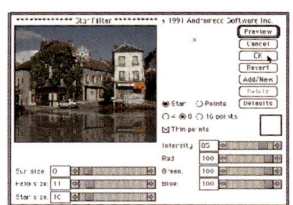

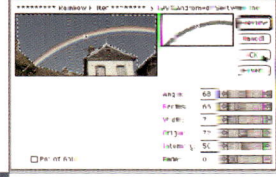

Starフィルタ Star Filter

光学的にはクロスフィルタとして知られているエフェクトを画像のどこにでも（効果的ではないがハイライト部分にも）かけることができる。線の数は4,8,16本の3種類、長さも個別に自由に変えることができる。ハローの強さも調節可能だ。これでもうすこしリアリティがあればかなり使えるフィルタなのだが。

This filter is like the photographic Cross Filter. It can be used anywhere, but is not effective in highlighted areas. Three types - 4, 8 and 16 lines - are possible, and length can be set to taste. The intensity of the Halo can also be varied. But these still require a bit more reality to become useful.

Rainbowフィルタ Rainbow Filter

人工的に虹を作り出すフィルタ。円弧と起点、虹の幅、角度、透過度を自由に設定できるので使い勝手が良い。完全な白以外の部分にかけることができるので、画像を選べばかなりリアリティのある虹を作ることができる。

This filter produces an artificial rainbow. The arc, origin, angle and transparency can be set freely; moreover, the rainbow can set against any backdrop but pure white, allowing for the creation of very realistic rainbows.

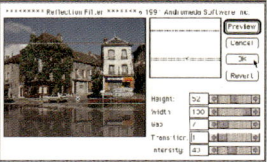

Reflectionフィルタ Reflection Filter

水面に反射しているようなイメージを作るフィルタ。Gap（間隔）スライダを調整して反射に使う部分を上下方向で特定することができるのでTransition（フェザリング）を適切に設定すると、自然な映り込みが作成できる。

A filter which produces a reflection on water. Adjust the Gap slider to position the reflection up or down on the surface; add Transition (Feathering) to achieve a very natural effect.

PaintThinner&PhotoSpot

ペイントシンナー／フォトスポット

開発元：Second Glance　　　　　　販売元：有限会社フォーチュンヒル　　　　　　　　　　　　　　Developer: Second Glance

PaintThinnerとPhotoSpotは２つで１セットのプラグインモジュールである。

テキスタイルデザインやシルクスクリーンなど数多くの特色版を必要とする作業にぴったりのソフトだ。

必要な作業画面を開いておいて**モードメニュー**の**インデックスカラー**を選択、作業目的と画像に合わせた色数を入力する。あまり少ない数にすると階調が飛んで後で苦労する。プラグインフィルタを使えるようにするために**RGBカラーモード**にファイルを戻して、フィルタメニューから**PaintThinner**を選択する。似通った色を全てクリックしておいて**Add**ボタンをクリックすると１色分の特色版ができる。予定した版数分に相似色を集めていく。必要があればピックアップした色を変えたり、加えたり、削除したり、編集作業を行うことができる。

*Selected*ボタンをクリックするとすでに選んだ部分が表示される。*Remaining*ボタンをクリックするとまだ選んでいない部分が表示される。*Thinned*ボタンをクリックすると結果が表示される。*Thinned*を選んで*Aply*ボタンをクリックするとPaintThinnerでの作業は終了する。

ファイルは開いたまま**ファイルメニュー**の**出力用プラグ**から**PhotoSpot**を選択すると分版用のダイアログボックスが開くので、各版に名前をつけて*Sep...*ボタンをクリック、次の画面で保存先やファイルフォーマットを決めて、*Make Seps*ボタンをクリックすると各版別に保存される。フォトショップだけでも特色版を作ることは不可能ではないが、このソフトほど簡単確実に作ることはできない。

PaintThinner and PhotoSpot are two plug-ins which come as a set. They are perfectly designed to assist in textile design, silk screen printing and other particular activities required by special printing techniques. **Open** the necessary work space on your monitor,then select index color from the **Mode** menu. Don't set the number too low, lest the gradation fly apart.

In order to make the plug-ins work return to **RGB** mode, as you would for other filters. Select **PaintThinnner** from the **Filter** menu. If you select all the colors you will be using and click the **Add** button you can create a special color separation. In this way you can collect all the differnt color film sheets you require. If needed, you can change, add or delete colors, editing as you wish. If you click the **Select** button the colors you have already selected will be displayed. If you click the **Thinned** button, the resulting blend will be shown. If you then click the **Apply** button, your work in **PaintThinner** will be finished.

If you leave the file open and select **PhotoSpot** from **Export** on the **File** menu a film separation dialogue box will be shown. You can then name each separation, and by clicking the **Sep**. button, convert to the file format of your choice. Click the **Make Seps** button to save the separations. It is not impossible to make separations on Photoshop alone, but this software makes it easier.

１．作業画像を開いておいてモードメニューから**インデックスカラー**を選択する。その他に目的の色数を入力。パレットは**使用中の色に合せて割り付ける**、ディザの種類はなしにして**OK**をクリック。モードメニューから**RGBカラー**を選択してフィルタが使えるようにする。

1. **Open** the image you are working on and select **Indexed color** from the **Mode** menu. Input the color you are using by **Other:**. Set **Palette** to **Adaptive**, **Dither** to **None**, and click **OK**. Then select **RGB color** from the **Mode** menu, and use the Filter.

２．ファイルメニューから**Second Glance**の**PaintThinner**コマンドを実行する。作業画面上で必要な色を拾ってから**Add**ボタンをクリックする。色集めが終わったら**Thinned**ボタンを選んで、**Apply**をクリックする。

2. Do the **PaintThinner** command under **Second Glance** on the **Filter** menu. From the Image select the color you require and click the **Add** button. After collecting your colors click **Apply**.

３．色集め作業終了後ファイルメニューの**出力用プラグ**から**PhotoSpot**を実行する。各版に名前をつけて**Sep...**ボタンをクリック、保存用のダイアログでフォーマット形式や保存先を決めて**Make Seps**ボタンをクリックすると各版別に保存される。

3. After selecting colors Choose **PhotoSpot** under **Export**. Execute. Name each separation and click the **Sep**. button. Decide your format in the dialog box, then click **Make Seps** to save your separations.

FASTedit/TIFF・FASTedit/CT

ファーストエディット／ティフ

開発元：Total Integration,Inc.　　販売元：有限会社フォーチュンヒル

Developer: Total Integration, Inc.

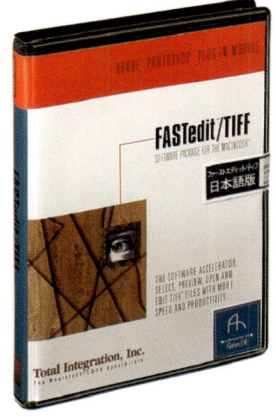

FASTedit/TIFFはソフト的にフォトショップの作業スピードを上げるためのプラグインでRGBとCMYKの非圧縮TIFFファイルのみに対応している。

スピードアップ以上に役立つのは搭載メモリも仮想記憶用のハードディスク容量も少ないマシンを使っている場合で、想像以上の効果を上げることができる。救いの神といっても良いかもしれない。

フォトショップの割り当てアプリケーションメモリ6MB、仮想記憶ディスク用の割り当てハードディスク容量10MB以下で36MB(4K)TIFFファイルのレタッチが多少の制約はあるもののスピード的にも問題なく行なえるのだから。

その秘密は単純なことで、元ファイルから必要な編集エリアだけを部分的に**開いて**作業後、元ファイルの元の場所に**ペースト**して保存しているだけだ。必要なメモリ量は選択した編集エリアに比例するので、メモリが少ない場合は小さめの編集エリアを選択すれば良い。

編集エリアは別に保存しておいて後から同ポジションに貼りこむこともできるので、バリエーションを保存するのにディスク容量が節約できて便利だ。ぜひ持っていたいプラグインの１つだ。

FASTedit/CTはサイテックスのCTフォーマットに対応したバージョンである。印刷がらみでサイテックスシステムを利用している人にはこちらの方が都合が良いだろう。

QusrkXressのDCSフォーマットに対応したFASTedit/DCS(EPS)バージョンも発売されている。DTPで利用する人にはこちらが便利だが、本当は３フォーマットを１本のソフトで利用できるほうがはるかに便利なはずだ。

FASTedit/TIFF is designed to speed up Photoshop, and works only with uncompressed TIFF files in CMYK and RGB.

Above and beyond speeding up the application, if you are using a machine with little on board or virtual memory, it will help performance vastly. You might even call it a Godsend.

Even with only 6MB of RAM and less than 10MB of hard drive scratch memory, a 36MB (4K) TIFF file can be retouched without too many limitations and very decent speed. The secret is simple. FASTedit opens only the portion of the file you are immediately working on; then, when you are finished, pastes it to the original image and saves it. Only enough memory to handle the edited area is required. Therefore, if you have little memory, you should select small areas to work upon.

Moreover, you can save an edited piece and then return it to the image later, which means, conveniently, that less disk space is required. This is a plug-in you should definitely have.

FASTedit/CT is the version for Sytech CTs. For those involved with Sytech CTs through printing work, this is the version to have.

A version for QuarkXpress is now in development. It's called FASTedit/DCS(EPS). For those in desktop publishing, this will be a big help. But it would be even better if all three versions were contained in the same plug-in.

１．ファイルメニューの**入力用プラグ**から**FASTedit™ TIFF...**を実行する。開きたいTIFFファイルをクリックしてプレビューイメージの編集エリアを選択、**Open**ボタンをクリックする。

２．選択した編集エリアがファイル名の後ろに座標情報を付記して**開く**。
元データよりサイズが小さいので軽快に作業を行なうことができる。

３．編集作業終了後ファイルメニューの**出力用プ**ラグから**Write or Update TIFF...**を実行する。Saveして**Replace**をクリックすると編集エリアが元ファイルの同位置に**ペースト**されて保存される。

1. Do **FASTedit** under **Acquire** on the **File** menu. Select the area to be edited on the TIFF preview file and click the open button.

2. Record information and the name of the edited area behind the file name, and **Open** the file. The size is smaller than the original, so you can work freely with it.

3. After finishing, choose **Write or Update TIFF** under **Export** on the **File** menu. Do Save and Replace to **paste** and save the edited piece in its original position.

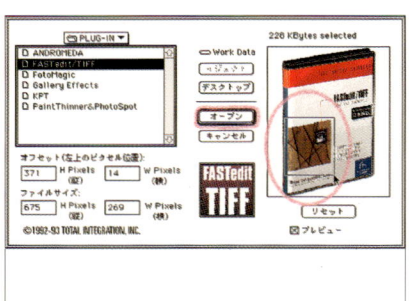

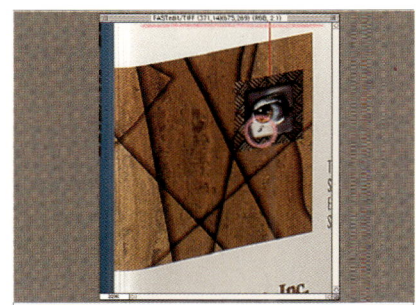

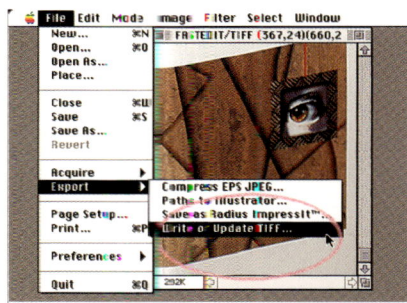

ツール／メニュー／パレット／ショートカット

Tools/Menus/Palettes/Shortcuts

ツールボックス

長方形選択ツール	長方形の範囲を選択
楕円選択ツール	楕円形の範囲を選択
なげなわツール	フリーハンドで範囲を選択
自動選択ツール	同じ色の範囲を選択
切り抜きツール	画像を切り抜く
文字ツール	文字を入力
手のひらツール	ウインドウ内でのスクロール
ズームツール	画像を拡大・縮小
塗りつぶしツール	選択範囲を描画色で塗りつぶす
グラデーションツール	階調をつけて塗りつぶす
ラインツール	直線を描く
スポイトツール	色のサンプルを採取
消しゴムツール	画像を消して背景色で塗りつぶす
鉛筆ツール	フリーハンド曲線または直線を描く
エアーブラシツール	画像にエアーブラシをかける
ブラシツール	画像をペイントする
スタンプツール	画像の一部をコピーする
指先ツール	画像の一部をにじませる
ぼかし・シャープツール	画像の一部をぼかしたり、シャープにする
覆い焼き・焼き込みツール	画像の一部を明るくしたり、暗くしたりする

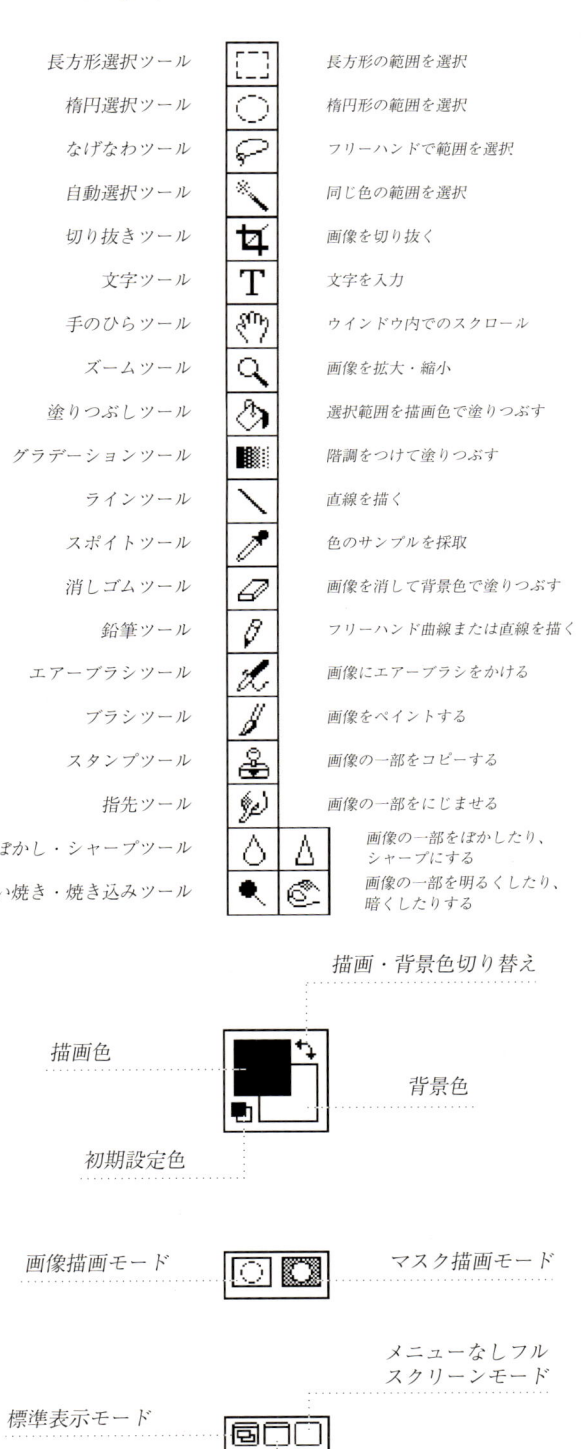

描画・背景色切り替え

描画色 / 背景色

初期設定色

画像描画モード / マスク描画モード

標準表示モード

メニューなしフルスクリーンモード

メニュー付きフルスクリーンモード

Toolbox

Rectangular marquee	Makes a rectangular selection
Elliptical marquee	Makes an elliptical selection
Lasso	Makes a freehand selection
Magic wand	Selects areas by color
Clopping	Crops an image
Type	Creates text in a image
Hand	Scrolls through a window
Zoom	Magnifies an image
Paint bucket	Fills areas with foreground color
Gradient	Creates a gradient fill
Line	Draws straight lines
Eyedropper	Takes a sample of a color
Eraser	Erases image to backgraound color
Pencil	Draws freehand or straght lines
Airbrush	Airbrushez an image
Paintbrush	Paints an image
Rubber stamp	Duplicates an area
Smudge	Smudges an area
Blur/sharpen	Blurs or shaepens an area
Dodge/burn	Lightens or darkens an area

Switch colors

Foreground color / Background color

Default colors

Standard mode / Quick Mask mode

Full screen without menu bar

Standard windows

Full screen with menu bar

ファイルメニュー

File Menu

ファイル

新規...	⌘N
開く...	⌘O
指定形式で開く...	
配置...	
閉じる	⌘W
保存	⌘S
別名で保存...	
復帰	
入力用プラグ	▶
出力用プラグ	▶
用紙設定...	
プリント...	⌘P
環境設定	▶
終了	⌘Q

メニュー

サブメニュー

File

New...	⌘N
Open...	⌘O
Open As...	
Place...	
Close	⌘W
Save	⌘S
Save As...	
Revert	
Acquire	▶
Export	▶
Page Setup...	
Print...	⌘P
Preferences	▶
Quit	⌘Q

Menu

Submenu

入力用プラグ ▶

EPS JPEG 解凍...
PICT リソース...
TWAIN対応機器から入力...
TWAIN対応機器の選択...
アンチエイリアシング PICT...

出力用プラグ ▶

EPS JPEG 圧縮...
Illustrator のパス...
ImageWriter カラー...

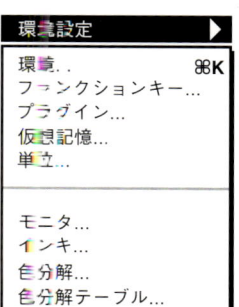

環境設定 ▶

環境... ⌘K
ファンクションキー...
プラグイン...
仮想記憶...
単位...

モニタ...
インキ...
色分解...
色分解テーブル...

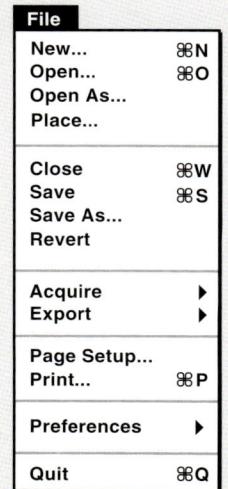

Acquire ▶

Anti-aliased PICT
Decompress EPS JPEG...
PICT Resource...
TWAIN Acquire...
TWAIN Select Source...

Export ▶

Compress EPS JPEG
Paths to Illustrator...

Preferences ▶

General...	⌘K
Function Keys...	
Plug-ins...	
Scratch Disks...	
Units...	
Monitor Setup...	
Printing Inks Setup...	
Separation Setup...	
Separation Tables...	

編集メニュー

編集

取り消し／やり直し	⌘Z
カット	⌘X
コピー	⌘C
ペースト	⌘V
選択範囲内へペースト	
選択範囲の後ろへペースト	
消去	
塗りつぶし...	
境界線を描く...	
切り抜き	
発行側の作成...	
発行側の設定...	
パターンの定義	
スナップショット	
合成のコントロール...	

モードメニュー

モード

モノクロ2階調
グレースケール
ダブルトーン
インデックスカラー
RGBカラー
CMYKカラー
Labカラー
マルチチャンネル
カラーテーブル...

Edit Menu

Edit

Undo/Redo	⌘Z
Cut	⌘X
Copy	⌘C
Paste	⌘V
Paste Into	
Paste Behind	
Clear	
Fill...	
Stroke...	
Crop	
Create Publisher...	
Publisher Options...	
Define Pattern	
Take Snapshot	
Composite Controls...	

Mode Menu

Mode

Bitmap
Grayscale
Duotone
Indexed Color...
RGB Color
CMYK Color
Lab Color
Multichannel
Color Table...

選択範囲メニュー

選択範囲

全画面の選択	⌘A
選択範囲の解除	⌘D
選択範囲の反転	
フロート	⌘J
選択範囲の拡張	⌘G
近似色の選択	
境界上の領域を選択...	
境界をぼかす...	
フリンジ削除...	
境界線の消去	⌘H
選択範囲の選択	
選択範囲の記録	

ウインドウ

新規ウインドウ	
ズームイン	⌘+
ズームアウト	⌘-
定規の表示	⌘R
ブラシの表示（消去）	
チャンネルの表示（消去）	
カラーの表示（消去）	
情報の表示（消去）	
パスの表示（消去）	
名称未設定1	

ウインドウメニュー

Select Menu

Select

All	⌘A
None	⌘D
Inverse	
Float	⌘J
Grow	⌘G
Similar	
Border...	
Feather...	
Defringe...	
Hide Edges	⌘H
Load Selection	
Save Selection	

Window

New Window	
Zoom In	⌘+
Zoom Out	⌘-
Show Rulers	⌘R
Show(Hide) Brushes	
Show(Hide) Channels	
Show(Hide) Colors	
Show(Hide) Info	
Show(Hide) Paths	
Untitled-1	

Window Menu

フィルタメニュー

Filter Menu

フィルタ
フィルタの再実行	⌘F

ぼかし	▶
ノイズ	▶
ビデオ	▶
シャープ	▶
変形	▶
表現手法	▶
その他	▶

メニュー

サブメニュー

変形 ▶
- 回転...
- 球面...
- 極座標...
- つまむ...
- シアー...
- ジグザグ...
- 置き換え...
- 波形...
- 波紋...

ぼかし ▶
- ぼかし
- ぼかし〈移動〉...
- ぼかし〈強〉...
- ぼかし〈ガウス〉...
- ぼかし〈放射状〉...

ビデオ ▶
- インターレース...
- NTSCカラー

ノイズ ▶
- ノイズを加える...
- 明るさの中間値...
- 輪郭以外をぼかす

シャープ ▶
- アンシャープマスク...
- シャープ
- シャープ〈強〉
- シャープ〈輪郭のみ〉

表現手法 ▶
- 押し出し...
- 拡散...
- 逆光...
- ぶれ
- モザイク...
- エンボス...
- カラーハーフトーン...
- ソラリゼーション
- 水晶...
- 点描...
- 風...
- 分割...
- 面を刻む
- 輪郭検出
- 輪郭のトレース...

その他 ▶
- カスタム...
- ハイパス...
- スクロール...
- HSL&HSB...
- 明るさの最小値...
- 明るさの最大値...

Filter
Last Filter	⌘F

Blur	▶
Distort	▶
Noise	▶
Sharpen	▶
Stylize	▶
Video	▶
Other	▶

Menu

Submenu

Distort ▶
- Displace...
- Pinch...
- Polar Coordinates...
- Ripple...
- Shear...
- Spherize...
- Twirl...
- Wave...
- Zigzag...

Video ▶
- De-Interlace...
- NTSC Colors

Stylize ▶
- Color Halftone...
- Crystallize...
- Diffuse...
- Emboss...
- Extrude...
- Facet
- Find Edges
- Fragment
- Lens Flare...
- Mosaic...
- Pointillize...
- Solarize
- Tiles...
- Trace Contour...
- Wind...

Blur ▶
- Blur
- Blur More
- Gaussian Blur...
- Motion Blur...
- Radial Blur...

Noise ▶
- Add Noise...
- Despeckle
- Median...

Sharpen ▶
- Sharpen
- Sharpen Edges
- Sharpen More
- Unsharp Mask...

Other ▶
- Custom...
- High Pass...
- Maximum...
- Minimum...
- Offset...

142

イメージ メニュー

Image Menu

イメージ
階調補正	▶
色調補正	▶
演算	▶
鏡像	▶
回転	▶
変形	▶
画像解像度...	
画像サイズ...	
ヒストグラム...	
トラップ...	

メニュー

サブメニュー

Image
Map	▶
Adjust	▶
Calculate	▶
Flip	▶
Rotate	▶
Effects	▶
Image Size...	
Canvas Size...	
Histogram...	
Trap...	

Menu

Submenu

階調補正 ▶
階調の反転	⌘I
イコライズ（平均化）...	⌘E
2階調化...	⌘T
ポスタリゼーション...	

鏡像 ▶
水平方向
垂直方向

Map ▶
Invert	⌘I
Equalize	⌘E
Threshold...	⌘T
Posterize...	

Flip ▶
Horizontal
Vertical

色調補正 ▶
レベル補正...	⌘L
トーンカーブ...	⌘M
明るさ・コントラスト...	⌘B
カラーバランス...	⌘Y
色相・彩度...	⌘U
バリエーション...	

変形 ▶
拡大・縮小
平行四辺形
台形
自由な形に

Adjust ▶
Levels...	⌘L
Curves...	⌘M
Brightness/Contrast...	⌘B
Color Balance...	⌘Y
Hue/Saturation..	⌘U
Variations...	

Effects ▶
Scale
Skew
Perspective
Distort

演算 ▶
加算...
合成（％指定）...
合成（マスク指定）...
一定値...
比較（暗）...
差の絶対値...
複写...
比較（明）...
乗算...
スクリーン...
減算...

回転 ▶
180度
90度時計回り
90度反時計回り
角度入力...
マウスで回転

Calculate ▶
Add...
Blend...
Composite...
Constant...
Darker...
Difference...
Duplicate...
Lighter...
Multiply...
Screen...
Subtract...

Rotate ▶
180°
90°CW
90°CCW
Arbitrary...
Free

カラーパレット

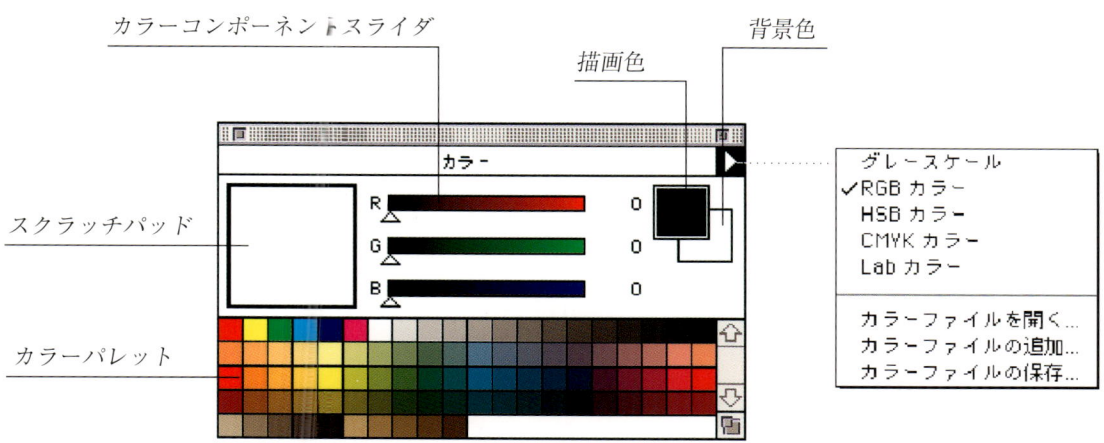

Color Palettes

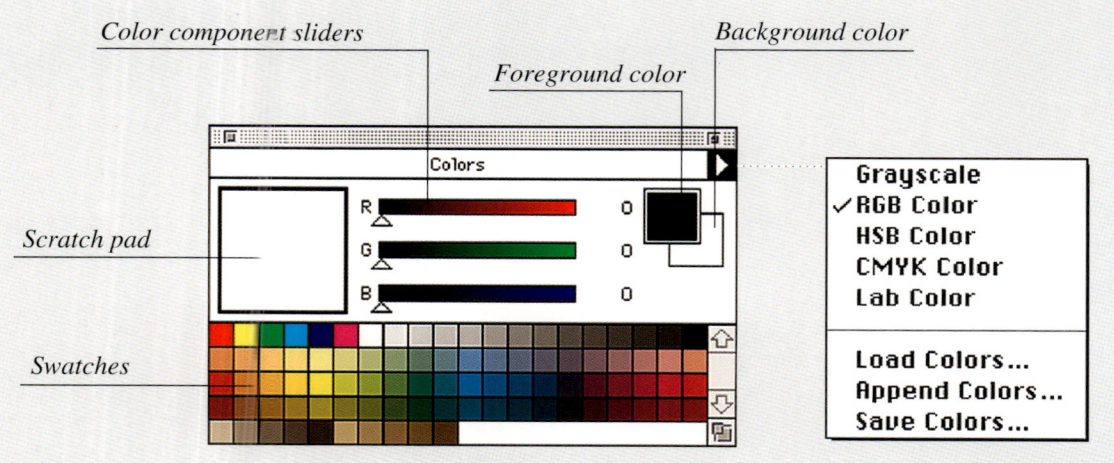

ブラシパレット

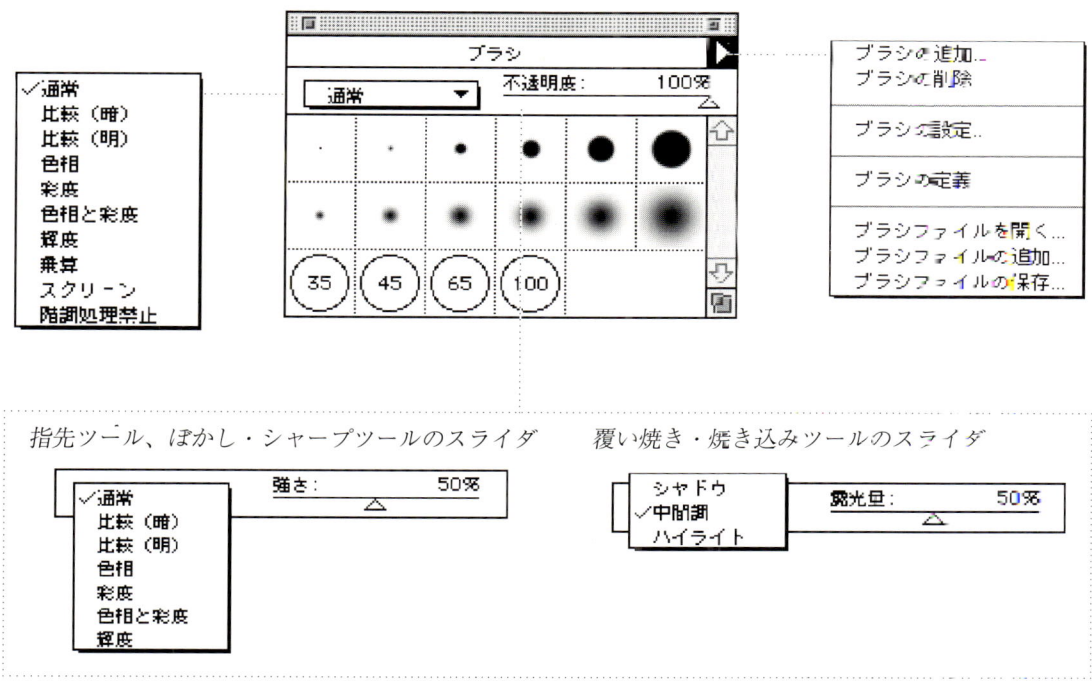

指先ツール、ぼかし・シャープツールのスライダ

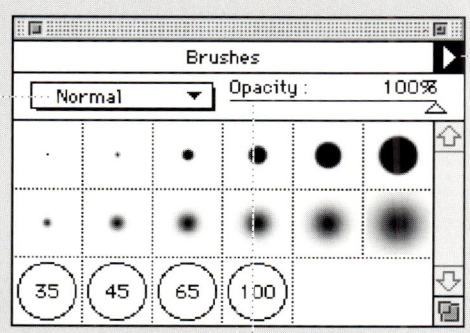

覆い焼き・焼き込みツールのスライダ

Brushes Palettes

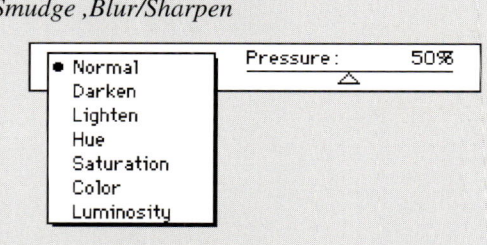

Smudge ,Blur/Sharpen

Dodge/Burn

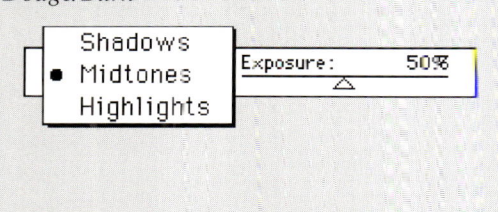

チャンネルパレット

パスパレット

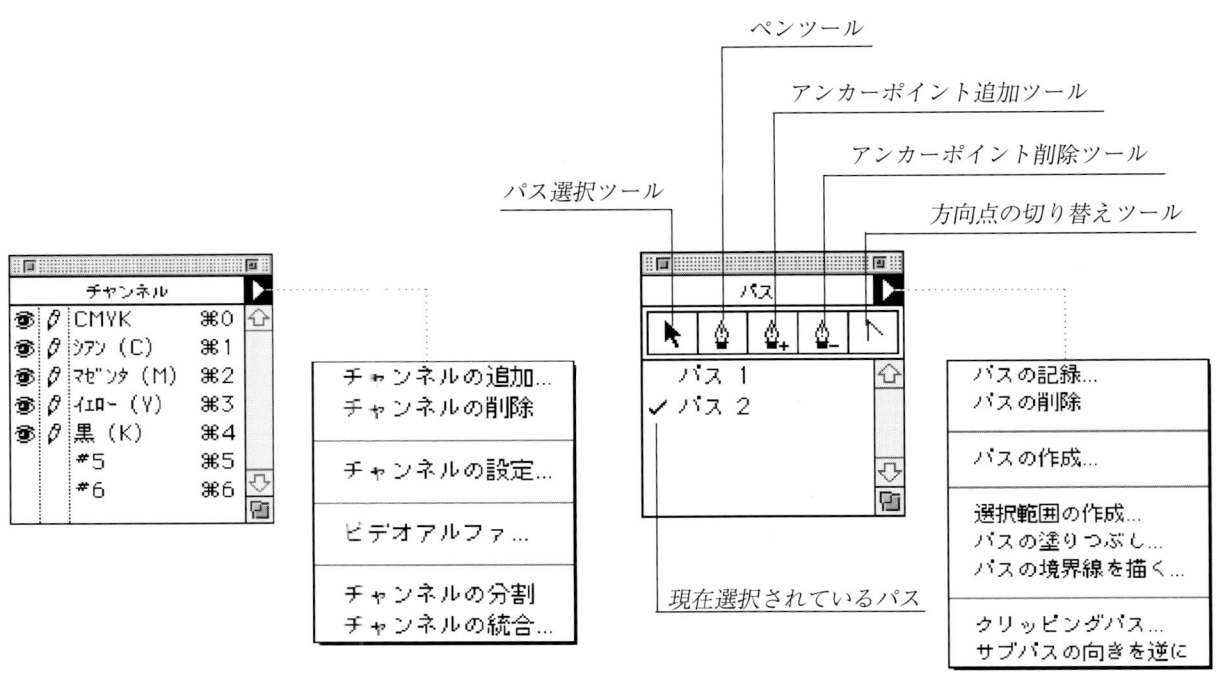

ペンツール

アンカーポイント追加ツール

アンカーポイント削除ツール

方向点の切り替えツール

パス選択ツール

チャンネル

		CMYK	⌘0
👁	𝄞	シアン（C）	⌘1
👁	𝄞	マゼンタ（M）	⌘2
👁	𝄞	イエロー（Y）	⌘3
👁	𝄞	黒（K）	⌘4
		#5	⌘5
		#6	⌘6

チャンネルの追加...
チャンネルの削除

チャンネルの設定...

ビデオアルファ...

チャンネルの分割
チャンネルの統合...

パス

パス 1
✓ パス 2

現在選択されているパス

パスの記録...
パスの削除

パスの作成...

選択範囲の作成...
パスの塗りつぶし...
パスの境界線を描く...

クリッピングパス...
サブパスの向きを逆に

Channels Palettes

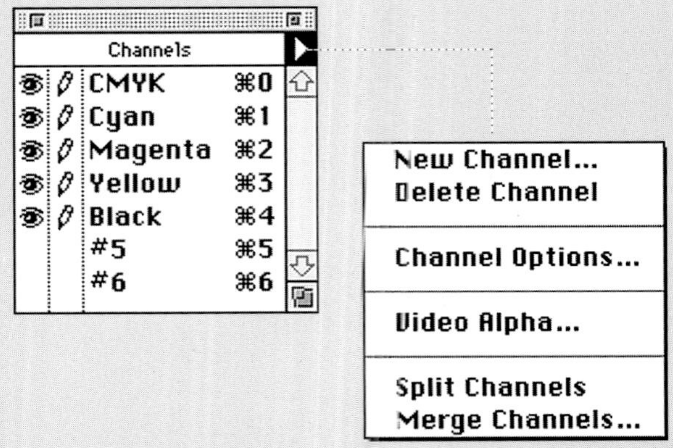

Paths Palettes

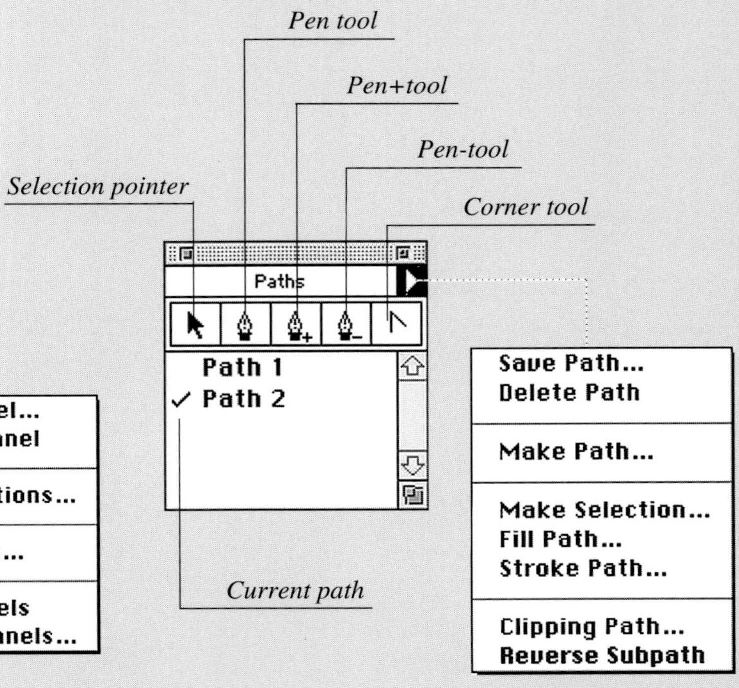

Pen tool

Pen+tool

Pen-tool

Corner tool

Selection pointer

Channels

		CMYK	⌘0
👁	𝄞	Cyan	⌘1
👁	𝄞	Magenta	⌘2
👁	𝄞	Yellow	⌘3
👁	𝄞	Black	⌘4
		#5	⌘5
		#6	⌘6

New Channel...
Delete Channel

Channel Options...

Video Alpha...

Split Channels
Merge Channels...

Paths

Path 1
✓ Path 2

Current path

Save Path...
Delete Path

Make Path...

Make Selection...
Fill Path...
Stroke Path...

Clipping Path...
Reverse Subpath

情報パレット

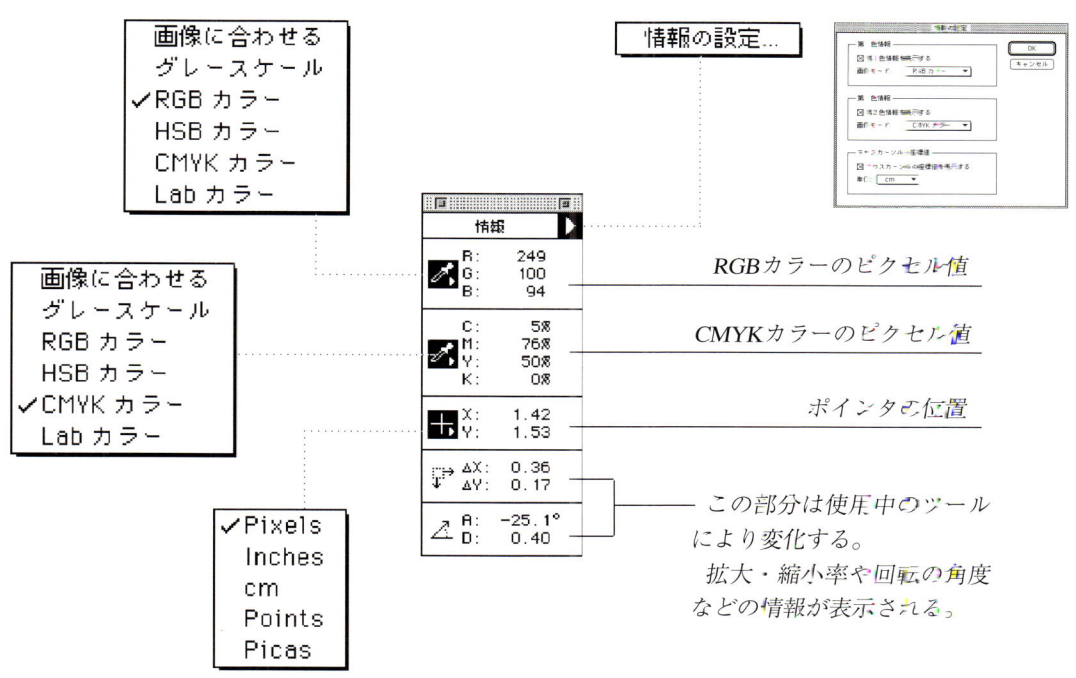

情報の設定...

画像に合わせる
グレースケール
✓RGB カラー
HSB カラー
CMYK カラー
Lab カラー

画像に合わせる
グレースケール
RGB カラー
HSB カラー
✓CMYK カラー
Lab カラー

✓Pixels
Inches
cm
Points
Picas

情報

R:	249
G:	100
B:	94

C:	5%
M:	76%
Y:	50%
K:	0%

| X: | 1.42 |
| Y: | 1.53 |

| ΔX: | 0.36 |
| ΔY: | 0.17 |

| A: | -25.1° |
| D: | 0.40 |

RGBカラーのピクセル値

CMYKカラーのピクセル値

ポインタの位置

この部分は使用中のツール
により変化する。
拡大・縮小率や回転の角度
などの情報が表示される。

Info Palettes

Options...

Actual Color
Grayscale
✓RGB Color
HSB Color
CMYK Color
Lab Color

Actual Color
Grayscale
RGB Color
HSB Color
✓CMYK Color
Lab Color

✓Pixels
Inches
Centimeters
Points
Picas

Info

R:	245
G:	104
B:	94

C:	0%
M:	70%
Y:	58%
K:	0%

| X: | 204 |
| Y: | 52 |

| ΔX: | 20 |
| ΔY: | 20 |

| A: | -45.0° |
| D: | 28.28 |

RGB color value of pixel

CMYK color value of pixel

Position of pointer

*Depending on tool in use,
Info pallette displays
additional information,
e.g.,scaling percentage
or angle of rotation*

147

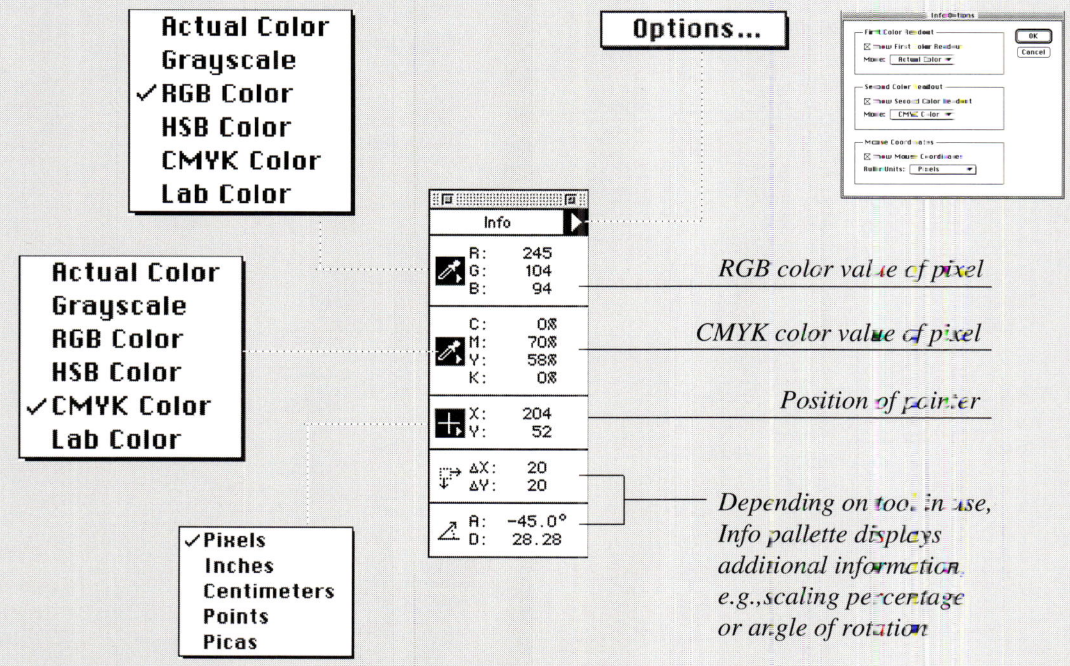

Shortcuts

Selecting

Tool or key	Plus	Result
⬚⬚	Shift key	Constrains Marquee to a circle or a square
⬚⬚	Option key	Draws marquee from center
⬚⬚ ⬚ ⬚ ✳	Shift key	Adds to a selection
⬚⬚ ⬚ ⬚ ✳	Command key	Subtracts from a selection
⬚⬚ ⬚ ⬚ ✳	Command+Shift and drag	Select the combined selected areas.
⬚	Option key	Rubber Band mode (selecting from point to point by clicking.)
⬚	Command&Option (while in progress)	Removing the area selected in Rubber Band mode.
⬚	Shift&Option (while in progress)	Adding to a selected area while using Rubber Band mode.
T	Command key	De-selecting a selected floating area.
Option key	Drag selection	Drag/Copy(moves a copy of selection)
Command+ Option key	Drag selection	Moves selection border only
Option key	Pasting.	Opening a control dialog box while pasting.
Cursol key(Arrow key)		Moves selection in 1-pixel increments

Painting

Tool or key	Plus	Result
✏	Option key	Selects background color
Option key	Delete	Fills selection with foreground color
Any painting/ editing tool	Command key	▸
Any painting tool	Option key	✐
Any painting/ editing tool	Number key	Sets paint opacity (0=100%;1-10%)
Any painting/ editing tool	Shift key	Constrains stroke to a straight line
Doge/Burn Blur/Sharpen	Clicking a tool with Option.	Switching tools.
Any painting/ editing tool	Caps Lock key	Cross-hair pointer

Viewing (right column, top)

Tool or key	Plus	Result
⌫	Double-click tool	Erases entire image
⌫	Option key	Magic eraser
Any tool	Command key	✂ Removes color from Colors palette
Any tool	Option key	Replaces color in Colors palette

Viewing

Tool or key	Plus	Result
🖐	Double-click tool	Fits artwork in window
🔍	Double-click tool	1:1 magnification
🔍	Drag	Magnifies selected area
Command key	[-][+] key	Zooms and resizes window
Any tool	Command key+ spacebar+click	Magnifies image,including when dialog box is open
Any tool	Option+spacebar +click	Zooms out of image,inclu-ding when dialog box is open

Pen Tool

Tool or key	Plus	Result
✒ ✒+ ✒- ⌐	Command key	▸
✒ ✒+ ✒-	Command+control key	⌐
▸	Control key	⌐
▸	Command+ Option key	Adds or deletes anchor point (if path is clicked)

Others

Tool or key	Plus	Result
Command key	F key	Applies last filter
Command + Option key	F key	Opens last filter dialog box
Command key	Period key	Cancels operation
Any painting/editing tool	Spacebar	🖐
Option key	Variations	Resets Variations setting to last adjustments

ショートカット

選択ツール

ツール・キー	キー・操作	結　果
⬭ ⬚	シフトキー	正円／正方形
⬭ ⬚	オプションキー	センターから描画
⬭ ⬚ ⌒ ✎	シフトキー	選択範囲に追加
⬭ ⬚ ⌒ ✎	コマンドキー	選択範囲から除外
⬭ ⬚ ⌒ ✎	コマンド＋シフト＆ドラッグ	選択された共通領域の選択
⌒	オプションキー	ラバーバンドモード（点から点とクリックしながら選択するモード）
⌒	コマンド／途中から＋オプション	ラバーバンドモード時の選択範囲内を起点とする除外
⌒	シフト／途中から＋オプション	ラバーバンドモード時の選択範囲内を起点とする追加
T	コマンドキー	フローティング領域の選択範囲をフロート解除する
オプションキー	選択範囲をドラッグ	ドラッグ／コピー（選択範囲のコピーを移動する）
オプションキー＋コマンドキー	選択範囲をドラッグ	選択範囲の境界のみを移動
オプションキー	ペースト	ペースト時に合成のコントロールダイアログを開く
カーソルキー（矢印キー）		1ピクセルずつ移動

ペイントツール

ツール・キー	キー・操作	結　果
🖋	オプションキー	背景色の選択
オプションキー	デリートキー	選択範囲全体を描画色で塗る
ペイント＆編集ツール	コマンドキー	▶
ペイント描画ツール	オプションキー	🖋
ペイント＆編集ツール	英数字キー	ペイントの不透明度を変更
ペイント＆編集ツール	シフトキー	直線で描く・角度を規定する
覆い焼き・焼き込み／ぼかし・シャープツール	オプションキー＋ツールをクリック	ツールの切り換え
ペイント＆編集ツール	caps lockキー	クロスポインタ

ツール・キー	キー・操作	結　果
🖋	ツールをダブルクリック	画像全体の消去
🖋	オプションキー	マジック消しゴム
任意のツール	コマンドキー	✂ カラーパレットから色を取り除く
任意のツール	オプションキー	🖌 カラーパレットの色を置き換える

表示

ツール・キー	キー・操作	結　果
🖐	ツールをダブルクリック	画像をウインドワにフィットする
🔍	ツールをダブルクリック	画像を1：1の拡大率で表示する
🔍	必要部分をドラッグ	ドラッグした選択範囲を拡大する
コマンドキー	⊟⊞キー	ウィンドワの縮小拡大
任意のツール	コマンド＋スペースバー＋クリック	ダイアログボックスが開いている時にも画像を拡大する
任意のツール	オプション＋スペースバー＋クリック	ダイアログボックスが開いている時にも画像を縮小する

ペンツール

ツール・キー	キー・操作	結　果
🖊 🖊+ 🖊- ⌐	コマンドキー	▶
🖊 🖊+ 🖊-	コマンド＋コントロールキー	⌐
▶	コントロールキー	⌐
▶	コマンド＋オプションキー	パスがアクティブな時にアンカーポイントを追加したり削除する

その他

ツール・キー	キー・操作	結　果
コマンドキー	Fキー	前回のフィルタを適用する
コマンド＋オプションキー	Fキー	前回のフィルタダイアログボックスを開く
コマンドキー	ピリオドキー	操作を取り消す
ペイント＆編集ツール	スペースバー	🖐
オプションキー	バリエーション	バリエーションの設定を前回の設定にリセット

149

Index

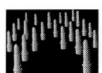

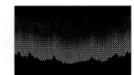

キ・ク   　　サ・シ

コ

ス

ヒ・フ

ヘ

ホ・マ

メ・モ

ラ・レ

実戦フロッピーディスクの使い方

Instructional disk内容............基礎実戦編 6 章分の実戦用素材データすべてと完成作例および取り扱い説明文日本語、英語、計24ファイル。

Chapter 2&3フォルダ...........●Image File:モニタキャリブレーション用のCMYKデータ。●Wrong File:カラーコレクション用の 4 点の写真の集合。●Pear-B&W:
人工着色実戦用の白黒写真データ●Curvesフォルダ:カラー補正用のカスタムデータ（詳細は下記に）

Chapter 4フォルダ.................Subject-1 (本文中では"オブジェクト素材"),Gold (本文中では"ゴールド素材"),Final-1 (完成作例) 計 3 ファイル、第 4 章実戦用の素材
ファイルと完成作例。

Chapter 5フォルダ.................Subject-2 (本文中では"オブジェクト用素材"),Background (本文中では"バック用素材"),Final-2 (完成作例) 計 3 ファイル、第 5 章実戦
用の素材ファイルと完成作例。

Chapter 6フォルダ.................Camera (本文中では"合成用素材-1"),ColorClassic (本文中では"合成用素材-2"),Face (本文中では"画面はめ込み用素材"),Jumbo eye (本
文中では"レンズ映り込み用素材"),Final-3 (完成作例) 計 5 ファイル、第 6 章実戦用の素材ファイルと完成作例。

Chapter 7フォルダ.................Subject-3 (本文中では"オブジェクト"),Sky (本文中では"空の写真"),Forest (本文中では"背景の森の写真"),Final-4 (完成作例) 計 4 ファ
イル、第 7 章実戦用の素材ファイルと完成作例。

Curvesフォルダ ....●Barley-Curve:Wrong File No.2画像のカラー補正用カスタムデータ。

（Chapter 2&3 フォルダ内）●Glass-Level:Wrong File No.1画像のカラー補正用カスタムデータ。
●Pasture-Green-Curve:Wrong File No.3画像のグリーン部分のカラー補正用カスタムデータ。
●Pasture-Blue-Curve:Wrong File No.3画像のブルー部分のカラー補正用カスタムデータ。

☆Curvesフォルダ内のカスタムデータは確認用のデータなので、最初から使わずにカラー補正を行ったあとで、確認のために利用すること。

☆第 8 章、第 9 章、第10章、応用編 3 章分は実戦素材、完成作例ともフロッピーディスクには添付されていない。読者の作品製作に掲載テクニックを応用、実
践していただければ幸いだ。

☆漢字TALK7.1＋フォトショップ2.51Jの環境下で作成、動作確認を行っている。漢字TALK6.07＋フォトショップ2.01Jでファイルを開く場合はファイルメニュー
の入力用プラグからAdobe JPEG 解凍コマンドを選択して開くことができる。

Contents of the Instructional Disk:

The disk contains 24 files, including all the data, completed works and Japanese and English explanatory notes found in Chap.2~7.

Chapter2&3Folder.●Image File: CMYK data for use in monitor calibration. ● Wrong File: Composite variation of 4 photographs. ● Pear-B&W: Black & White film data for artificial colorization work. ● Curves Folder: Custom data for color supplementation work (for details see below)

Chapter 4 Folder.... Three files: Subject 1 (referred to as "subject material" in text), Gold (referred to as "gold material" in text), and Final 1 (finished example). Material files and finished examples for Chap. 4.

Chapter 5 Folder.... Three files: Subject-2 (referred to as "subjet maerial" in text), Background (referred to as "background material" in text), and Final 2 (finished work). Material files and finished examples for Chap. 5.

Chapter 6 Folder.... Five files: Camera (referred to in text as "composite materials 1"), Color Classic (referred to in text as "composite materials 2"), Face ("composite paste-on materials" in text), Jumbo Eye ("lens reflection material" in text), and Final 3 (finished work). Material files and finsihed works for Chap. 6.

Chapter 7 Folder.... Four files: Subject 3 (referred to as "subject" in text), Sky (referred to as "Sky Photo" in text), Forest (referred to as "Background Forest Photo" in text) Final 4 (finished work). Material files and finished works for Chap. 7.

Curves Folder.... ●Barley-Curve : Wrong File No. 2. Custom data for color additions.
●Pasture-Green-Curve: Wrong File No. 1. Custom data for image color additions.
●Pasture-Green-Curve: Wrong File No. 3. Custom data for green part image corrections.
●Pasture -Blue-Curve: Wrong File No. 3. Custom data for blue part image corrections.

☆The data in the Curves folder is for comparison. First, do the corrections yourself, without referring to the Folder. Use the Folder only to check your work.

☆The materials for Chapters 8, 9 and 10 are not contained in the disk. Use your own techniques to experiment with these works.

☆These files were created and mastered under System7.1 and Photoshop 2.51. When opening the files with System6.07 and Photoshop2.01 choose the **Adobe JPEG Decompress** command from the **Acquire** on the **File** menu.

ハードディスクへのインストール　Installing to a Hard Disk

1．Instructional diskをスーパードライブに挿入してInstructional disk アイコンをダブルクリックする。

2．保存先のハードディスクを選択するためにデスクトップボタンをクリックする。

3．データ保存先のハードディスク名をクリック、選択してOpenボタンをクリックする。

4．Extractボタンをクリックするとデータがハードディスクに解凍保存される。

1. Insert the Instructional Disk to a Superdrive and double click the disk icon.

2. Click the **desktop** button to select the destination hard disk.

3. Click the name of the destination hard disk, then select the **Open** button and click.

4. Click the **Extract** button to decompress and save the files to the destination hard drive.

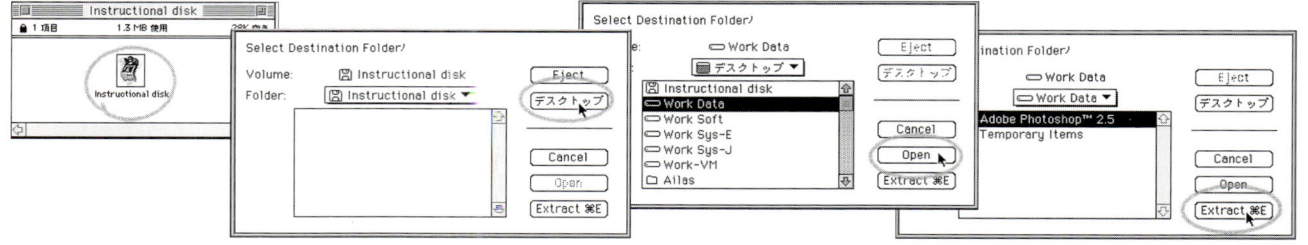

Using the Instructional Disk

まず最初に２ＨＤディスクの読めるドライブに実戦フロッピーディスクを挿入してInstructional diskアイコンをダブルクリック。コピー先のハードディスクを指定して**Extract**ボタンをクリック、全てを解凍コピーする。ハードディスクの空き容量が約1.3メガバイト必要。

「必ず読んでください！」ファイルにはこの解説と、その後あらたに付け加えられた最新情報が書き込まれている。この文章を読んだ人も必ず確認しておいてほしい。

ファイルは全てフォトショップのJPEG圧縮ファイルとして保存されている。フォトショップVer.2.5の**ファイル**メニューから**開く**コマンドで開くことができ、ファイルアイコンのダブルクリックでも開くことができる。

一度開いて加工したファイルはそのまま保存せずに、必ず**別名で保存**コマンドでJPEG圧縮せずにPhotoshop2.5フォーマットで保存すること。その後作業を繰り返しても画像を劣化させずにすむ。

ハードディスクにコピー後Chapter2&3フォルダに入っているWrong Fileをオープンして各コマの下にふってあるフィルムナンバーにしたがって、画像を４つに分割してWrong File No.1からWrong File No.4まで別々に名前を変えて保存する。分割のしかたは**切り抜きツール**を使ってNo.1を切り取り後、別名で保存、再度Wrong Fileを**開いて**No.2を切り取り後**別名で保存**という手順を踏むか、**長方形選択ツール**でNo.1を選択して**コピー**、新規で新しいファイルを作って**ペースト後別名で保存**という手順を繰り返すか、どちらでもかまわない。

Chapter2&3フォルダ内のImage FileはCMYKカラーモードで作成保存されている。その他のカラーファイルは全てRGBカラーモードで作成保存されている。白黒の画像はグレースケールモードで保存されている。白黒の画像はすべてカラー化するので、実習に使用する際には**モード**メニューでグレースケールモードからRGBカラーモードに変換して利用する。

Image Fileはキャリブレーション用に添付されており、モニタに表示してフォトショップ添付のガンマコントロールパネルデバイスを調整して、第２章冒頭の印刷結果に近づければ標準印刷用のキャリブレーションが取れる。

Wrong Fileはわざとカラー補正を狂わせてスキャニングした画像だ。Image Fileの色に近づくように第２章のカラー補正実習を行う。どうしても思うようにならない時の為にカスタムデータをCurvesフォルダのなかに添付してある。使い方は簡単で補正するファイルを**開い**てから、実習内容に合せて**イメージ**メニューの**色調補正**で**トーンカーブ**又は**レベル補正**コマンドを選択、**読み込み**ボタンをクリックして添付ディスク内のCurvesフォルダから必要なカスタムデータファイルを**開く**だけだ。

フォトショップのカラー補正コマンドのほとんどで、カスタムデータの保存と**読み込み**が実行できる。カラー補正をした後、OKボタンをクリックする前に**保存**しておくだけで他のファイルに対してそのカスタムデータを**読み込ん**で利用することができる。

カラーコレクションの実習が終わったファイルは別名で保存して、第３章のセレクションテクニック実習に使用する。

添付の素材画像はなるべく圧縮率を低めて解像度を高めにしたつもりだが、参考用の完成画像はディスクの容量の都合で、高圧縮低解像度になっている。JPEG特有の画像の乱れは意図的なものではないので、製作の参考にしないでほしい。

First of all insert the Instructional Disk in a 2HD drive and double click the Icon. Indicate the destination hard drive and click the **Extract** button, unfreezing the files. You will require about 1.3MB of open space on your hard drive.

In the "Read me first!" file are contained this explanation and additional new information added thereafter. The person who reads this explanation is not exempt from reading this file.

All files are saved as Photoshop compressed JPEG files. You can open them by choosing **Open** from the **File** menu on Photoshop 2.5, or by double clicking the file icons.

Once opened, the files cannot be saved until they are renamed. They will then be saved as normal Photoshop files, not as compressed JPEG files.

Next, open the folders of Chapter 2&3 where you will find four files each, named Wrong File No.1 to Wrong File No.4. Open and again rename each of these. Do this by using the **Cropping Tool** to cut out the image of No.1, and saving it under a new name, through all the four files, or by using the **Marquee Tool** to select and save each of the four files under a new name. Either method will do.

The Image Files in Chapter 2&3 are saved in CMYK Color mode. Black and White images are saved in Grayscale mode. All the black and white images will eventually be colorized, at which time the mode on the **Mode** menu will be changed from Grayscale to RGB Color.

The Image File is for calibration, and should be used in conjunction with the gamma control panel device attached to Photoshop. By adjusting the color to match the image at the head of Chapter 2 you will have achieved industry standard calibration.

Wrong File is deliberately scanned in distorted color. To approximate the coloration of the Image File use the techniques in Chapter 2. If you just can't get the right effect, refer to the custom data in the Curves Folder. They are easy to use. Just open the file, then choose **Curves** or **Level** command under **Adjust** on the **Image** menu. Then click the **Load** button for the attached Curves Folder and select the required custom data

With almost all of Photoshop's color correction commands you can **Save** and **Load** custom data. After making color corrections, save them before clicking the **OK** button. then you can use the same custom data to repair other files.

After finishing color corrections save the file under a new name; they will be used again in Chapter 3, "Selection Techniques."

The supplementaryu materials were intended to be high-resolution, lightly-compressed files, but space limitations on the attached disk resulted in the opposite, namely high-compression, low-resolution materials. The distortion seen in htese files should not be seen as characteristic of JPEG performance.

あとがき

　このところコンピュータによる画像処理の普及度には目を見張るものがある。数年を経ずして少なくとも印刷対象の写真はデジタル化してしまうのではないかと思われる勢いである。デザイナー向けの画材屋さんがマッキントッシュの出力センター兼、販売店になったと思ったら、今は主だったプロ写真機材商が軒並マッキントッシュの画像処理システムを扱うようになった。プロの写真家のなかに商売になるほどマッキントッシュが浸透し始めているという事なのだろう。

　マッキントッシュの写真画像処理ソフトでフォトショップの右に出る物は現在の所まだない。*Fitts Imaging* の『*Live Picture*』はフォトショップの初登場以来久々の期待感を抱かせる、将来の画像処理ソフトの定番になりそうな予感のするテクノロジーだが、生熟度はまだ低くフォトショップほど手軽ではない。当分フォトショップの天下は続くだろう。

　日進月歩のハードに比べソフトの進化はゆっくりしている。今フォトショップを完全にマスターしておくことは、将来のより優れたソフトを使いこなすためにも、決して無駄にはならないはずだ。

　フォトショップ実戦マスターを読んで実践実習した読者は、フォトショップで何ができて何ができないのか充分に理解できたことと思う。そしてデジタル処理で、できないことはソフトやハードの問題以上にオペレータの創造力と理解力、習熟度不足によるのだということも。

　一人でも多くの読者が、この本に触れたことでフォトショップを自由自在に駆使するようになり、素晴らしい作品を生み出すきっかけとなることを願ってやまない。

　最後に、１年間にわたるプロジェクトに御協力いただいたスタッフの皆様、協力会社の皆様、影に日向に支え励ましてくれた編集の大田さん、ボランティアに近い仕事にもかかわらず我儘を認め支えてくれた経理担当の妻、節子に心よりの感謝を捧げつつ…………

１９９４年１月 吉日　　　早川廣行

　この本はマッキントッシュQuadra900を使い、大日本スクリーン製造株式会社のDTS-1015AIスキャナによりスキャニングしたデータをフォトショップVer.2.5で加工処理後、350ppiのハイレゾデジタルデータをページメーカー4.01Jでレイアウト、サイテックスシステムで分解フィルム出力、完全デジタル入稿処理により印刷しています。

　表紙カバーはフォトショップVer.2.5で加工処理した4000×3000ピクセルの個々の画像データを日本イマプロ株式会社のQCR-Ziフィルムレコーダーで4×5ポジフィルムに出力、従来通りの紙版下レイアウト＆製版システムによって印刷されています。

Postscript

The popularity of image manipulation by computer is just astonishing these days. Some say that in the near future the photographic data for printing material will be completely digitalized. For example, art supply shops for graphic designers now have the facility of the computer output service, and/or work as sales representatives for computer software and hardware. And photographic equipment supply stores are now beginning to employ a Macintosh image manipulation systems. Macintosh has even begun to make sales to professional photographers.

As of now nothing surpasses Photoshop in terms of image manipulation sofware. There have been increasing expectations for Live Picture, by Fitts Imaging, since Photoshop arrived on the market. In the future, this technology is likely to become standard as the manipulation software. However, the demand remains low at this moment and its operation is not easy as Photoshop, which is likely to continue its reign for the time being.

Compared to the rapid progress of hardware, the development of software is going at arelatively slow pace. It is not a waste of time and effort to learn all about Photoshop now, since you can apply the knoweledge and experience to operate even more superior software in the future.

Those who have read, experimented and practically learned from "Photoshop: A Designer's Guide" sufficiently undertand what they can and cannot do with the Photoshop software. In most cases, they also come to understand that things that cannot be achieved in the digital process are due to the lack of operator's imagination, understanding and experience rather than accidents or problems relating to software and/or hardware.

I hope most of those who read this book will learn how to use Photoshop independently and efficiently to create great photographic works.

Lastly, I would like to thank the project staff for their cooperation as well as the people at our affiliated companies, and Mr. Ota, the editor of this book, for his professional help and moral support in so many ways. Special thanks should be given to my wife, Setsuko, for her patient and hard work as my own accountant manager.

January 1994　　Hiroyuki Hayakawa

This book is created using a Macintosh Quadra 900. All data except the image in the jacket are scanned in by DTS-1015AI scanners produced by Dainippon Screen Mfg. Co., Ltd. Scanned data is manipulated by Photoshop Version 2.5 and transferred to 350ppi high resolution data. Those high resolution data are laid out using PageMaker 4.01J, input to MOs, and output to the separation films on the Scitex system.

The indivisual 4000×3000 pixel data is manipulated and processed by Photoshop Version 2.5E and is output to the 4×5 positive transparency by QCR-Zi film recorder made by the Imapro Corp. for the image of the jacket. The jacket is printed under the traditional and conventional method.

著者略歴

早川廣行 （Hiroyuki Hayakawa）
1945年生 東京都出身
1966年東京総合写真専門学校卒
1966年より広告写真家早崎治氏に師事
1971年～1973年欧州遊学
1973年帰国後ハヤサキスタジオ入社
1985年独立ハヤカワスタジオ設立
1986年マッキントッシュの広告写真撮影に参画
　　　　そのコンセプトに感銘してマッキントッシュを導入
1990年フォトショップと出会い画像処理を始め現在に至る
ハヤカワスタジオ・デジタルダークルーム
デジタルデザイン研究所・代表取締役
日本広告写真家協会会員・日本写真芸術学会会員

フォトショップ実戦マスター
Photoshop : A Designer's Guide
〈A Comprehensive, Step-by-Step Manual for Adobe Photoshop〉

発行　1994年3月25日初版第1刷発行
　　　1994年5月15日　　第2刷発行
　　　1995年4月15日　　第3刷発行

著者　　　　　　　早川廣行（ⒸHiroyuki Hayakawa）
装丁　　　　　　　株式会社エムズスペース（箕浦 卓）
本文デザイン　　　早川廣行／デジタルダークルーム（白川雅子）
編集担当　　　　　大田 悟
翻訳　　　　　　　スコット・ブラウス
編集協力　　　　　アドビシステムズジャパン
テクニカル校正　　アレフ（川　忠博）／上野俊一

発行者　　　　　　久世利郎
発行所　　　　　　株式会社グラフィック社
　　　　　　　　　〒102 東京都千代田区九段北1-9-12
　　　　　　　　　Tel.03-3263-4318 Fax.03-5275-3579
印刷・製本　　　　恒美印務有限公司
データ変換　　　　凸版印刷株式会社
カバー写植　　　　イノックス

ISBN4-7661-0768-3 C3072